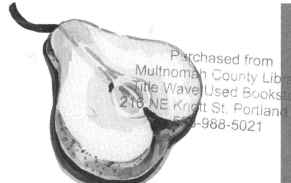

Th...
to...

Dried
Foods

**Preserve Fresh Fruits,
Vegetables, Herbs,
and Meat with a Dehydrator,
a Kitchen Oven, or the Sun**

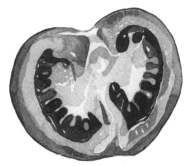

Teresa Marrone

The mission of Storey Publishing is to serve our customers by
publishing practical information that encourages
personal independence in harmony with the environment.

EDITED BY Margaret Sutherland
ART DIRECTION AND BOOK DESIGN BY Carolyn Eckert
TEXT PRODUCTION BY Tina Henderson

FRONT COVER PHOTOGRAPHY AND ILLUSTRATION © Dietlind Wolf
BACK COVER AND INTERIOR ILLUSTRATIONS © Holly Exley, except for diagrams pages 56–61 courtesy of the author

INDEXED BY Nancy D. Wood

STOREY PUBLISHING
210 MASS MoCA Way
North Adams, MA 01247
www.storey.com

Printed in the United States by R. R. Donnelley
10 9 8 7 6 5 4 3 2 1

Library of Congress Cataloging-in-Publication Data

Marrone, Teresa.
  The beginner's guide to making and using dried foods / by Teresa Marrone.
      pages cm
  Includes index.
  ISBN 978-1-61212-179-6 (pbk. : alk. paper)
  ISBN 978-1-60342-927-6 (ebook) 1. Food—Drying. 2. Dried foods. I. Title.
TX609.M29 2014
641.4'4—dc23
                              2014011269

Acknowledgments

This book would not have been possible without the inspiration and information from Phyllis Hobson's ground-breaking book *Making & Using Dried Foods* (originally published way back in 1983 as *Garden Way Publishing's Guide to Food Drying*). Ms. Hobson's work has taught several generations of home cooks how to dehydrate foods, enabling them to preserve the bounty from their gardens and orchards.

Contents

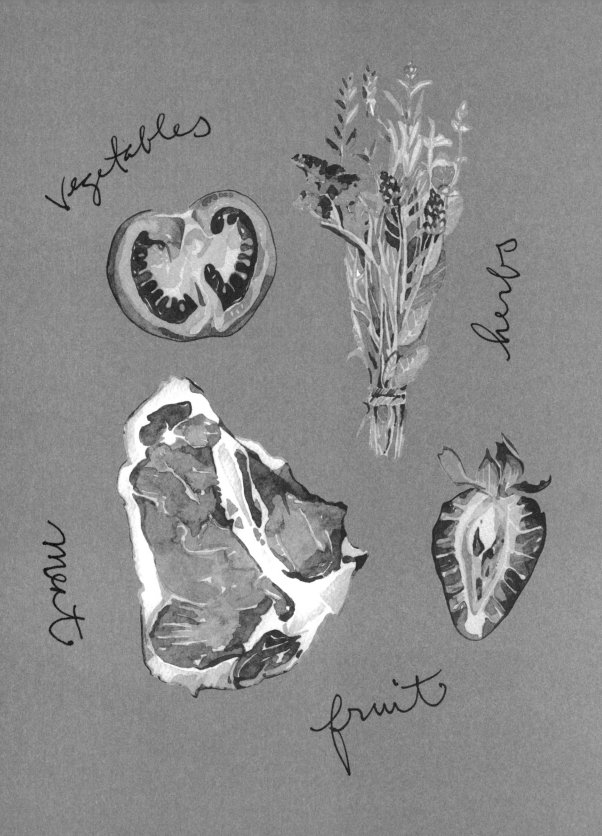

vegetables

herbs

meat

fruit

CHAPTER 1

Drying Foods at Home: An Introduction

DRYING FOODS is a natural alternative to canning and freezing and benefits the family on a tight budget. This time-honored method of food preparation and preservation benefits the hiker, the camper, or the angler looking for a compact food supply light enough to carry in a backpack. It benefits the homemaker looking for delicious, healthful snacks to offer the family, and it benefits vacationers with two homes because drying is a safe way to store food over the winter. Drying is also an ideal way of storing foods for those who live in isolated locations where electricity to operate a freezer may be undependable or nonexistent, and it is a good way to stockpile an emergency food supply in a small storage area.

The goal of dehydrating is to remove excess moisture, reducing the water content to between 10 and 20 percent for most foods, so bacteria that cause decay cannot survive. Since dried foods are only one-half to one-twelfth the weight and bulk of the original food, a small, dry, cool closet can provide all the storage space needed for a winter's supply of food.

Because drying is a more natural method of preservation than canning and freezing, many people believe drying foods preserves more of the nutritional values present in raw foods, and a USDA study backs up this belief. While it is true that vitamins are lost in blanching, a pretreatment recommended for some vegetables before drying, this nutritional loss can be kept to a minimum if the foods are steam-blanched for no more than the specified time.

Almost any food can be dried by following the instructions in this book, which are aimed at preserving as much of the nutrients and flavor of the food as possible.

Will your dried food be as good as what you can buy on the market? Commercial manufacturers have the advantage of expensive freeze-drying equipment, but you have the advantage of sweet, tree-ripened fruit and just-picked, garden-fresh vegetables. Your own homegrown fruits and vegetables, or those bought at local farmers' markets or roadside stands, should be more delicious and nutritious than those the food processors have.

Why Dry Foods at Home?

In addition to the benefits described above, home-dried foods are a great option in many situations. Here are some of the reasons home-dried foods are prepared and used by so many people.

To Save Money

Drying is a safe, easy way to preserve foods. It can also save money when compared to other food preservation methods. You don't have to buy canning jars (or replace them when they break), and even if you do store your dried foods in canning jars, the lids can be washed and reused many times. You can store dried foods also in jars that are not suitable for canning, such as well-cleaned glass jars that originally held peanut butter, mayonnaise, and other prepared foods. Most dried foods can be stored at room temperature, a significant energy saving over frozen storage. And if you live in an area that has plenty of clear, dry, sunny weather, you can dry foods outdoors in the sun, which provides more free energy.

You will save the most money, of course, by drying fruits and vegetables from your own garden. Even if you don't plant a garden, though, you can still economize by drying foods at home. During the harvest season, fruits and vegetables can be purchased cheaply at farmers' markets, orchards, and roadside stands. Shares in a CSA (community-supported agriculture) program usually provide a bounty of dawn-fresh, locally grown vegetables and fruits throughout the growing season, at reasonable prices. Produce and meats are surprisingly inexpensive when bought in bulk quantities at co-ops and warehouse clubs. Choose only top-quality fresh produce and meats, and keep an eye on the place of origin if you're concerned about purchasing foods that have been shipped long distances. Watch also for specials on supermarket produce. Bananas flecked with brown, which often sell for half price, make excellent fruit leathers. Often, produce is marked down when a new shipment is due; this bargain-priced produce will work fine for drying as long as it is still wholesome.

Drying can also save you money by avoiding waste. Finely chop leftover cooked meat or vegetables and dry until crumbly; use another time to enrich soups, casseroles, or stews. Spread leftover sauces or thick soups on a solid liner sheet and dry until leathery, then rehydrate later for a quick meal when time is short. Purée excess cooked fruits in the blender, then make delicious homemade leathers as described in chapter 8.

Specialty grain products such as flax crackers, flavored pasta, and whole-grain cereals are expensive to buy, but you can make your own for far less — and control the ingredients as well. Unlike fruits and vegetables, flour, flax seeds, and cornmeal are available all year, so making homemade grain products is a good winter project that will pay handsome rewards later. To get some ideas of the possibilities, see chapter 9.

To Preserve the Harvest

When your garden is overflowing with tomatoes, the apples are piling up in the orchard, and the neighbors are leaving zucchini on your porch, get out your dehydrator and roll up your sleeves. Even if you plan to can or freeze some of your bounty, you'll find that drying offers an additional option that produces some very useful foodstuffs.

Plum tomatoes and other small varieties can be cut in half and dried, then used in place of purchased (and expensive) sun-dried tomatoes; larger tomatoes can be sliced and dried, then used in the same way. Dried apple slices make great lunchbox treats, and your home-dried apples won't be loaded with preservatives like most commercial versions. Zucchini slices, when dried, become a delightful, low-calorie snack, perfect for dipping; they also make a nice salad topper when crumbled. And of course, most of your dried fruits and vegetables can be rehydrated and used like fresh or canned foods.

To Save Space

Fruits and vegetables have very high water contents. Apples, apricots, and blueberries are approximately 85 percent water by weight, ripe tomatoes are almost 95 percent, and even firm, solid vegetables like carrots are over 85 percent. Dehydrating reduces the water dramatically, generally to 10 to 20 percent by weight. As the water is reduced, the food shrinks in size. Three pounds of fresh rhubarb (about 3 quarts of cut-up pieces) weighs just 3 to 4 ounces after drying, and measures about 2 cups (1 pint). The same amount of rhubarb would typically require four or five 1-pint jars if sliced and canned. So your pantry shelf may hold up to four times as much food that's been dried vs. food that's been canned — and dried foods take up even less room when vacuum-sealed in plastic storage bags.

For Selective or Restricted Diets

A small but growing number of people choose to eat foods that are uncooked, basing their diets primarily on vegetables, fruits, seeds, nuts, grains, sprouts, and other foods such as seaweed and coconut or nut milk. **Raw-food and living-food diets** often make extensive use of home-dried foods. A clear benefit of dried foods in the raw diet is that fruits and vegetables can be dehydrated when in season, for use during cold months. Dehydrated foods also offer textures and forms that add variety to the diet: vegetable crisps, for example, can replace baked crackers or fried tortilla chips as an accompaniment to raw dips. Crackers made from recipes designed specifically for dehydrating, kale or collard chips, and other dehydrated vegetable snacks also add variety to the raw-food diet.

If you are on a **sodium-restricted diet**, dehydrating can help. Many commercially processed foods are high in sodium, and it can be hard to find low-sodium products such as canned vegetables, crackers, convenience mixes, and even breakfast cereal. With a dehydrator, you can fill your pantry with healthful, home-dried vegetables, low-sodium snack foods, homemade veggie burger mix, powdered broth mixes that replace high-sodium bouillon, home-packed mixes for soup and other foods, and even homemade breakfast cereal — and *you* control the amount of sodium.

For the growing number of people who are allergic to **gluten** — a type of protein found in cereal grains — the supermarket shelves are a land mine because a surprising number of commercial products contain gluten. Home-dried vegetable crisps, as well as gluten-free crackers and chips prepared in your dehydrator, are a great alternative to commercial products made with cereal grains. Powdered vegetable flakes, broths made from dehydrated vegetables, and homemade veggie burger mix take the place of purchased versions. Home-packed soup and snack mixes replace supermarket versions that have hidden gluten.

It goes without saying that dehydrated vegetables fit perfectly into the **vegan diet**. Most home-dried fruits do, too, as long as you don't use honey dip. As noted above, homemade broth powders and veggie burger mix are healthful alternatives to commercial versions, and work well with the vegan diet. So too do many of the tasty vegetable snacks in chapter 9.

For Special Uses

Many people keep **emergency supplies** for times of adverse weather, power failures, or other catastrophes, and dried foods should always be included. When you're housebound in a blizzard, or facing empty shelves at the supermarket because of a hurricane or other natural disaster, you'll be glad to have a supply of wholesome dried foods and ready-to-cook mixes in the pantry or basement.

If there is a baby at your house, you can bypass the expensive jars of baby food on the grocer's shelf by making **homemade baby food** from fresh fruits and vegetables. You will also appreciate knowing exactly what goes into the food you're feeding to your baby, and preparing it yourself is the best way to ensure it meets with your approval. See chapter 8 for instructions on making and using home-dried baby foods.

Campers and backpackers often pack dried foods to save weight and space, and also to avoid the need for refrigeration. Home-dried fruits, vegetables, sauces, and even meats can be used to create a wonderful variety of meals. Dried mixes you pack yourself are far less expensive than commercially packaged freeze-dried foods and can be customized to suit your own tastes and appetites. See chapter 10 for recipes and packing instructions.

Dried foods also make wonderful, unique **gifts**. See chapter 10 for pantry gift ideas including soup, cookies, teas, and other edible goodies from your kitchen. You'll also find instructions for potpourris, sachets, and fragrance jars in chapter 11.

double boiler

cutting board

mason jar

colander

CHAPTER 2

The Basics of Drying Foods

DEHYDRATING, OR FOOD DRYING, is an ancient method of food preservation in which moisture is removed from food so its final water content is generally 10 to 20 percent (depending on the food). Since the goal is to dry rather than to cook, gentle heat is used; most dehydrating is done well below 150°F. Circulating air helps move moisture away from the food; without air movement, the food may spoil before it becomes dry. The basic concepts haven't changed for centuries — but the specific techniques and equipment have.

Until the advent of food dehydrators at the end of the eighteenth century, drying food was a somewhat crude procedure. The food was harvested (or hunted), cut into smaller pieces if necessary, and, in the oldest days, simply set out in the sun to dry; typically it was spread out on mats, hung from poles, or laid on rocks. Sometimes, it was exposed to the smoke and mild heat of a fire, either inside a dwelling or in the open. American Indian tribes near the coasts often soaked fish or meat in salt water before drying, a technique that added flavor and also helped prevent spoilage. As wood- or coal-burning stoves became common in houses, foods were often strung on cords and hung near the stove to dry, which worked well since the stoves often were warm through the night.

The results of these early methods weren't always perfect. Sometimes the food spoiled before it was dry enough to store, or it wasn't quite dry enough and became spoiled during storage. Critters made off with foods that were in the open; sometimes the foods were contaminated with dust and dirt. Dried foods weren't as tasty and enjoyable as fresh foods: many fruits turned brown and became hard, vegetables were often tough and stringy, and meats were so hard that they were almost impossible to chew.

Today, we know a lot more about food safety and have a much better understanding of enzymes, bacteria, and other factors that affect food preservation and storage. Pages 15 and 16 show eight basic steps in modern-day dehydrating, from food selection and preparation, to pretreating, to drying, testing, and storing the finished product. Dehydrating equipment is covered in chapter 3, starting on page 35.

It's impossible to give an exact time for drying foods, regardless of the method used. Total time will be affected by the relative humidity and temperature the day you're drying; moisture content of the food will vary a bit too, and fruits or vegetables that were frozen often seem to contain more moisture than fresh produce. Each dehydrator works just a bit differently, and the more food you put in any dehydrator — manufactured or home-built — the longer it will take to dry everything. If you're sun-drying, you're subject to the vagaries of the weather. A range of times is given for each food in the chapters that follow. Check the food at the shortest time noted, and if it is not yet dry, check every 30 minutes or so, until it is done. Also be aware that some pieces in a batch may dry, more quickly than others; simply remove individual pieces as they are dry and continue drying the rest until all are done.

Drying Foods at Home

Step 1.

Choose fresh, wholesome foods at the proper ripeness. See general information in Food Selection and Preparation (pages 18–20), and information on specific foods in chapters 4 through 8 on Fruits, Vegetables, Herbs and Spices, Meat and Poultry, and Leathers, Baby Food, and Prepared Foods.

Step 2.

Prepare your equipment and any necessary trays, racks, screens, or liners. For specific information, see Manufactured Dehydrators (pages 36–41), Sun-Drying (pages 41–46), Oven-Drying (pages 46–52), and Home-Built Dehydrators (pages 52–67), all in chapter 3. Unless you are sun-drying, you will also need a quick-read thermometer, small remote probe thermometer, or remote probe thermometer (see page 47) that measures temperatures between 90 and 160°F.

Step 3.

Assemble your tools, including sharp knives, cutting boards, a vegetable peeler, a wire-mesh strainer or colander, and clean towels. Depending on your pretreatment methods, you may also need measuring cups and spoons, glass or other nonreactive bowls, a stainless steel or other non-reactive saucepan or pot, tongs, a slotted spoon, kitchen parchment,

and nonstick cooking spray. Also see Storing Dried Foods on pages 29–32 for information about supplies and equipment needed for storing your finished dried foods.

Step 4.

Clean your work surface and wash your hands. Wash all fruits and vegetables, even if they will be peeled later. Prepare the food according to the instructions for each specific food in the chapters listed in step 1, taking care to cut each type of food (apples or carrots, for example) into uniform pieces so the batch dries evenly. If pretreating is recommended, refer to Pretreating Methods on pages 21–26 for detailed instructions.

Step 5.

Spread the prepared food evenly on the trays (or racks, screens, or liners as appropriate) as directed in the specific instructions, keeping space between pieces and avoiding overlaps if possible. As each tray is filled, place it in the dehydrator (or other equipment/method) and start drying. Continue preparing food and filling trays until you have a full load or have prepared all the food you've selected. It is fine to combine different foods of a similar type and size, such as two fruits or vegetables, in the same load; however, don't dry strongly flavored foods such as onions in the same load with mild foods such as fruits.

Step 6.

Once all the trays have been started, make a note of the time and check foods as directed in the specific instructions. Some foods need turning or stirring occasionally during drying; depending on your equipment and method, you may also need to rotate trays and switch positions occasionally as directed in the instructions for each type of equipment or method listed in step 2. Don't add additional fresh food to a load that's been drying for longer than about 30 minutes; moisture from the fresh food may transfer to the partially dried food, increasing the time needed to complete drying. Test foods for dryness at the shortest time indicated in the instructions for each specific food; also see Testing for Dryness and Other Final Steps, on pages 26–28. To check the food, remove a few pieces and allow them to cool to room temperature, then inspect the pieces to see if they pass the doneness test given with each type of food. Dried foods feel softer when they're warm, so it's important to cool the food pieces before judging doneness.

Step 7.

Remove individual pieces of food as they become dry, if practical (particularly when drying slices or large pieces). When all food of one type is dry, condition the dried food as described on page 28; sun-dried food must be pasteurized as described on page 28 after conditioning, and some experts recommend pasteurizing all fruits and vegetables that were dried without peeling, regardless of the drying method used. Wash all your trays, racks, screens, and other equipment after dehydrating each batch of food.

Step 8.

Package the dried, conditioned food as described in Storing Dried Foods on pages 29–32. Store in a cool, dark location, or as directed for individual foods.

Temperatures Used for Dehydrating

When you use a dehydrator or oven to dry foods, you must decide on a *target temperature*, which is the setting you're trying to maintain throughout dehydrating. This is not simply a matter of setting the temperature dial on a dehydrator or oven and forgetting about it, however, because the actual temperature inside the device changes throughout the dehydrating process unless adjustments are made, either by you or by a sophisticated thermostatic control found in a few top-end dehydrators. During the first hour or two, the fresh food is producing a lot of moisture. The moisture-laden air absorbs much of the heat produced by the heating element, and the food doesn't start to warm up until both the air and the food begin to dry; once the air has less moisture, the temperature inside the dehydrator usually rises. In addition, some manufactured dehydrators, and all ovens, cycle on and off, causing fluctuations in the actual temperature. So although you set your dehydrator or oven at, say, 135°F, the temperature inside the device may range from 130 to 140°F — and often, the range is much wider than that.

Most authorities agree that different target temperatures should be used for various types of foods. Meats, for example, are dehydrated at higher temperatures to dry them quickly before they spoil; herbs are dehydrated at very low temperatures to prevent the loss of heat-sensitive oils that give herbs their fragrance and flavor.

In this book, a target temperature of 140 to 145°F is used for meats and poultry. Fruits, which are high in moisture as well as natural sugars, have a target temperature of 135°F. Vegetables are dehydrated at a target temperature of 125°F to prevent "case hardening," premature drying of the outside that prevents the interior from drying properly. Herbs are dehydrated at 100 to 105°F to preserve their fragrant oils. Some people use higher settings for the first hour or two of dehydrating to speed the process.

You may choose to use different target temperatures for other reasons. Perhaps you're using a home-built dehydrator that doesn't reach 145°F. Maybe you're choosing a lower temperature because you want to leave a manufactured dehydrator running overnight and don't want to overdry the food. Temperatures that are 10 to 15 degrees lower than the temperatures recommended here will work fine; it will just take longer than the times indicated. If the temperatures are *too* low, however, the process may take so long that the food begins to spoil before it is dry; this is a particular concern with meat and poultry.

People who follow raw-food diets use a setting of 105 to 110°F for fruits and vegetables to avoid destroying healthful but heat-sensitive enzymes present in the raw food. Although some authorities feel that bacteria present in the food might pose a health risk in foods dried at these low temperatures, raw foodists counter that if the produce has been grown naturally and is well washed before drying, the risk is minimal to nonexistent. Some raw foodists dehydrate food at 145°F for the first few hours, and then reduce the setting to 105–110°F; this method is recommended for raw-food diets by Excalibur, a top manufacturer of box-style dehydrators. The higher starting temperature shortens the drying time, improving safety, and as noted above, the food doesn't reach that temperature because the air is absorbing much of the heat.

Food Selection and Preparation

Just as with canning and freezing, top-quality fresh foods produce the best dried foods. Fruits, vegetables, and herbs to be dried should be picked when they are at their peak of flavor. You'll get better results with produce that's in season and locally grown, rather than buying out-of-season produce that has been shipped in from a faraway state or another country.

Most fruits should be left to ripen thoroughly before picking. Apricots, cherries, peaches, and plums are sweeter and more flavorful when tree-ripened (note, however, that pears are picked when still underripe and kept in cold storage, then removed from storage and ripened as needed). Berries will be plump with flavorful juices if allowed to ripen on the plants.

Unlike fruits, most vegetables are best picked while they are still slightly immature. Harvest beans when the pods are still tender, before the seeds swell. Pick spinach and other leafy vegetables before the leaves reach full size. Most root vegetables should be pulled while still somewhat undersized. Harvest corn before the natural sugars turn to starch, while the kernels are succulent enough to squirt out juice when punctured with the thumbnail. Most vegetables in the cabbage family — including broccoli, cabbage, and kohlrabi — should be picked after the vegetable is well formed, but before it becomes strong tasting; Brussels sprouts, however, are best after the first frost.

In general, the faster a food is dried, the better its quality, but temperatures can't be so high that the food is cooked. To speed drying, the food should be free of surface moisture before dehydrating begins. If you're picking foods from your garden, spray them in the garden the night before to wash them, then pick the next day in late morning, when the sun has dried off the morning dew. If you're drying purchased produce, wash it well and blot dry before proceeding. If foods will be pretreated by soaking prior to dehydrating, keep soaking times to the minimum time recommended. Foods that have been partially cooked by water-blanching or steam-blanching should be well drained before loading onto the dehydrator trays.

Fruits and vegetables with tough skins or rinds should be peeled to permit the air to reach the tender inner flesh. Drying will go more quickly when more of the food surface is exposed to the air. To do this, cut food into smaller pieces: for example, cut strawberries and apricots into quarters, slice apples and zucchini, and cut cabbage into shreds. Use a very sharp blade that slices cleanly; a dull blade bruises the food or makes ragged cuts. A serrated tomato knife does a great job with tomatoes, plums, and other tender, thin-skinned fruits. Use a stainless steel or ceramic knife rather than one made from carbon steel, which may discolor the food. Some vegetables such as onions, carrots, and turnips may be coarsely grated with a food processor or hand-held grater. A food processor does a great job of keeping slices evenly thick. A mandoline is also excellent for quick and even cutting. This specialty kitchen tool looks like a board with a razor-sharp blade in the middle; the food is pushed across the blade with a special pusher, and falls out underneath. Slice thickness can be adjusted easily, and a special insert cuts thin julienne pieces — squared strips that are thicker than shreds, but thinner than anything you're likely to cut by hand. *Always use the blade guard* when slicing on a mandoline.

Hygiene is very important when preparing foods to be dehydrated. Scrub your hands frequently, both before and while handling food. Wash

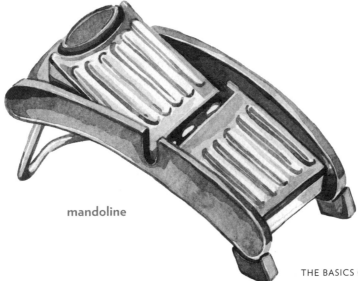

mandoline

cutting boards with hot, soapy water, then rinse them well; it's not a bad idea to spray a solution of ¾ teaspoon chlorine bleach combined with 1 quart of water onto the cutting board, then let it sit for a few minutes and rinse before proceeding. If you have long hair, tie it up (or wear a hairnet) to prevent stray hairs from getting into the food. Wash your hands after touching your hair, sneezing, or coughing. Also make sure that any bowls, spoons, or measuring cups you use are spotlessly clean.

Pretreating

All fruits and vegetables contain *enzymes*, biological catalysts that cause certain reactions to occur. Enzymes cause seeds to sprout and then continue to help the sprout develop a stem, leaves, and so on. Eventually, enzymes cause the edible portion of the plant to mature, or ripen, and this is the stage we're interested in. The enzymes continue to work after the fruit is picked or the vegetable is harvested, however; if this enzymatic action isn't halted, the food will continue to mature, bacteria will grow, and the food will finally decay, a process we call *spoiling*.

Dehydrating foods does not stop enzymatic action completely; like freezing, dehydrating only slows it down. Some dried foods keep well without pretreatment, but others will continue to deteriorate in color, flavor, texture, and nutrients after they are dried unless they are treated before dehydrating. Certain vegetables dried with no pretreatment may become tough and strong-flavored after a period of storage. Without pretreatment, some fruits — apples, apricots, bananas, peaches, pears, and nectarines — darken during drying, and they will continue to darken considerably during storage. While this darkening does not spoil the fruit, it is an indication that there is still enzymatic action at work.

Many vegetables are pretreated before drying, just as they are before freezing, by blanching in boiling water or steam. Blanching is a form of quick, partial cooking; foods are cooked just long enough to halt the natural enzymatic action. Most fruits are not blanched; instead they may be soaked in any of several solutions to prevent enzymatic darkening. Descriptions follow, and the individual fruit listings in chapter 4 include recommendations for pretreatment. Some fruits such as blueberries and cranberries, however, require blanching to *check*, or break, a waxy coating on the skin that prevents moisture from escaping.

Some people prefer to dehydrate foods with no pretreatment. They contend that foods retain more nutrients and digestive enzymes when they are dried without pretreatment, arguing that blanching cooks the foods and that other methods, such as sulfiting, add undesirable chemicals to the foods. Certainly, fruits and vegetables can be dehydrated with no pre-treatment, as long as they are exposed to good air circulation and enough warmth to prevent spoilage before they're fully dry. Darkened fruits and strong-tasting vegetables have been eaten for centuries, and there's no danger in continuing that today; it's a matter of personal preference.

Pretreating Methods

Pretreating methods include blanching; soaking in acidulated water, sulfite solution, or fruit juice; dipping in any of several mixtures; and spraying with lemon juice. These methods will increase the drying time as compared to that for the same foods that have not been pretreated.

BLANCHING

Blanching in steam or water is a method of partially cooking the food, typically just to the point of inactivating the enzymes; as noted, it's also used to break the skins of fruits that have a waxy coating. Steam-blanching preserves more of the food's natural vitamins and minerals than water-blanching, but requires a slightly longer processing period. Water-blanching requires no special equipment.

Syrup-blanching is similar to water-blanching, but a sweetened mixture is used rather than plain water; this is used strictly for fruits (not vegetables). Fruits that have been syrup-blanched are softer and more brightly colored than those pretreated by other methods and are less likely to darken during storage; of all the methods used to pretreat fruits, syrup-blanching is best for producing dried fruits that are similar in texture and appearance to commercially dried fruits. Candying is similar to syrup-blanching, but the sugar solution is more concentrated, producing dried fruit that is much sweeter and firmer; see pages 117–118 for instructions.

Steam-blanching: For best results, use a steamer pan. This specialty piece of cookware looks somewhat like a double boiler, but the upper pan has holes in the bottom. To use for steam-blanching, add about 2 inches of water to the lower pan and place over high heat. Place a thin layer of prepared food in the upper pan, spreading evenly; cover the upper pan tightly. When the water is boiling in the lower pan, position the upper pan over the lower pan and begin timing. Steam for the length of time specified for each food; for blanching times longer than 3 minutes, stir the food once, being careful to avoid the steam that will billow out of the pan when you remove the lid. After blanching, transfer the food immediately to ice water to stop the cooking action. Drain and place on drying trays (or proceed as directed). For high altitudes, add 1 minute to the blanching time specified for each 2,000 feet of elevation above sea level.

A collapsible steamer basket is another option. These consist of a perforated base with legs that hold the food above a shallow layer of water; the base is surrounded by overlapping, fold-in leaves that adjust to fit many pot sizes. It's worth it to shop around for a quality model; the leaves often fall off cheaper models or become difficult to fold in.

As another alternative, you can improvise with a metal colander that sits on top of a deep pot; the base of the colander must be suspended at least 2½ inches above the bottom of the pot. Place a thin layer of prepared food in the colander, spreading evenly; cover the top and sides of the colander with foil, leaving the bottom exposed. Add about 2 inches of water to the pot and heat to boiling over high heat, then place the colander on top of the pot and begin timing as directed above.

Water-blanching: Fill a large pot two-thirds full of water; use about 1 gallon of water per pound of food. Heat the water to a rolling boil over high heat. Place the prepared food in a wire basket and lower into the water, or add the food directly to the boiling water. Cover and boil for the length of time specified for each vegetable or fruit. After blanching, transfer the food immediately to ice water to stop the cooking action. Drain and place on drying trays (or proceed as directed). For high altitudes, add 30 seconds to the time specified for each 2,000 feet of elevation above sea level.

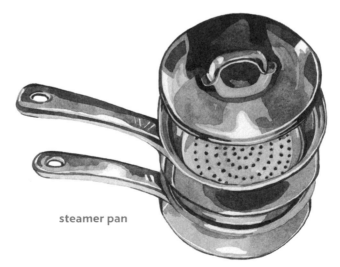

steamer pan

Syrup-blanching: Combine 1 cup sugar, 1 cup corn syrup, and 2 cups water in a nonreactive saucepan (as an alternative to corn syrup, use a total of 1½ cups sugar and 2½ cups water). Heat to boiling, stirring until the sugar dissolves completely. Add the prepared fruit. Adjust the heat so the mixture simmers but does not boil, and cook for the length of time specified in the directions (for high altitudes, add 30 seconds to the time specified for each 2,000 feet of elevation above sea level). Remove the fruit with a slotted spoon and drain; for less sticky dried fruit, rinse briefly in cold water and drain.

This amount of syrup holds 2 to 3 cups of prepared fruit. The syrup can be used for three batches; after that, add a half-quantity of ingredients and heat to boiling before proceeding. If you're syrup-blanching several types of fruit, start with the lightest color first, since the syrup will pick up the color of the fruit and may stain subsequent batches. If you like, you may strain the syrup after you've blanched all your fruit, and refrigerate it to use as a light, fruit-flavored syrup.

SOAKS, DIPS, AND SPRAYS

Soaking in acidulated water: This is a fancy term to describe water that has lemon juice or some other acidic ingredient added to it. To *each quart* of water, add *one* of the following:

- 1 to 3 cups lemon or lime juice (bottled is fine)

- 1 to 3 teaspoons citric acid powder (available at wine-making supply stores and some drugstores)

- 2 to 6 teaspoons ascorbic acid crystals or powder (from the drugstore or health food store)

- 6,000 to 18,000 milligrams of vitamin C tablets, crushed with a mortar and pestle (you may see some white residue in the water; this is from binders used in the tablet manufacture and can be ignored)

Acidulated water reduces, but does not eliminate, browning in apples, apricots, bananas, nectarines, peaches, and pears, as well as in potatoes and turnips. It is not as effective as sulfite (below); just-dried fruits pretreated with acidulated water will be somewhat darker than fruits that were pretreated with sulfite, and the fruits treated in acidulated water will continue to darken during storage. However, acidulated water has less potential to cause allergic reactions and is considered a more natural treatment.

Solutions made with the lowest amount listed for each type of acid will provide some protection against browning, and do not need to be rinsed off. The highest amount provides more protection, but also adds a sour or bitter flavor; you may wish to rinse the food very briefly in cold water after soaking. You may use any amount between the two measurements; try a batch and see what you prefer. Soak the food for 5 to 10 minutes in the prepared solution (or as indicated in the directions for specific fruits), then remove with a slotted spoon and drain well. This amount of solution will hold up to 2 cups of prepared produce. After two or three batches of food have been soaked, add another half-quantity of acid to the water before using again. Discard the solution after using.

Soaking in sulfite solution: Sulfuring is a somewhat controversial treatment method. People with asthma may react adversely to sulfite compounds; others may choose to avoid this chemical for health reasons. Sulfuring is used by commercial fruit producers before drying because the fruit remains soft and vibrantly colored after drying; it also retains its freshness for a long time during storage. Most commercially dried apples, apricots, pears, peaches, and raisins have been sulfured, and sometimes other fruits are sulfured as well. Traditionally, this is done by exposing the fruit to sulfur dioxide fumes produced by burning powdered sulfur. Although this can be done at home, it is a messy, smelly process that can cause respiratory problems. It's easier to soak fruits briefly in a solution containing sodium metabisulfite. This compound is used in most wine to prevent bacterial growth.

Sodium metabisulfite powder is available at stores that sell winemaking supplies and from online sources. Be sure you are not getting sodium bisulfite or sodium sulfite (they are more potent and require different mixing instructions). To prepare the sulfite solution, mix 1 tablespoon of sodium metabisulfite with 1 quart of water, stirring until the powder dissolves. Soak prepared fruit for 5 minutes, or as directed in the individual instructions. Use a slotted spoon to transfer the fruit to a colander; rinse briefly with cold water if you like. Drain and place on drying trays. This amount of solution will hold up to 2 cups of prepared fruit, and may be used for up to four batches on the same day; mix up a fresh batch if you have more than four batches to process. Don't save the solution to use another day; discard it when you're done. Note: If you use sodium metabisulfite, mark the storage containers to indicate that the fruits contain sulfite so anyone who's allergic to it is aware of its presence.

Soaking in fruit juice: Soak prepared fruit for 5 minutes in undiluted pineapple juice or orange juice. Drain and place on drying trays (or proceed as directed). You may soak two batches of fruit in the juice before replacing it with fresh juice. When you're done pretreating, you can drink the juice.

Dipping in pectin: Powdered pectin (found with the canning supplies at the supermarket) can be used to prepare a thin syrup that is used as a dip before drying apricots, bananas, blueberries, cherries, huckleberries, nectarines, peaches, and strawberries. Fruits treated this way retain more of their fresh flavor, color, and texture. To prepare the pectin syrup, stir together 1 box (1.75 ounces) of powdered pectin and 1 cup of water in a saucepan. Heat to boiling over medium heat and boil for 1 minute, stirring constantly. Add ½ cup sugar; continue to cook, stirring constantly, until the sugar has dissolved, 30 to 45 seconds longer. Remove from the heat and stir in 1 cup cold water; stir for about 1 minute longer. Cool completely. Put cleaned and prepared fruit in a mixing bowl and add enough pectin syrup to glaze the fruit with a thin film. Gently stir the fruit to coat each piece with the syrup. Drain well and place on drying trays (or proceed as directed). Store unused syrup in the refrigerator until needed. This amount of syrup treats up to 5 pounds of fruit.

Lightly dipping in honey: Honey contains a compound that works in the same way as the acid in citrus juice to inhibit browning of fruits such as apples, pears, bananas, and, surprisingly, potatoes. The honey dip does not add perceptible sweetness, although the dried foods may have a crisper surface than foods treated with other methods.

Prepare the dip by mixing ½ to ¾ cup honey with 1 quart lukewarm water, stirring until well combined. Dip fruit in small batches and remove with a slotted spoon. Drain well before drying. This amount of solution will hold up to 2 cups of prepared fruit. After two or three batches of fruit have been soaked, add another half-quantity of honey to the water before using again. Discard the solution after using.

Using a commercial fruit protector: If you look on the supermarket shelf with the canning supplies, you'll find commercial products designed to inhibit browning of cut fruit. Fruit-Fresh is one brand; it's a combination of ascorbic acid, citric acid, and dextrose (a type of sugar). Use these products according to the directions on the package. The powder can be sprinkled over fruit or mixed with water and used as a soak. Limit soaking time to no more than 10 minutes, otherwise the fruit will absorb too much water. Drain the treated fruit well and place on drying trays.

Spraying with lemon juice: This one's just like it sounds — simply arrange foods on the dehydrator trays and spray with lemon juice. This pretreatment is simple but adds a tart taste that may not be desirable. Orange juice may also be used, but it has only about one-sixth the citric acid content of lemon juice so is not as effective at reducing browning.

Testing for Dryness, and Other Final Steps

You've chosen produce or other food at the perfect stage, carefully prepared it for drying, and, finally, started dehydrating it by the method of your choice (see chapter 3 for specifics on various dehydrating methods and equipment). But how do you know when it's done?

First, it's important to cool foods to room temperature before you test them for doneness, because the texture is different when the food is still warm from the dehydrator. When you think the food is nearing completion, take a few pieces out of the dehydrator and let them cool for a few minutes. Hold a piece of the cooled food in your hands and compare it to the description noted in this book for each type of food.

In many cases, the description will say that the food should be leathery or supple. This means that the food should be dry on the surface, and you should be able to bend a piece without breaking it. Often, you'll want to cut (or bite) into the thickest portion, and then squeeze it firmly to ensure that no moisture is still present in the center. Some foods are described as brittle when done; this means that a piece will break or snap when you try to bend it. Some listings specify that the food feels springy when pressed. This means that it will yield to pressure and will feel somewhat elastic, bouncing back when you release it; if the food feels squishy rather than springy, it isn't dry enough. If the food fails to pass the doneness test, return the pieces to the dehydrator and check again later. It is always better to overdry food than to underdry it. Note also that individual pieces in a batch of food often dry at different rates. Simply remove pieces as they are done, cool to room temperature, then transfer to a jar and seal it tightly; as additional pieces are done and cooled, continue to add them to the jar until all is done.

Some foods take a long time to dry. If you've been drying the food in a dehydrator or oven all day and the pieces are nearly done when you're ready for bed, you can turn off the dehydrator or oven and just leave the food on the trays; chances are good that it will be done in the morning.

If the food isn't close to done at the end of the day and you are using a manufactured dehydrator, you can reduce the temperature to 90–100°F and let the dehydrator run overnight. This isn't recommended with home-built dehydrators or with most oven-drying. However, if you are oven-drying in a gas oven that has a pilot light, simply turn off the oven and let the food sit in the oven overnight; the warmth from the pilot light will provide enough gentle heat to continue dehydrating at a very slow pace.

Although it's not ideal, you can use a stop-and-start technique if the food has been drying all day but isn't done at night. Sun-drying is a time-tested method that is always done on a stop-and-start basis, since the drying action stops once the sun goes down and foods are brought inside overnight. With other methods, fruits and vegetables generally can be left on the trays overnight at room temperature as long as they are partially dry (however, if you're drying meat, if the weather is extremely humid, or if the food isn't already somewhat dry, it's best to refrigerate the pieces overnight). Ensure that the food is protected from pets; you may also want to put a thin cloth over the trays to discourage insects. Restart the dehydrating process promptly the next morning.

Continuous drying (rather than stopping and restarting) provides the best results and is the best from a food-safety standpoint. Some people who use a manufactured dehydrator prefer to start dehydrating in the evening, allowing the dehydrator to run overnight at lower temperatures; this way, you can check the food in the morning and continue drying if needed during the day, when you'll be around to check the progress. If you run the dehydrator overnight in a remote room, you also avoid having to listen to the dehydrator fan all day.

Conditioning Dried Foods

Before you package and store your dried foods, you must be certain that enough moisture has been removed to make it impossible for mold and bacteria to grow and cause decay. The best way to do this is to place the dried food in a glass jar (with just one type of food per jar) and seal it tightly, and then set it aside at room temperature. Some pieces of the food may be a bit overdry while others might still contain a bit of excess moisture, and when they're all sealed together in a jar, the moisture will equalize so all pieces have the same moisture content. This is referred to as *conditioning* and is really the final step in determining if the food is dry enough.

Place the jar out of direct light and check it every day for three or four days. If you see any moisture beads in the jar, or if the inside of the jar looks hazy, return the entire batch to the dehydrator for a few hours, then cool and try again.

Conditioning is especially important with foods that are somewhat soft when properly dried, because it can be difficult to judge the doneness properly. Fruit — particularly that which is candied or has been syrup-blanched before drying — and jerky may still have too much moisture to store safely, even when you think it is properly dried. Although conditioning takes a few days, it's well worth doing; it's much better to spend a bit of time at this stage than to have to toss out an entire batch of food because it spoiled during storage.

Pasteurizing Dried Foods

After conditioning, sun-dried foods must be pasteurized before storing; some food-safety experts also recommend pasteurizing any fruits or vegetables that were not peeled prior to drying, regardless of the method or equipment used for dehydration. During sun-drying, insects may infiltrate the screens, depositing eggs that are nearly invisible. The heat of sun-drying isn't always enough to kill these eggs, so pasteurizing is used to ensure that the food won't be compromised by insects that hatch during storage. Two methods are used by home cooks to pasteurize dried foods: heat-pasteurization and freezer-pasteurization.

Heat-pasteurization is done in your oven, before the foods are packaged. Heat the oven to 175°F. Spread the food loosely on rimmed baking sheets, or in a loose layer no more than 1 inch deep in a large roasting pan. Bake the food for 15 minutes, then cool completely before packaging.

Freezer-pasteurization is generally done after the foods have been packaged. Foods that have been pasteurized by freezing retain some heat-sensitive vitamins that are lost during heat-pasteurization. For adequate pasteurization, your freezer must reach a temperature of 0°F or below; not all freezers are this cold, so check yours with a freezer thermometer before proceeding. Place the foods, packaged or simply put in freezer storage containers or bags, in the coldest part of the freezer and freeze for 48 hours.

Storing Dried Foods

Airtight, insect-proof containers should be used to store dried and conditioned foods. Glass or plastic jars that have a soft ring inside the lid work best. Feel free to reuse jars that originally held peanut butter, jelly, or other foods; make sure they are absolutely clean and completely dry before using. Although it isn't strictly necessary, you may want to sterilize glass jars and metal lids in boiling water, particularly if you're packaging foods that will be stored for a long time. When packaging a large quantity of dried food, it's wise to divide it up and store it in several smaller batches; that way, if problems develop in a particular batch, you haven't lost the entire amount.

Dried foods will lose color, flavor, and nutrients when exposed to light and heat. *Keep containers in a dark, dry, cool place.* This doesn't mean they need a special storage area. A closed, unheated closet anywhere in the house will serve the purpose; a cool, dry, dark room in the basement is even better. If you're storing foods in an area that receives natural or artificial light, keep glass jars in the dark by inverting a cardboard box over them, or covering them with a bushel basket or a sheet of black plastic. Metal containers keep their contents dark; cookie tins, shortening or coffee cans, and the big metal canisters used for popcorn all work well.

Be sure to label jars and plastic packages with the name of the food and the date it was dried. Create labels on a home or office printer, or simply write the information on a piece of masking tape. If you're packing ready-to-use recipe mixes for camping or gifts (both covered in chapter 10), also list the number of servings in the package and directions for preparing the food. If the dried food was pretreated with a sulfite solution, include that information on the label so anyone who's allergic to sulfites is aware of its presence. When using dried foods, always choose the package with the oldest date on it so that your stock is as fresh as possible.

Electric vacuum-sealing appliances can be used to pack dried foods. The best systems are those that draw out the air with an electric pump, then use a built-in heat strip to seal the special heavyweight bags designed to work with the system. The bags aren't cheap, but they tend to hold the seal better than less-expensive systems that use a hand pump to draw air out of a zipper-style bag that has a permeable round seal. Once sealed, the bags can be stacked in a box for storage. Some vacuum-sealing systems have a flexible hose and a special attachment that can be used to pull the air out of canning jars (or other specialized containers) to create a

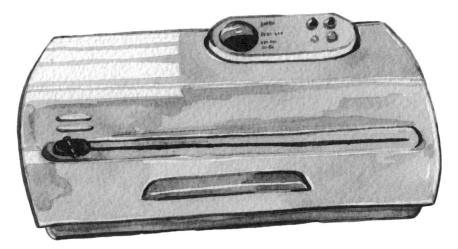

vacuum sealer

vacuum. This greatly extends the shelf life of dried foods, and as a bonus, you can reseal the jars each time you take food out.

Regarding safety and vacuum-packing foods, it should be mentioned that when using vacuum-sealing methods, you must be certain your food is properly dried to prevent the growth of *Clostridium botulinum*, the bacteria that causes botulism, a life-threatening illness. Unlike most other bacteria that cause food spoilage, *C. botulinum* grows in an oxygen-free environment; however, it requires low-acid conditions and adequate moisture. Fruits have enough acid to prevent growth of *C. botulinum* when properly dried, but vegetables and meats are low-acid and therefore more likely to permit growth if not properly dried. If your vacuum-sealed jars have bulging lids, or if there are off odors or other signs of spoilage when you open the jar, *discard the contents without tasting*. Food-safety experts also recommend that all vegetables or meats that have been vacuum-packed — even if they show no signs of spoilage — should be boiled for 10 minutes (plus one additional minute per each 1,000 feet above sea level) before tasting; and if the food has an off odor, appears foamy, or otherwise seems spoiled during cooking, it must be discarded.

Oxygen absorbers are another option that works well with canning jars. These little packets are filled with powdered iron oxide, which absorbs oxygen and creates a vacuum inside the jar (always use a new lid when using oxygen absorbers, so the rubber seal is fresh). Although the iron oxide is inedible, it is harmless when contained in its packet, which is made from food-safe material. Look for oxygen absorbers online or at stores that carry supplies for emergency preparedness; follow the usage instructions that come with the packets. It's best to buy oxygen absorbers in pouches that contain a fairly small number of packets, since each time the pouch is opened, all of the packets will start absorbing oxygen and will eventually lose their effectiveness. Work quickly once the pouch is opened, sealing the jars promptly. Some users transfer unused packets to a small canning jar, sealing it as quickly as possible after opening the pouch. The packets in the canning jar will vacuum-seal the jar shortly after it's closed, and should remain in good shape for future use.

Silica gel is less high-tech than oxygen absorbers, but easier to find. It works by absorbing moisture but it does not create a vacuum. Look for silica gel crystals at florists and hobby shops. For a one-quart canning jar, put about 2 tablespoons of silica gel crystals in the center of a paper coffee filter, then gather the filter around the crystals and tie the neck tightly with kitchen twine. (You can also sew small muslin bags to hold the gel, or use a new child-size 100 percent cotton sock; tie either of these tightly with kitchen twine.) Place the packet on top of the food, and then seal the jar. You can also pack about ½ cup silica gel into a larger cloth bag, then put that into a large storage container that is holding rolled-up plastic bags of dried foods. When you're using silica gel, check the crystals occasionally; if they turn pink, they have absorbed as much moisture as they can hold. Spread them out on a solid liner sheet and dehydrate at 140°F until they turn white, then repack into a clean coffee filter (or repack into the muslin bag or sock). Silica gel is not edible; you may want to put a note on the outside of any container that includes silica gel to alert other people that the crystals are not some sort of seasoning powder!

Freezer-weight food-storage bags can be used to store dried fruits and vegetables, especially for short periods. Pack the dried food into the bags, then roll tightly to expel air before sealing. Watch for any signs of moisture, such as moisture beads or a foggy appearance inside the bags, for the first few days. If moisture appears, either the food is not dry, or the bag was not properly sealed and moisture has entered. If there are no signs of mold, return the food to the dehydrator for further drying (moldy foods should be thrown out). For long-term storage, additional protection is advised when using plastic bags. Once you're sure the food is properly dried, you can store multiple rolled-up bags of food in a larger, tightly sealing canister or jar, perhaps with the large packet of silica gel as noted above. Don't combine packages of onions or any strong-flavored food with other foods, because their flavors will blend. For storage in vacation homes, where insects and critters might be a problem, store the freezer bags inside glass or metal containers with tight-fitting lids.

Because their flavors are easily lost, herbs, herb mixtures, and herb teas are best stored separately in very small containers, such as clean, dry spice jars or vitamin bottles. Be certain, though, that the bottles and lids are odor-free. Herb leaves that are to be used within a few months may be crumbled before storing to save space, but for the best flavor retention in long-term storage, herb leaves should be stored intact, then crumbled just before using. See Storing and Using Herbs in chapter 6 for more information.

Jerky should be cut in serving-size sticks and sealed in jars. Other dried meats may be stored in glass or plastic jars, but the jars should be small because dried meat is a very concentrated food and is used in small amounts. Every time the jar is opened, moisture in the air enters the jar — and the food. It should be remembered, too, that dried meats, including jerky, will keep for only a short period at room temperature because any fat in the meat will turn rancid. For long-term storage, dried meats should be refrigerated or, preferably, frozen. See chapter 7 for additional storage tips.

Fruit and vegetable leathers should be rolled in plastic wrap or waxed paper when they are removed from the dehydrator trays (see page 273 for wrapping tips). Stand the rolls in a glass or metal container — clean, dry coffee cans work well — and seal with a tight-fitting lid. Leathers can also be refrigerated or frozen to retain freshness; bring them to room temperature before eating them.

Large batches of grain may be stored in metal containers that have tightly fitting lids. One to two cups of the grain should be sealed in plastic freezer-weight bags or brown bags and then stacked inside the can. Different grains may be stored in one can, but don't mix packages of grain and other dried foods in one container.

Ready-to-cook mixes for camping and backpacking are best sealed in plastic freezer-weight bags or vacuum bags, both of which are lightweight and waterproof; see Mixes for Camping and Backpacking (pages 315–317) in chapter 10 for more information.

How to Use Dried Foods

Many dried foods are ready to eat as is, as an out of hand snack. Dried fruit is particularly suited to this use and is also used in the dry form in baked goods and other recipes. Some dried, sliced vegetables make unusual and delicious snacks, served plain or with dips; dried zucchini slices are very good, as are cucumber, radish, and parsnip. Dried herbs are ready to use in the same ways you'd use purchased dried herbs. Strips of meat that have been dried to make jerky are typically eaten with no further preparation.

Many dried foods, however, are rehydrated before use. *Rehydrating* is a process that adds water back to the dried food. Most dried fruits or vegetables can be rehydrated by soaking; they are then used much as you would use the fresh produce. The texture of most rehydrated food will be softer, more like cooked or canned food; for example, rehydrated apple slices are tender, not crunchy like a fresh, raw apple. Dried meats, on the other hand, are usually quite firm — often tough — when rehydrated. In addition to soaking, some dried foods can also be added in their dried state to soups and stews; you'll need to add more liquid than you would if using fresh produce, so until you're comfortable with this, it's best to follow recipes written specifically for dried foods.

Rehydrating Dried Foods

Dried foods are generally rehydrated in water. Fruit juice, broth, or other liquids may be used instead; the liquid must be unsalted, because salt slows water absorption. Two methods are used for rehydrating.

Hot-soaking is the quickest method. To hot-soak, place the dried food in a *heatproof* bowl; Pyrex or stainless steel is recommended. Pour boiling water or other boiling liquid over the food just to cover, or as directed for individual foods; some dried foods require additional liquid, and some are better with warm rather than boiling water. Stir and let stand until the food is tender, stirring occasionally. This may take as little as 15 minutes or as long as several hours.

Cold-soaking takes longer because cold water works more slowly than hot water, but fewer vitamins are lost in cold water than in hot. To cold-soak, place the dried food in a bowl or plastic food-storage container, then add room-temperature or cold liquid just to cover, or as directed for individual foods; some require additional liquid. Stir the food, then cover the bowl or container and refrigerate overnight.

The water used for rehydrating contains both flavor and nutrients and makes a great addition to soups, stews, or casseroles. Water from rehydrating fruits is often flavorful enough to drink as a beverage; sweeten to taste if needed.

grapes

raisins

CHAPTER 3

Equipment

WHEN YOU BECOME INTERESTED in dehydrating foods, your first decision will involve the method and equipment you'll use. Although most herbs can be dried at room temperature with no specialized equipment, you'll typically need some supplies or equipment to get started with other foods. Many people do their first "real" dehydrating in their home oven. This allows you to try a batch or two of food with little or no initial investment. Oven-drying is generally not a good long-term solution, however, because it costs more to operate an oven over the extended periods needed for most dehydrating than to operate a manufactured or home-built dehydrator. To calculate the operating cost of a manufactured dehydrator, divide the wattage of the dehydrator by 1,000, and then multiply the result by the local rate per kilowatt hour. For example, a 600-watt dehydrator in a 10-cent-per-kilowatt-hour area would cost 6 cents per hour to run. Oven costs are more difficult to calculate, but as a general rule, an electric oven will cost about twice as much to operate as a dehydrator; gas ovens typically cost less than electric ovens, depending on fuel costs in your area.

Manufactured Dehydrators

Like other kitchen appliances, manufactured food dehydrators for home use are available in several styles, with a variety of features. There are small-batch dehydrators styled for the apartment kitchen, and floor-model dehydrators big enough for the farm garden. The size of the heating element varies from 200 to 1,000 watts or more. Some have built-in fans; others don't.

When purchasing a manufactured dehydrator, you may have to make your choice without seeing the models in a store. Many dehydrators are sold only by mail, not by your local appliance dealer, and few brands offer a no-risk trial period. It isn't even possible to depend on the reputation of a company you know and trust, since you may not be familiar with the companies that manufacture dehydrators.

The good news is that you can find a wealth of information online that compares features and performance of various dehydrators. Manufacturers' websites are just the start; some mail-order companies have extensive comparison charts and even videos showing operation of the different brands and models. Many individuals have also posted online videos that show the techniques they use. All of these can be very helpful in evaluating equipment.

Look for information on materials, construction, the wattage of the heating element, and the power and positioning of the fan. Compare features such as placement of the controls, the number of trays included as well as their size and construction, the footprint of the unit, and the design of the door (if applicable). The food capacity of the unit (the total size of the drying area) is another big factor to consider. Do you want four trays or ten trays in the same footprint? How much food will you be drying? As a rule of thumb, 12 square feet of drying area is sufficient for a half-bushel of vegetables. Also check into warranties offered, considering not only the length of the warranty but how problems will be resolved. If you have to pay to ship a defective unit back, and then wait several months for the repaired unit to be returned, you may miss the entire harvest season.

A quality dehydrator has an adjustable heater, preferably one designed to operate at controlled temperatures between 90 and 150°F. Consider the design and placement of the heat controls; some dehydrators position them in a location that might be difficult to access in your specific situation. A three-prong plug ensures proper grounding and safety. Also look for the Underwriters Laboratories (UL) seal. Found on either a hangtag or decal, the UL seal means the appliance has met the Laboratories' safety standards and that it is safe from fire and shock hazard. Some manufactured dehydrators also have an automatic shutoff device in case the unit overheats or suffers an electrical malfunction.

Trays in manufactured dehydrators are generally plastic, with solid rims around an open grid that allows warm air to flow through, carrying moisture away from the food. Some trays are designed with grids that are close enough to allow you to put sliced food directly on the grid without danger of it falling through. Others have widely spaced grids that always require the use of mesh liner sheets (screens), which have a grid with about ⅛-inch spacing. Most manufactured dehydrators include screens; even models that can hold sliced foods directly on the trays will require screens for berries and foods that are cut into smaller pieces.

For making leathers (roll-ups) or dehydrating other loose mixtures, solid liner sheets are required. These are generally sold as an add-on item, and it's a good idea to purchase a few that are designed specifically for your dehydrator model when you're starting out. Both the solid and the mesh liner sheets (screens) are washable and reusable, and with proper care they should last as long as the dehydrator. Trays, screens, and solid liner sheets are generally dishwasher-safe.

The size of the unit, the constant noise of the fan, and the humidity added to the air in an already humid room can be a little overpowering in a small kitchen. Most manufacturers' directions specify that their dehydrators should not be used outdoors, but you might be able to find a spot on an enclosed back porch, in a utility room, or even in a spare bedroom. A small utility table on casters is ideal for holding a dehydrator and for moving it from one room to another.

Manufactured dehydrators for home use come in two styles: those with stackable trays, and those that are solid boxes with removable trays. Here's some information that compares the differences, as well as the strengths and weaknesses, of each design.

Stackable-tray dehydrators are the easiest to find and can often be inspected at large discount stores, cookware shops, and discount farm-supply stores. They are composed of individual plastic trays that stack on top of one another; most models have round trays, but some have square trays that make more efficient use of the space. The stacked trays rest on a base unit that typically contains a heating element and a fan, although some models have the heating element and fan in the top. (Do not even consider models that don't have a fan; these units, although very inexpensive, are inadequate because moving air is critical to proper dehydrating.) Units with top-mounted elements are nice because if food pieces fall between the grids on the tray, or if liquids drip, they land on a smooth base plate that's easy to clean. Dehydrators with the elements in the base have openings in the base for ventilation and heat, and if food falls into the openings, the base can be difficult to clean.

A big advantage to stackable models is that they are expandable. Most come with four to six trays, and you can purchase additional trays to increase the capacity of the dehydrator, simply stacking them up. A disadvantage to stackable models is that the heated air must blow through the trays closest to the elements before reaching the other trays. Quality stackable dehydrators are designed with vents in the rims to move fresh air over each tray, but they are still generally less efficient than solid-box styles,

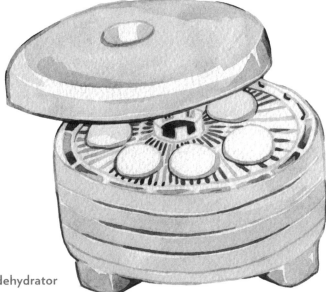

stackable-tray dehydrator

which have the elements mounted on the back wall so that fresh heated air blows horizontally across all trays. With stackable models, you may have to rotate the trays from top to bottom several times during dehydrating to ensure that all trays are exposed to the full heat and ventilation. Solid liner sheets also impede airflow, so if you plan to make a lot of fruit leathers or to dehydrate foods such as thick soups and sauces, you may find that a box-style model is a better choice.

Solid box-style dehydrators are rigid cabinets with a door for access; the trays slide in from the front. They can be difficult to find in stores, so you may have to buy one without seeing it in person. They are also more expensive — often a *lot* more expensive — than stackable models, and hold only a set number of trays. With box-style dehydrators, the fan and heating element are generally mounted on the inside back wall of the unit, so fresh heated air blows across all trays rather than through a stack of trays as with stackable models. Most box-style dehydrators have plastic walls and trays; others have metal components, and some are entirely built from stainless steel. (Never consider aluminum or galvanized metal for dehydrator trays; these corrode from acids in food and also can leach chemicals into the food during drying.)

Box-style dehydrators are generally more efficient and easier to regulate than stackable models; many models are also insulated to prevent heat loss. With well-designed models, you can dehydrate a full batch of food without rotating the trays, making them a good choice if you plan to run

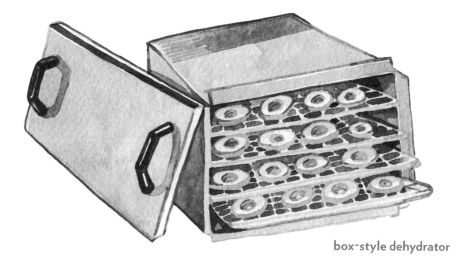

box-style dehydrator

the dehydrator overnight or when you're away from the house. They are usually bulkier than stackable units and take up more countertop space. As noted, they hold only a set number of trays so the capacity can't be expanded as it can with stackable dehydrators. Another point to consider is the rigidity of the trays; some are flimsy and can twist or bend when loaded with food, making it difficult to slide them into the dehydrator. Look for solidly constructed trays that are at least 1 inch apart.

Tips for Using a Manufactured Dehydrator

When you buy a manufactured dehydrator, read through the enclosed manual, but take some of the advice with a grain of salt. Here are some suggestions to help you produce top-quality dehydrated foods.

- The best temperature for dehydrating specific foods may not be the one recommended by the manufacturer. For example, if you're dehydrating foods for a raw-food or living-food diet, you will want to keep the temperature at 118°F or below, regardless of what the manufacturer recommends. You may have other reasons for using a temperature that's different from what's recommended by the manufacturer — or what's recommended in this book. Keep notes of temperatures used and the results produced as you gain experience in dehydrating, and let that be your guide.

- Don't rely on the dehydrator's temperature setting. The dial may be set to, say, 135°F, but the dehydrator may actually be running anywhere from 120 to 150°F. Factors that may affect the actual temperature include the amount of food you've placed in the dehydrator, the room air temperature, the quality of the dehydrator's heat source, and the accuracy of its thermostat. Insert the stem of a small remote probe thermometer or a remote probe thermometer into an opening, or slip it between the trays. Check the temperature after the dehydrator has been running for about 20 minutes, and then adjust the setting if necessary. Continue to check it periodically throughout drying, if possible, because the actual temperature changes as the food loses moisture (warm air holds more heat than cool air). Be aware also that some manufactured dehydrators cycle frequently from higher to lower heat, so you may see fluctuations due to that. Either adjust the setting so the actual operating temperature never exceeds your top limit, or go for an average of the high and low temperatures (for example, a range of 130 to 140°F averages to 135°F).

- Don't automatically follow the manufacturer's advice if it says you don't need to rotate trays or move foods around. The first few times you use your new dehydrator, check the food on the trays every hour or two. You may find that the food is drying unevenly from tray to tray or even within the same tray. Trust the evidence of your senses. If the food is drying unevenly in a stackable-tray dehydrator, periodically switch positions of the trays, moving the top tray to the bottom of the stack each hour so that all trays spend time directly next to the heat source. If food is drying unevenly in a box-style dehydrator, periodically rotate trays from front to back and also move them from top to bottom. With either style, move individual pieces of food from the center of the trays to the edges if foods are drying unevenly on individual trays. (On the other hand, if you're lucky you may discover that your dehydrator really does produce even heat and ventilation, and you won't have to fiddle around moving trays!)

- Some manufacturers' screens and solid liner sheets have a very slick surface that cleanly releases even sticky foods. Others are not so easy to work with. If you find that fruits or other foods tend to stick to the trays, screens, or liner sheets, simply coat them lightly with nonstick cooking spray. Always use nonstick cooking spray when drying syrup-blanched or candied fruits.

Sun-Drying

Sun-dried fruits are delicious; indeed, most raisins you buy in the store have been sun-dried, and commercial producers also sun-dry apricots, peaches, and other fruits. If you are blessed with clean air, low humidity, and an abundance of hot, sunny days, sun-drying is the least expensive method of dehydrating fruits (chapter 4) and leathers (chapter 8). The advantages to sun-drying are obvious. The energy of the sun is absolutely free, requiring no outlay for electricity. There is no investment in equipment and just a handful of other expenses, since all the necessary materials can be assembled at home. Unlike other drying methods, there is no capacity limit in sun-drying. The only limit to the amount of food that can be dried at one time is the number of trays available and space to set them.

For reliable sun-drying at home, daytime temperatures must be 90°F or above and the relative humidity must below 60 percent — the lower, the better. If the temperature is too low, the humidity too high, or both, spoilage will occur before the foods are adequately dry. The Southwest region of the United States has an ideal summer climate for sun-drying, but other regions are not so fortunate; for example, sun-drying should not be attempted in the humid Southeast. Summer conditions in the Northwest, Midwest, and Northeast are better but may still be marginal. Even if your location is marginal, however, you can use the sun when conditions are good, then fall back on a dehydrator or the oven to finish off a batch on those days when a sudden rainstorm or a low cloud ceiling hampers your sun-drying operation.

Although sun-drying vegetables, meats, and fish is a technique that was used for centuries, modern food science tells us that sun-drying at home should be used only for fruits, which are high in natural acids and sugar. (The exception to this is hot chile peppers, which can simply be strung together and hung in the sun; see page 184 for details.) Instructions are not given in this book for sun-drying vegetables, meats, or fish; should you choose to do so, the basic techniques are the same as those used for fruits. Remember that tomatoes are a fruit — not a vegetable — so they are safe for sun-drying.

To dry fruit in the sun, you'll need drying trays and something to cover the fruit to protect it from insects and dirt. Baking sheets or homemade wooden trays may be used as drying trays, but drying is much more efficient if air can circulate freely around the fruit. Wooden frames covered with screens or other mesh-type material are a better choice. Many people use window frames that are being removed during remodeling projects;

ALTERNATIVE SPACES FOR SUN-DRYING

If you have a greenhouse, solarium, or sun space that isn't currently filled with plants, you can set up drying trays inside it. The food will be protected from critters, and the clear roof allows plenty of sunlight in. As with all sun drying, if the weather turns cloudy or rainy, you may have to finish drying in a dehydrator or your oven.

Some people also put small amounts of food on trays, or even baking sheets, and then place them in the back window of an automobile that won't be moved for a few days.

these can be cleaned up and fitted with new screens to use as your drying trays. If the windows date to 1978 or earlier, however, they may be painted with lead-based paint and should not be used unless you can confirm that the paint is lead-free. You can also make simple wooden frames, sealing the wood with food-grade mineral oil for durability.

The weight of the fresh food will cause large screens to sag, so keep openings fairly small — a foot square, or slightly larger — when building frames. For larger openings in existing frames, screw wooden strips into the frames at 2- to 4-inch intervals, or add a network of criss-crossed twine to the frame for additional support, stretching it tightly and stapling it to the frame before adding the screen.

Choosing material for the screens is the most challenging part of building the drying frames. Polypropylene screening sold for use in manu-factured dehydrators is the ideal choice, but you'll probably have to mail-order it; search online for "dehydrator screens" and look for polypropylene that is sold in rolls or rectangular pieces. Material used for replacement window screens is available at any big-box home center and most hard-ware stores, but not all of it is safe to use for food. *Never* use aluminum or galvanized screening or hardware cloth; these metals react with acids in fruits and will contaminate your dehydrated products. Nylon, plastic, and stainless steel screens are often available, but it can be hard to determine if they're food-safe. The National Center for Home Food Preservation at the University of Georgia reports that Teflon-coated fiberglass window screen is safe for use in sun-drying racks; if the Teflon coating gets damaged, however, the fiberglass may shed minute particles, so keep an eye on it. As a final option, you can use a double layer of fine-mesh nylon fabric netting. This inexpensive material is sold by the yard at fabric stores (it is used for crafts, particularly for making "scrubbies" for dishwashing and shower-ing). Nylon netting needs more support than other materials and is a bit more difficult to wash if it is permanently attached to the frames (however, if it's simply lying on another screen that's used for support, the netting can be removed and washed in the washing machine).

Stretch your screening material tightly over the frames and staple it in place; if using nylon netting, roll-fold the edges so you're stapling through a heavier layer. You'll have to wash the screens with a hose and soft brush after each use, and if you're not careful you can easily pull out the staples or rip the material. For additional security, nail strips of wooden molding over the edges of the screens.

Because sun-drying takes days rather than hours, the fruit will be exposed to potential bacterial growth for a longer period of time, so pre-treating is more important than when drying in a dehydrator. Pretreating instructions are found in chapter 2, and recommendations for individual types of fruit are included in chapter 4.

After pretreating, spread the fruit in a single layer over the drying trays and place them in a well-ventilated spot in full sun. The trays need to be raised off the ground for ventilation and cleanliness; it's also easier to tend to the trays when they're not down on the ground. Cement blocks work well as supports; so do benches, sawhorses, or stacked bricks. If you have large sheets of aluminum or tin, lay them on the ground under the raised trays; the sunlight will reflect off the metal and radiate back up to the trays. A concrete surface also provides some radiant heat.

The trays must be covered with a layer of material that lets light and moisture pass through but keeps out insects, twigs, dust, and other unwanted materials. The easiest option is to set another screen-covered tray of the same dimension on top of the one that is holding the fruit; set the top tray upside-down to prevent its screen from touching the fruit. If there are gaps between the frames of the two trays, weight the corners with bricks to keep them pressed together tightly.

Another covering option is to drape open-weave fabric over the entire tray, propping the fabric up so it isn't resting directly on the fruit and wrapping it around the edges so insects can't sneak through gaps in the side. Cheesecloth is often recommended for this use, but it can be difficult to work with because it gets caught on rough surfaces, unravels and leaves threads on the fruit, and wads up into a hopeless ball when laundered. Fine-mesh nylon netting discussed above is a better choice; it's cheap, doesn't fray, and doesn't tangle up during washing. If the netting seems too open and insects are able to get through, use a double layer.

Stir or turn the pieces of fruit several times a day (or as directed in the instructions for specific fruits in chapter 4) to expose all surfaces to the sun. Take the trays inside at night to prevent the fruit from absorbing moisture from dew and to discourage nocturnal critters.

All drying times given in chapter 4 for sun-drying specific fruits are rough estimates, since the time required will vary depending on the temperature, the amount of sunshine, the humidity in the air, the amount of air movement, and the amount of moisture in the food. Any time out of the sun, of course, is "down time" and is not included in the drying-time estimates. Sun-dried fruit should always be pasteurized as described on page 28 to kill any minute insect eggs that may have been deposited on the fruit while it was outside. Also be sure to wash your drying screens and any fabric you used to cover them.

Tips for Sun-Drying

- You may want to try sun-drying a test batch of fruit to see how it works in your area. For a quick and easy setup, use a cake-cooling rack set over a rimmed baking sheet rather than worrying about building a large screen. Place your prepared fruit on the rack, using a screen, cheesecloth, or nylon netting if necessary to keep it from falling through. Wrap cheese-cloth or nylon netting over the setup to keep out insects, propping it up with jars, cans, or blocks of wood to prevent it from touching the fruit.

- If you do use wooden trays, sand them well and seal them with food-grade mineral oil; also note that the odors of such woods as pine and cedar will transfer to the food being dried on them.

- You may be able to buy a used dehydrator that no longer works at a yard sale or online auction site and then use the trays for sun-drying. After

cake-cooling rack set over a rimmed baking sheet

adding the fruit, cover the trays with screening material as described above.

- If you're using cheesecloth to cover your drying trays, buy it at a fabric store. The material will be wider than the kind sold in small packages at the supermarket, and it will also cost a *lot* less per yard.

- To intensify the sun's heat, prop a pane of glass above the drying tray, allowing enough room for adequate ventilation. Take precautions to prevent the glass from getting bumped or knocked off, and remember that the edges may be quite sharp. For even more efficiency, combine the pane setup with the aluminum reflectors mentioned above.

Oven-Drying

Some modern ovens have a built-in convection system in which a fan circulates the air inside the oven, speeding cooking time and reducing hot spots to provide more even baking. Most convection ovens have a special cycle for dehydrating, and can be set to run at temperatures as low as 100°F. If you're lucky enough to have an oven like this, you can use it just like a manufactured dehydrator. All you'll need are racks to hold the food and a thermometer to monitor the temperature. Follow the instructions that came with your oven; also see Setting Up Your Oven on the following page for more information.

Most ovens, however, don't have convection and are not the best choice if you plan to do a lot of dehydrating. For one thing, most use more energy than a dehydrator, and few have more than three racks so the amount of food you can dehydrate at one time is limited. Many can't be set at the low temperatures used for most dehydrating, so they cook the food rather than dehydrating it. The oven also needs to run for many hours, heating up the kitchen and preventing you from using it for other cooking (this applies to convection ovens, too). Finally, non-convection ovens lack a good method to circulate the air, which is critical to proper dehydrating.

However, if you're just getting started with dehydrating and want to try it without investing in new equipment, you can use your non-convection oven for foods that don't require lengthy dehydrating times; the oven is also a good backup if the weather turns foul when you're sun-drying. If your oven can't be set to 150°F or below, however, it really isn't suitable for dehydrating unless you're willing to turn it off frequently (and back on, after it cools) to keep it from getting too hot.

Setting Up Your Oven

First, you'll need something to hold the food. Suggestions for racks and screens are given in Racks for Oven-Drying or Home-Built Dehydrators on page 50. Once you have racks and screens figured out, you need just a few more things to complete your setup; except for the fan, these instructions apply to both convection and non-convection ovens.

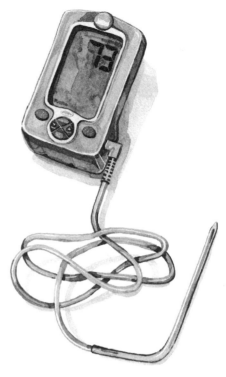

A thermometer is necessary to monitor the actual oven temperature. Don't rely on the temperature setting of your oven, as it may not be accurate (especially at the lower temperatures used for dehydrating). You'll also have the door propped open a bit, and this might cause the temperature to vary from that indicated on the controls. A **remote probe-type thermometer** is the best choice; these handy gadgets have a metal temperature probe connected to a thin, strong cable that plugs into a readout that sits outside the oven. If you don't have a remote probe thermometer, it's worth the relatively small investment to get one; you'll find it useful for lots of other cooking and grilling chores as well. You could also use a standard oven thermometer — a metal-cased thermometer with a stand that allows it to sit on the oven rack — but these are more difficult to read, typically requiring you to open the door to check the temperature (and thus losing your heat).

You'll also need something to hold the oven door open an inch or two, to allow moist air to escape. A ball of foil can be used; a clean, empty flat can like that used for tuna fish or canned pineapple works great too. If you're drying in a standard (non-convection) oven, you'll also need a fan of some sort, and a stool to set it on so it's blowing into the slightly open oven door.

Whether you have a convection or standard oven, it's a good idea to turn the oven on and let the temperature stabilize before you prepare the food to be dehydrated; you may have to adjust the temperature setting several times before it settles in at the level you want. To get started, position your thermometer. If you have a remote probe model, place the probe onto a middle shelf and position the readout next to the oven (not inside it!); if you are using a standard oven thermometer, place it on the edge of a middle shelf. Prop the door slightly open with the ball of foil or the flat can, positioning

oven door and thermometer position

it so it will depress the oven light switch when the door is closed; the door should be open by a gap of an inch or a bit more. Turn the oven on to your desired temperature; if you're using a standard (non-convection) oven, position the fan so it is blowing towards the opening on one side.

Monitor the temperature for at least 20 minutes. Ovens cycle on and off frequently; this cycling is less noticeable when the door is closed in normal operation, but will be more frequent during dehydrating because the door is slightly open (and the fan, if you have a standard oven, is blowing warm air out the gap on the other side). Don't be surprised if you need to adjust the temperature setting. The actual temperature will vary as the oven cycles but should be as near as possible to your desired temperature.

Once you have the setting adjusted so the temperature is within your range, prepare the food and place it on the racks, using screens if necessary. Place the racks on the oven shelves; it's also a good idea to place an empty baking sheet on the lowest rack or the bottom of the oven to catch any drips or food that may fall off the racks. Check the temperature after about 15 minutes and adjust if necessary.

Ovens dry more unevenly than do dehydrators. The thick walls retain and radiate heat, so pieces around the edges of the trays will dry more quickly than those in the middle; the temperature at the top of the oven is also different from that at the bottom. When oven-drying, it's important to switch positions of the racks every hour or two, also rotating them from front to back. You should also reposition food on the trays occasionally, moving pieces from the center to the edges and vice versa. Monitor and adjust the temperature periodically to maintain your desired temperature.

If the food is not completely dry at the end of the day, you may simply turn the oven off, leaving the trays in place with the oven door still propped open a bit. If you need to remove the trays from the oven, place them on a countertop, allow to cool, and cover loosely with a towel until the next day. You may find that the food is fully dried by morning. (Note that meat or foods that are still fairly moist should be refrigerated overnight.)

Convection ovens with a dehydrating setting work well, and drying times will be similar to those listed for dehydrators. Non-convection ovens are less predictable. Because situations vary so widely, this book provides only very broad guidelines for the time it might take to dehydrate foods in a non-convection oven. If your setup is efficient, with well-controlled temperatures and good ventilation, your drying times will be similar to those listed for dehydrators. On the other hand, it may take close to twice as long in your non-convection oven than it would in a dehydrator. Keep notes when you dehydrate in your oven; eventually you'll know if your oven-drying time is likely to be similar to the times listed for dehydrators — or a lot longer.

Note: Foods that take longer than 18 hours to dry are not recommended in a non-convection oven.

Tips for Oven-Drying

- For sturdy drying racks, look at appliance-recycling outlets for used oven racks that are a bit smaller than your oven; they are usually cheap or even free. Add nylon netting or screens as described on page 43; you could also sew a pillowcase-style cover from nylon netting.

- Oven-drying may not be suitable for homes with small children or large pets. The open oven door can be dangerous for toddlers.

- Most standard-size ovens will hold about 5 pounds of fresh food, so they aren't the best option for large-scale dehydrating.

Racks for Oven-Drying or Home-Built Dehydrators

Whether you're dehydrating in your oven or using a home-built dehydrator, you'll need racks to hold the food. Baking sheets can be used, but they are inefficient because the air circulates only on the top side. Metal cake-cooling racks are a better choice; these allow circulation from both the top and the bottom. The best racks have two sets of bars that cross at right angles to form a grid, which is better at preventing foods from falling between the bars (however, racks with only parallel bars can also be used). Ideal bar spacing, whether your racks are grid-style or parallel, is ½ inch or less. If your racks have wider spacing, you can set two racks on top of one another, offsetting the top one slightly to make narrower gaps (use wire or twist ties to secure the racks together in this position). Another option that works with small square racks is to lay one rack on top of another at a right angle, creating a grid. You can also add screens to widely spaced racks as described below.

Some foods will fall through even ½-inch spacing, so you'll need to add a screen. The best option is to buy polypropylene mesh that is made for use in manufactured dehydrators. Search online for "dehydrator screen" and you'll find numerous choices. Buy either roll material that can be cut or precut rectangular pieces; the circular screens made for round dehydrators don't work well with square or rectangular racks. Clip the screens to your racks with small metal binder clips from the office supply store.

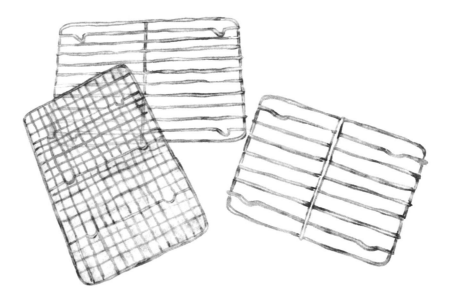

Another screen option is nylon fabric netting, which can be purchased very cheaply by the yard from a fabric store. It is sold for crafts, and is often used to make "scrubbies." Buy the kind that's safe to iron, which means it will stand up to the mild heat of dehydration. The netting is easy to wash by hand or in the machine, and the edges won't fray. Cut a piece that's as wide as your rack is long and almost three times as long as the depth of your rack (so for an 18- by 12-inch rack, cut a piece that's 18 inches wide and about 30

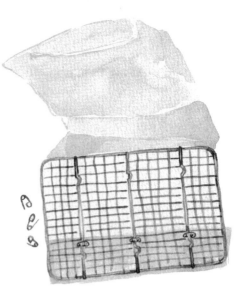

inches long). Place the rack upside down on the netting, with a 3-inch band of netting towards you. Fold the edge of the band over so you have about an inch of double netting, then use three safety pins to secure it to the rack, stretching it taut. Roll the rack over twice so it's covered with a double thickness of netting and the bottom side is again facing you. Pull the netting taut, then fold the edge and pin it. A double layer of cheese-cloth may be used in the same way as the nylon netting, but it is harder to work with; it clumps up, sticks to many foods, and frays during handling and washing.

Material sold for window screening works great — if you can find the right type. See page 43 for more information on window screening. Cut the screening material to the same size as your rack, tape the edges with freezer tape if necessary for protection from scratches, and use metal binder clips around the edges to hold the screen in place on the rack.

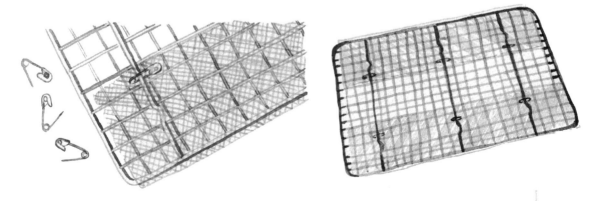

When drying blueberries, cranberries, and other round foods that might roll off the racks, place strips of clean, unpainted wooden screen molding around the edges of the trays and use binder clips to secure them in place, creating a small railing.

Another option that works really well for home-built dehydrators is to buy a used manufactured dehydrator that no longer works at a yard sale or online auction site, and then use the trays. These are really nice because they have edges that prevent the foods from rolling off and will generally have mesh liner sheets so you don't have to worry about screening materials. If you're using your oven as a dehydrator, it's probably not a good idea to use plastic trays from a manufactured dehydrator. Ovens may cycle briefly to a temperature that's too hot for the plastic trays.

For fruit leathers or other loose foods, you'll need solid sheets; see Solid Sheets to Hold Purées on page 272.

Home-Built Dehydrators

There are numerous ways to build a homemade dehydrator; search online and you'll find many ideas. When considering plans, remember that the two most important factors are appropriate heat and adequate moving air; one without the other is not a recipe for success. You'll find many plans that rely on a bank of incandescent 100-watt lightbulbs to produce the necessary heat, but these lightbulbs have been phased out and replaced with other styles that don't generate as much heat.

It should be pointed out that home-built dehydrators can be bulky and may be as expensive as a manufactured stacking-tray dehydrator if you have to buy all the materials. However, if you have room for a somewhat large box, can scrounge up some of the materials, and enjoy building things, a home-built dehydrator might be a good project.

In the following pages, you'll find plans for a dehydrator that I designed, built, and tested for this book (for simplicity I'm going to slip into first-person mode here). Dimensions are based on full-size (13- by 18-inch) cake-cooling racks and baking sheets; you can adjust the dimensions to suit your own cookware. (See Racks for Oven-Drying or Home-Built Dehydrators on page 50 for information.) The heat source is a 250-watt heat lamp, the same as those used in bathroom fan/light fixtures. These were readily available at home centers and hardware stores at the time of this writing and are not currently part of the phase-out program.

If these become unavailable in the future, other heat sources such as halogen lights may be used but will require some experimentation.

Airflow is provided by a computer case-cooling fan, available from stores that sell computer components or electronic gadgets; these fans are also used to cool media cabinets and are available at stores specializing in audio/video components. (You might be able to pick up a used case-cooling fan for little to nothing from a computer-repair shop.) These fans are small and quiet, and most are designed to work at temperatures of 150°F or higher, so they are a better solution than a small tabletop fan that's not designed to stand up to the heat. Look for a fan with high air-flow; the one I used is rated at 65 cfm and it works really great.

The dehydrator shown on the following pages holds five racks, contained in a box built from ¼-inch plywood. To hold the drying racks and baking sheets, I used pairs of ½-inch wooden dowels, which slip through holes drilled in the sides of the box; the racks and sheets that hold the food sit on top of the dowels. The dowel setup also allows me to use small racks and bakeware as well as my full-size ones.

Home-Built Dehydrator

GENERAL MATERIALS

- 8-inch square metal (non-Teflon) baking pan (for heat shield; see p. 67)
- Four nail-on nylon glide feet, ½ inch thick
- Computer case-cooling fan, preferably AC powered (see note, opposite)
- 250-watt incandescent heat lamp (for dehydrating above 120°F, buy a 375-watt heat lamp instead)
- One probe-style thermometer
- Twenty medium-weight rubber bands
- One 3-foot-long piece of strong kitchen twine
- Heavy-duty aluminum foil
- Freezer tape or duct tape

ELECTRICAL

- 4-inch metal octagonal electrical box, 1½ inches deep (for the lamp holder)
- 4-inch metal 2-gang square electrical box, 1½ inches deep (for the dimmer switch)
- Rectangular metal 1-gang electrical box, 1½ inches deep (for the fan wiring)
- Five screw-in clamp connectors for NM cable*
- One ½-inch EMT (electrical metallic tube) screw-in box connector
- About 2 feet *each* of plastic-sheathed 14/3 and 14/2 NM cable*
- One 14/2 (with ground) power tool replacement cord (with male plug on one end and stripped wires on the other), length as desired
- Wire nuts as needed
- Push on-off dimmer switch and matching face plate
- Porcelain keyless lampholder (a light socket with a wide circular base)
- 4-inch-square metal 1-gang cover plate (for the dimmer switch)
- Rectangular metal 1-gang cover plate (for the fan wiring)

BUILDING MATERIALS

- One 4x8 sheet of ¼-inch plywood
- Four 4-foot lengths of ¾-inch-square (actual dimension) pine or other wood molding
- Five 4-foot lengths of ½-inch round pine dowels
- One 2-foot length of ¾-inch quarter-round pine molding

FASTENERS

- 50-count box of #6 x ¾-inch zinc construction screws
- Four #8-32 x 2-inch zinc machine screws (to hold the heat shield above the light)
- Twelve #8-32 zinc machine screw nuts (for the heat shield)
- Twelve #6-32 x ¾-inch zinc machine screws (to attach the electrical boxes)
- Twelve #6-32 zinc machine screw nuts (for the electrical boxes)
- Three #10-32 x ⅜-inch green hex-head grounding screws (to fit into the electrical boxes)
- Four 3-inch zinc machine screws that fit through the mounting holes in your fan (mine required #8-32 screws)
- Four washers and twelve machine screw nuts compatible with the 3-inch machine screws

Note: If your case-cooling fan is DC powered, you'll also need a DC-to-AC power converter. These are available at stores that sell computer components or electronic gadgets; if you're handy with electrics, you can use an old power converter from a small electronic device. For simplicity, run the fan's power cord out through a hole in the box and plug it into the converter outside the dehydrator, then plug the converter directly into a wall outlet rather than trying to wire the fan and converter into the light socket as shown in the plan here.

---

* If you're skilled with electrical work, you may choose to use flexible metal conduit to contain the wires between the electrical boxes. Doing so would improve the safety of the dehydrator (see page 67). If using conduit, replace the clamp connectors with EMT screw-in box connectors; also replace the 14/3 NM cable with individual insulated wires and the 14/2 NM cable with stranded wire.

Assembling the Home-Built Dehydrator

I've made the assumption that anyone building this has basic carpentry skills, as well as a working knowledge of basic electrical wiring. If you don't feel comfortable with these procedures — particularly the electrical work — get help from someone who does. Standard building tools are required, including a measuring tape, carpenter's square, circular saw, power drill and bits, clamps, screwdrivers, wrenches or pliers, wire stripper, and wire cutter. Study the diagrams on pages 58–60 before beginning to be sure you understand the construction.

18 inches	18 inches	18.5 inches	18.5 inches	Preliminary cuts
side 18 x 24	side 18 x 24	top 18.5 x 24.25	bottom 18.5 x 25.25	
				scrap wood
back 18 x 18.5		door 18.5 x 18.25		

Cutting Diagram

Step 1.

Cut the plywood according to the cutting diagram. Cut the square molding into four 24-inch lengths and four 16½-inch lengths. Cut the dowels into 20½-inch lengths; you will have a total of 10. Cut the quarter-round molding to 18½ inches in length. Sand the ends of all molding and dowels.

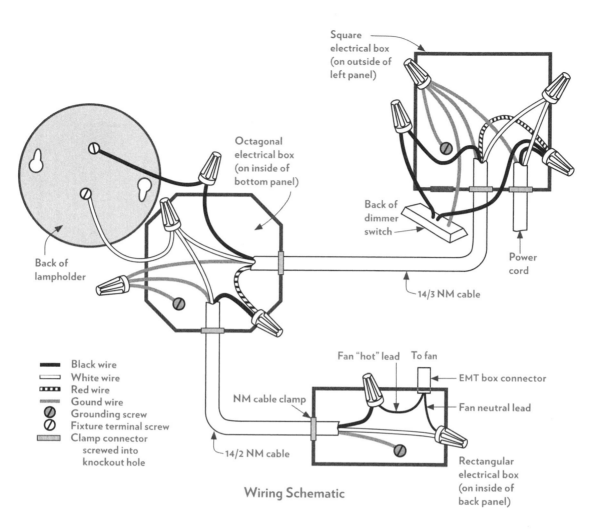

Square electrical box (on outside of left panel)

Octagonal electrical box (on inside of bottom panel)

Back of dimmer switch

Power cord

14/3 NM cable

Back of lampholder

Fan "hot" lead   To fan

EMT box connector

NM cable clamp

Fan neutral lead

— Black wire
▭ White wire
▥ Red wire
▦ Gound wire
⊘ Grounding screw
⊘ Fixture terminal screw
▥ Clamp connector screwed into knockout hole

14/2 NM cable

Rectangular electrical box (on inside of back panel)

Wiring Schematic

Step 2.

Clamp the two side panels together with the smoothest sides facing each other. Use a ½-inch spade bit to drill holes according to the panel diagram on page 58. Unclamp the panels, then drill a small hole in one side panel for the thermometer probe in the position indicated on the diagram; the hole should be just big enough to insert the stem of your thermometer. Sand the edges of the holes.

Step 3.

Drill four holes in the bottom of the baking pan, close to the corners; the holes should be just large enough for the #8-32 screws. Position the pan on the inside of the top panel as indicated on the panel diagram; mark and drill holes through the pan and then the plywood. Set the pan aside for now.

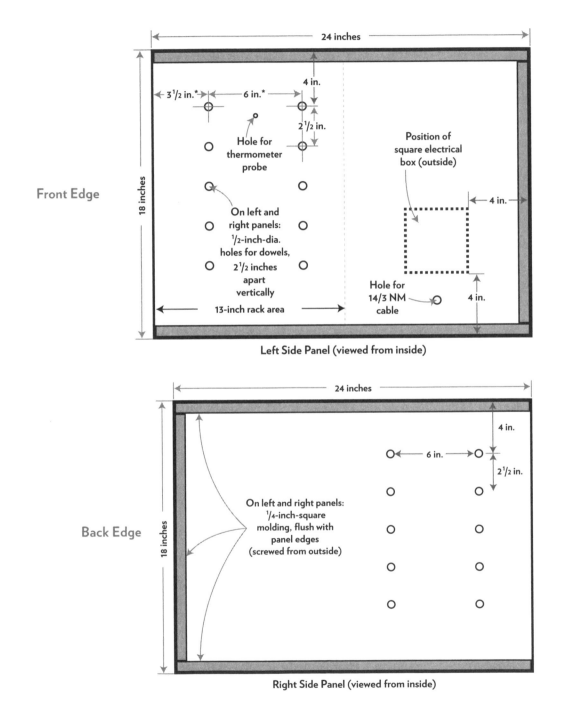

24 inches

18 inches

Front Edge

3 1/2 in.*   6 in.*   4 in.

2 1/2 in.

Hole for
thermometer
probe

Position of
square electrical
box (outside)

4 in.

On left and
right panels:
1/2-inch-dia.
holes for dowels,
2 1/2 inches
apart
vertically

Hole for
14/3 NM
cable

4 in.

13-inch rack area

Left Side Panel (viewed from inside)

24 inches

18 inches

Back Edge

4 in.

6 in.

2 1/2 in.

On left and right panels:
1/4-inch-square
molding, flush with
panel edges
(screwed from outside)

Right Side Panel (viewed from inside)

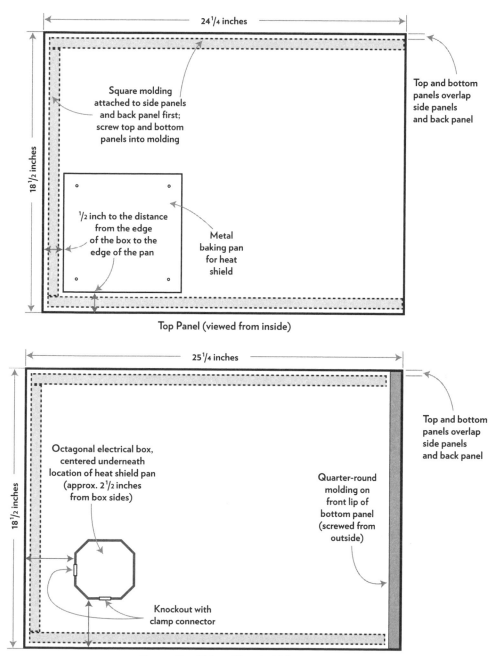

24¼ inches

Square molding
attached to side panels
and back panel first;
screw top and bottom
panels into molding

Top and bottom
panels overlap
side panels
and back panel

18½ inches

½ inch to the distance
from the edge
of the box to the
edge of the pan

Metal
baking pan
for heat
shield

Top Panel (viewed from inside)

25¼ inches

Top and bottom
panels overlap
side panels
and back panel

18½ inches

Octagonal electrical box,
centered underneath
location of heat shield pan
(approx. 2½ inches
from box sides)

Quarter-round
molding on
front lip of
bottom panel
(screwed from
outside)

Knockout with
clamp connector

Bottom Panel (viewed from inside)

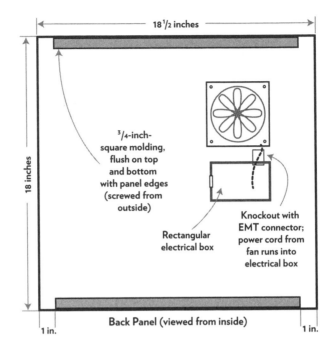

18 ¹/₂ inches

18 inches

³/₄-inch-square molding, flush on top and bottom with panel edges (screwed from outside)

Knockout with EMT connector; power cord from fan runs into electrical box

Rectangular electrical box

1 in.

Back Panel (viewed from inside)

1 in.

Step 4.

Assemble the box by screwing the plywood panels, with the smoothest face inward, to the square molding. First, screw the molding to the side panels according to the panel diagrams, aligning the molding flush with the outside edges of the panels and driving the #6 x ¾-inch construction screws in from the outside (predrill the holes to prevent splitting the molding, and use five screws per long edge and three per short edge). Screw the two remaining pieces of 16½-inch molding to the back panel according to the panel diagram above, insetting them 1 inch from the left and right edges. Have a helper

hold the back panel in position with one of the side panels so the molding butts together in the corners; the back panel should overlap the side panel. Predrill and drive a screw into each corner, screwing the corners of the back panel into the ends of the square molding on the side panel. Attach the other side panel in the same fashion; don't drive in more than just the corner screws, because you'll be removing the back panel later to work on the wiring. Attach the top panel by driving screws through the panel into the square molding attached to the side panels, aligning all outside edges; the top panel should overlap the side and back panels (this is not a temporary connection, so use five screws per long edge and three per short edge, being careful to avoid the existing screws in the side panels). Now attach the bottom panel in the same way; the bottom panel is deeper than the box, so there will be a 1-inch lip in the front. Attach the glide feet to the bottom corners of the box.

Step 5.

Punch out two knockout plugs in each of the three electrical boxes, according to the Wiring Schematic on page 57. Insert and tighten clamp connectors into both holes of the octagonal and square boxes, and into one hole of the rectangular box; screw the EMT box connector into the other hole of the rectangular

box. Screw a green grounding screw into the designated hole at the bottom of each box. Mount the square and octagonal boxes in the positions shown on the diagrams, using four of the #6-32 x ¾-inch machine screws and nuts for each box; set the rectangular box aside for now. Note that the square box goes on the outside of the left side panel.

Step 6.

Remove the back panel; this makes it easier to install the fan and to work on the wiring connections in the octagonal electrical box. Drill holes in the back panel to align with the mounting holes in the fan, positioning it as indicated on the panel diagram; the holes should be just large enough to fit the 3-inch machine screws you'll

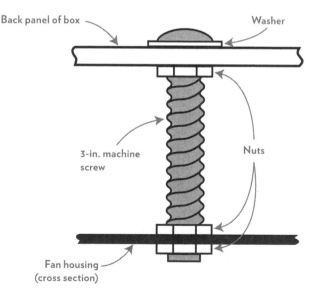

Cross Section of Fan Mounting

be using to mount the fan. Place the washers over the screws, then slip the screws into the holes from the outside of the panel. Thread two nuts onto each screw on the inside of the panel; one nut should be fairly close to the panel and the other should be about ½ inch away. Slide the fan onto the screws. Tighten one nut on each screw against the back panel. Adjust the fan's position so about ¼ inch of each screw is exposed on the outside of the fan. Thread one nut onto the end of each exposed screw. Slide the fan forward, against the nuts you just added, then tighten the nuts that are behind the fan until the fan is locked in position (see cross section diagram on page 61. Use the four remaining #6-32 x ¾-inch screws and nuts to mount the rectangular electrical box, positioning it so the end of the EMT connector is about ½ inch away from the edge of the fan where the power cord is. Slip the power cord through the connector and into the rectangular box.

Step 7.

Attach the baking pan to the inside of the top panel in the same manner as the fan, using the #8-32 x 2-inch machine screws and one washer and three nuts per screw. The inside of the pan should be facing down into the box, so the bottom of the pan is about 1¾ inches from the top of the box.

Step 8.

Drill a hole just large enough for the 14/3 NM cable in the left panel of the dehydrator, aligning the hole with the cable clamps in the square and octagonal electrical boxes. Run the 14/3 cable between the square box and the octagonal box, then tighten both cable clamps. Feed one end of the 14/2 cable into the octagonal box and tighten the cable clamp; leave the other end free for now. Shorten the 14/3 cable if necessary so you have just enough to work with. Strip the plastic sheath off both ends of the cables in the square and octagonal boxes, then strip the ends of the individual wires. Insert the stripped end of the power cord into the second hole on the square box and secure it with the cable clamp.

Step 9.

Use wire nuts to connect all wires in the square and octagonal boxes as shown in the Wiring Schematic. **Inside the square box** you'll be connecting the wires from the lamp, the power cord, and the dimmer switch; you'll need to add a pigtail of bare copper wire to the ground wires, then connect the pigtail to the grounding screw. **Inside the octagonal box** you'll be connecting the wires from the dimmer switch, the fan, and the lampholder; add a pigtail of bare copper wire to the ground wires from the NM cables, then connect the pigtail to the grounding screw. Tuck all wires neatly into each box. Screw the porcelain lampholder to the octagonal electrical box. Screw the 1-gang box cover to the square electrical box, then screw the dimmer switch to the box cover. Attach the face plate to the dimmer switch.

Step 10.

Reattach the back panel with the four corner screws. Run the 14/2 NM cable from the octagonal box into the rectangular box on the back panel, shorten if necessary, and tighten the clamp. Strip the sheathing and ends of the individual wires. Connect all wires with wire nuts. If your fan has a ground wire (most don't), use a wire nut to connect it with the ground wire from the NM cable, adding a pigtail of bare copper wire and attaching the pigtail to the grounding screw on the electrical box; otherwise, connect the ground wire from the NM cable directly to the box's grounding screw. Screw on the rectangular metal cover plate. Twist the heat lamp into the lampholder. Plug in the cord to test the wiring; the fan should run whenever the cord is plugged in, and the light is controlled by the dimmer switch. Once you're sure everything is wired correctly, finish attaching the back panel of the box, adding additional screws as needed (remember to predrill the holes). Tape a 15-inch–long piece of aluminum foil, shiny side facing out, to the inside of the left side panel next to the light; tape another to the inside of the back panel behind the light.

Step 11.

Set the door panel into position against the opening in the front of the box. Position the quarter-round molding on the lip of the bottom panel so the molding is pushed tightly against the door panel, *with the round edge against the door (facing the inside of the dehydrator).* Have a helper hold the molding in place while you predrill one screw hole at each end, drilling from the underside of the bottom panel into the quarter-round molding. Drive two #6 x ¾-inch screws, then add two more screws to securely hold the molding in place.

Testing and Adjusting the Temperature of the Home-Built Dehydrator

Before you put any food in the dehydrator, run it for a few hours. This allows you to check the temperature, and also helps eliminate odors from the freshly cut wood. Insert the dowels and secure with rubber bands as described in step 1 of Using the Home-Built Dehydrator on the next page. Close the door tightly as described in step 3. Insert the stem of a small remote probe thermometer or a remote probe thermometer into the hole you drilled in the side panel. Plug in the power cord and turn the dimmer switch to the highest level, then check the temperature in about 30 minutes. If the dehydrator is hotter than you want for the food you'll be drying, use the dimmer switch to lower the light intensity a bit and check again in 20 minutes or so.

On the other hand, if the dehydrator is not as warm as you want, you may have to switch to a 375-watt heat lamp (I had to order mine from an online source). This lamp is hotter than the 250-watt lamp, so you need to watch it carefully; start with the dimmer switch at about halfway and check the temperature after 30 minutes, rather than starting with the switch on high. For safety reasons and to protect the fan, the home-built dehydrator should not be operated above 145°F.

The dehydrator we built operates at 125 to 130°F with a 250-watt bulb at full intensity; I can lower the temperature by using the dimmer switch, and it maintains that temperature once it stabilizes. With the 375-watt bulb, the temperature goes up to 150°F but the light can be dimmed for any desired temperature below that. Temperatures are surprisingly even throughout the box, and the dehydrator is quieter than any manufactured dehydrator I've ever been around — a credit to the quality of the fan we used.

Using the Home-Built Dehydrator

Step 1.

Tightly wrap a rubber band near one end of each dowel. Slip the other end through one set of the holes in the side panels, then wrap another rubber band around the second end to keep the dowel from sliding out during use (this works surprisingly well). Repeat with all dowels.

Step 2.

Place an empty baking sheet or a piece of heavy-duty foil on the floor of the dehydrator underneath the tray area to catch drips. Place racks (or baking sheets) of prepared food on the dowels; you'll have room for up to five racks. Slip the stem of the thermometer into the hole on the side panel.

Step 3.

Tie a loop in one end of the kitchen twine, and slip it onto the top, front-most dowel on the left side. Position the door panel against the opening, slipping the bottom of the door between the quarter-round molding and the edges of the box; it should fit snugly. Bring the twine around the door panel, and then wrap it a few times around the top, front-most dowel on the right side. Observe that you can pull the door tightly against the opening, or allow a gap at the top to provide ventilation; the quarter-round molding allows the panel to angle out as needed while preventing the door from falling out. When you're starting a fresh load of foods, angle the door so there is a gap of about an inch at the top to permit moisture to escape.

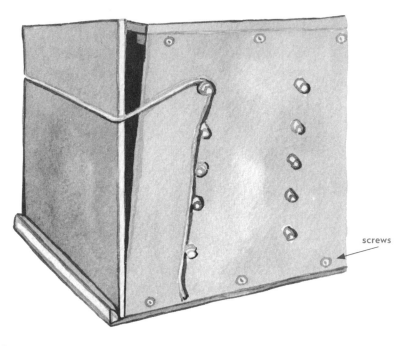

The door is left
partially open
to allow moisture
to escape

screws

Step 4.

Confirm that the dimmer switch is
off, then plug in the power cord; the
fan should start up immediately. Turn
on the dimmer switch and adjust for
the highest intensity; because the
door is open at the top, the dehydrator will run cooler at the beginning
than it will once the door is pulled
closed. Check the temperature in 30
minutes and turn down the light if the
temperature is hotter than you want.
If the temperature is a bit lower than
you want and the light is at full intensity, don't worry about it; once you
pull the door shut it will get hotter.
NOTE: Never leave the home-built
dehydrator unattended, and do not
run it overnight.

Step 5.

After an hour of running time, check
the foods to see if they're drying
evenly from rack to rack; you may
need to rotate the racks from front
to back and switch positions. When
the air coming out of the gap at
the top of the door no longer feels
moist (generally 60 to 90 minutes),
pull the door closed and secure with
the twine. Monitor the temperature
periodically, adjusting the light intensity as needed; as the food dries,
the temperature will rise, so you may
need to turn the light down. Continue
running the dehydrator until all food
is properly dried, moving and rotating racks if needed and removing
individual pieces as they become dry.
Wash the racks after use; also hand
wash the dowels as needed.

Variations, Options, and Tips for the Home-Built Dehydrator

If the dehydrator is built as described here, there is a very slight chance of damaging some of the wiring when you use or move the dehydrator — particularly the NM cable that runs on the outside of the dehydrator into the square electrical box. (To put it in perspective, the risk is about the same as damaging the cord from a table lamp.) Always take care not to damage the plastic sheathing. If you're comfortable doing electrical work, you may prefer to use flexible metal conduit to contain the wires between the electrical boxes to improve the safety.

The plans here have 2½ inches between each of the racks. You can tighten that to 2 inches or a bit less so you have room for more racks, but don't put the holes too close or you will weaken the panels. You can also set a rack or baking pan of food on the bottom of the dehydrator.

The dehydrator is bulky and difficult to move. To make moving it easier, add handles to the top panel, supporting them well on the underside. You may also put knobs on the side panels so you have a more permanent place to wrap the kitchen twine securing the door, or you may come up with another way to secure the door (although the kitchen twine system works just fine, it isn't very glamorous). To make the dehydrator less raw-looking, you could build a chase around the switch box on the outside.

- Don't spend a lot on the baking pan that acts as a heat reflector above the heat lamp. Check at a thrift store; the pan can be beat up and it will still work fine. Teflon isn't recommended; a plain aluminum or steel pan works best, and the heavier the pan, the better.

- Try to scrounge the NM cable; so little is needed that it doesn't make sense to buy a package. Also buy the cheapest dimmer switch you can find; prices range widely, and a no-frills model works fine.

- To judge the moisture level inside the dehydrator so you can determine when to pull the door closed, hold your hand above the opening. If the air is laden with moisture, you'll be able to feel it on your hand, and if you're wearing a watch, you may notice condensation on the face.

- Moist air seems to escape pretty well around the door even when it's pulled closed all the way and also through gaps in the construction all around the box. But if you want additional ventilation, use a hole saw to drill one or two 1-inch holes near the top of the door panel.

orange

slices

CHAPTER 4

Fruits

IF YOU'RE JUST getting into dehydrating foods, fruits are a great place to start. They're easy to dry, and the finished product is similar to familiar store-bought dried fruits — although you'll be able to make a variety of home-dried fruits that far exceeds what you'll find at the grocery store. Most are great eaten out of hand as a snack, and they are also easy to rehydrate for use in pies, cobblers, and other familiar fruit-based dishes. Dried fruits are easy to store, too, requiring no refrigeration (although for long-term storage, dried fruits are best when frozen).

Many fruits can be dried without any pretreatment: simply wash well, then cut up as needed, load onto the dryer trays, and proceed with drying. Other fruits are best with pretreatment, ranging from a quick dip in acidulated water or another solution, to blanching with steam or boiling water, to syrup-blanching. The individual listings below indicate any pretreatment that is recommended; full instructions for pretreatment are given in chapter 2. Note that pretreatments are optional; the recommended pretreatments will produce the best results, but this step can be skipped if you prefer to avoid the added steps or additional ingredients.

In the following pages, you'll find specific instructions for more than 25 types of fruit, including recommendations for pretreatment where appropriate. Fruits are listed in alphabetical order, with a few exceptions. Some fruits are combined with others because both dehydrating information and uses are the same. These include blueberries and huckleberries; cantaloupe and honeydew melons; oranges, lemons, and limes; and peaches and nectarines. Approximate drying times are given for a dehydrator or oven using a target temperature of 135°F, which works well for most fruit drying (note, however, that candied fruit uses a target temperature of 145°F). If you dehydrate at a higher or lower temperature, your times will change accordingly; variables such as humidity and the total amount of food in your dehydrator will also affect drying time, sometimes dramatically, so use the times given as a general guideline.

Each listing also includes suggestions for using the dried fruit, followed by a list of recipes in this book that use the fruit. Check the index to locate the specific recipe.

Finally, most fruits can be used to make tasty fruit leathers (also called roll-ups). Chapter 8 includes complete instructions and also explains how to make homemade baby foods from fresh fruit. Many fruits also lend themselves to "sun jam," a delightful treat that can be made in the dehydrator as well as by the traditional sun-cooking method; see pages 301–302 for details.

REHYDRATION REMINDER

To hot-soak, place the dried fruit in a *heatproof* bowl and add boiling water or fruit juice to just cover or as directed. Stir and let stand at room temperature until softened.

To cold-soak, place the dried fruit in a mixing bowl and add room-temperature or cold water, or fruit juice, to just cover or as directed. Stir. Cover the bowl and refrigerate overnight.

Drying Fruits: From Apples to Watermelon

Apples

Apples are an excellent choice for dehydrating and are particularly good for beginners to experiment with. Slices, rings, and chunks can also be candied; see page 116. Fruit leathers made from apples, alone or in combination with other fruits, are delicious; see chapter 8 for instructions.

Select fully ripe but still-firm apples. Wash well. Peel or not, as you prefer; the peels will be tougher than the apple flesh after drying but offer good fiber and extra nutrition. Cut away and discard any bruised or damaged portions. For sliced apples, cut into quarters, then cut away the cores and slice the quarters lengthwise into ¼-inch-thick half-moons; you may also slice the cored quarters crosswise, but the dried pieces will be smaller and you may need to use a screen. For apple rings, use a round corer to remove the cores from whole apples, then slice the cored apples crosswise into ¼-inch-thick rings; the rings can be dried whole or cut into half-rings for nicely shaped slices that are the same thickness across the slice (half-moon slices are thinner at the inside, and dry a bit unevenly).

Another option is a countertop apple peeler/corer gadget. It has a central screw to hold the apple and a crank handle. Turning the handle spins the apple, bringing it into contact with knives and a coring system that peels and cores the apple. Most peeler/corers can be set to cut the fruit into a continuous spiral as it's being peeled and cored or to simply peel and core it with no spiral cutting. If you want to dry rings, set the device to peel and core the fruit without spiral cutting, then cut the fruit crosswise for rings. If you want to dry half-rings, set the device for spiral cutting, then cut the cored spiral in half from top to bottom. A good peeler/corer can process an apple in about 30 seconds, so they are great if you have a lot of apples to dry (and as an added bonus, kids love operating them). Note that it's worth it to spend a bit more to get a solidly built peeler/corer with a good warranty; inexpensive ones often fail after just a few apples.

Recipes in this book featuring dried apples:

- Apple Skillet Bread
- Cooked Applesauce
- Crumb-Topped Dried Apple Pie
- Curried Winter Squash Soup Mix in a Jar
- Dried Fruit Snack Mix
- Fruit Smoothie
- Ham and Apple Dumplings
- Hot Cereal with Fruit

More recipes
in this book
featuring dried
apples:

- Overnight
  Oatmeal with
  Fruit and Nuts

- Quick Bread
  with Dried
  Fruits

- Slow-Cooker
  Pork Chops
  with Root
  Vegetables

- Swedish Fruit
  Soup Mix in a
  Jar

- Sweet and
  Tangy Cabbage
  with Apples

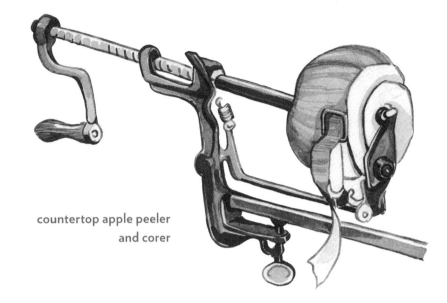

countertop apple peeler
and corer

Home-dried apples that have not been pretreated are usually golden or
tawny in color when first dried, but they will continue to darken in storage
unless vacuum-packed or frozen. To reduce the darkening, pretreat slices
with a light honey dip, acidulated water, or commercial fruit protector;
for snow-white dried apples that remain white even in storage, use a sulfite
solution. It's also helpful to place trays in a preheated dehydrator as each
is filled, rather than waiting until all trays are filled to begin. Sun-drying

DRYING METHODS: APPLES

DEHYDRATOR/ CONVECTION OVEN

Preheat dehydrator or convection oven to 135°F. As
each tray/rack is filled, place
it in the preheated dehydra-
tor/oven before loading
the next one. Apple slices
generally take 5 to 10 hours
at 135°F.

SUN-DRYING

Turn and rearrange slices
several times each day.
Apple slices will prob-
ably take 2 to 4 days to dry
completely.

OVEN (NON-CONVECTION)

Preheat the oven to 135°F.
As each rack is filled, place
it in the preheated oven
before loading the next rack.
During drying, rotate racks
every hour. At 135°F, apple
slices may take as little as
4 hours to dry, or as long as
15 hours.

takes longer than drying in a dehydrator or oven, so all apples should be pretreated with one of the above methods to prevent excessive browning and possible spoilage.

DONENESS TEST: Leathery to crisp, with no moisture in the thickest part.

YIELD: 5 pounds of whole apples will yield about 2 quarts of dried slices. When rehydrated, 1 cup of dried apple slices yields about 1¼ cups.

TO USE: Dried apple slices are a delicious out of hand snack; they also may be cut up and used in dried fruit blends and trail mixes. To rehydrate, hot-soak for 30 to 45 minutes, or cold-soak overnight. Rehydrated apples are soft rather than crunchy like raw apples. Use drained, rehydrated apples in pies, sauces, cobblers, or any other recipes in which the apples will be cooked.

Apricots

If you live in an area where apricots are grown, they are an excellent fruit to dehydrate. However, if you must purchase apricots that have been shipped in from afar, you will probably find them prohibitively expensive; the quality might not be worth the investment, either, because apricots destined for shipping long distances are shipped when still underripe and may never attain full sweetness.

Pick or buy apricots when perfectly ripe but not mushy. Any size or variety will work, as long as you choose those with bright color and sweet flavor. Canned apricots also dry well and need no pretreatment other than patting dry with a paper towel; they may not be an economical choice, though, and also take longer to dry. Apricot slices and chunks may also be candied; see page 119.

Apricots have very thin skins and don't need to be peeled; the skins help hold the fruit together and prevent the fruit from sticking to the dehydrator trays. (If you prefer to peel them, dip them in boiling water for 30 seconds, then plunge into cold water for 1 minute; the skins will slip off easily.) Use a paring knife to cut the apricot in half, following the natural seam and cutting just until the knife encounters the pit. Hold the apricot in both hands and twist in opposite directions; if the apricots are freestone,

one half should pop away from the pit. Now remove the pit from the other half; if the pit doesn't come out easily, use the tip of your knife to carefully cut the flesh close to the pit until you can separate them. If the pit doesn't separate easily after you try with a few fruits, you probably have a clingstone variety; in this case, it's best to simply cut the fruit away from the pits as best you can.

As an alternative for slices or chunks (particularly when working with clingstone varieties), ignore the pit and simply cut the apricot from top to bottom into ⅜-inch slices (½-inch slices if you want to dry the fruit in chunks), cutting parallel to the natural seam and skimming the knife along the edge of the pit when you get towards the center of the fruit. When you've sliced off the sides of the apricot, cut off the flesh around the pit in the center section that remains. Cut each slice in half so you have two half-round pieces, or cut all slices into chunks if you prefer. This method of slicing makes it easier to avoid mangling the flesh of clingstone fruits, which is likely if you try to remove the pits as described for freestone fruit.

Halves dry more quickly if the fruit is flattened before pretreating and drying. Hold a half in your fingers, cut-side up, and push the skin side upward with your thumbs to "pop" the fruit. If you prefer, cut the halves (unflattened) into ⅜-inch slices or ½-inch chunks.

Drying untreated apricots is not recommended; they will become unappealingly dark and hard when dried. Pretreating apricots with acidulated water, pectin dip, light honey dip, or commercial fruit protector will minimize this, but your home-dried apricots will still be darker and harder than purchased, sulfured dried apricots. A sulfite solution is the most effective pretreatment to prevent darkening and is a good choice unless you need to avoid sulfites. Another option that produces softer, more brightly colored fruit is syrup-blanching halved apricots. Simmer halves, slices, or chunks in the syrup-blanching solution for 5 minutes, then remove from the heat. If you're preparing halved apricots, let them soak in the solution for 15 minutes, then drain and rinse briefly before spreading on trays. Slices and chunks don't need to soak: simply drain, rinse briefly, and spread on trays. If you're drying canned apricots, simply drain them and pat them dry and cut into chunks if you like; home-dried canned apricots are soft and brightly colored and are very similar to commercially dried apricots. Always use one of the pretreatments recommended above if you're sun-drying apricots.

Recipes in this book featuring dried apricots:

- Best-Ever Fruitcake
- Chocolate-Dipped Fruit Treats
- Couscous with Fruit and Nuts
- Dried Fruit Bars
- Dried Fruit Snack Mix
- Fruit Smoothie
- Hot Breakfast Nuggets
- Hot Cereal with Fruit
- Overnight Oatmeal with Fruit and Nuts
- Pumpkin and Peach Cookies
- Swedish Fruit Soup Mix in a Jar

DEHYDRATOR/ CONVECTION OVEN

Use a screen when drying chunks. Coat trays, racks, or screens with cooking spray if you're drying syrup-blanched or canned apricots. When drying halves, position them on trays with the cut side up; turn once the top half no longer looks wet. Apricot halves and slices generally take 12 to 20 hours at 135°F. Chunks will dry in less time.

SUN-DRYING

Coat drying screens with cooking spray if you're drying syrup-blanched or canned apricots. When drying halves, position them on drying screens with the cut side up. Turn pieces at the start of the second day. Apricot halves and slices will probably take 2 to 4 days to dry completely. Chunks will dry in less time.

OVEN (NON-CONVECTION)

Apricots take longer than 18 hours and are not recommended.

DONENESS TEST: Leathery, with no moisture in the thickest part; slices may be somewhat brittle. Halves will be somewhat springy; if they feel mushy rather than springy, they are not dry enough. Syrup-blanched or canned apricots will be rich orange and somewhat glossy, with a pleasantly chewy texture; they are close in appearance and texture to purchased dried apricots.

YIELD: 1 pound fresh, whole apricots yields about 1¼ cups of dried slices, chunks, or halves. When rehydrated, 1 cup of dried apricot slices yields about 1⅓ cups.

TO USE: Eat halves and slices out of hand. Add chopped pieces to baked goods, or use them in dried fruit blends and trail mixes. Simmer halves over low heat in water just to cover for 30 to 45 minutes, then cool and serve in a fruit compote. To rehydrate slices or chunks, hot-soak for 1 to 1½ hours, or cold-soak overnight. The rehydrated apricots may be puréed with the remaining soaking liquid, sweetened as needed, and used as a sauce. Use drained, rehydrated apricots in pies, sauces, cobblers, or any other recipes in which the fruit will be cooked.

Bananas

Although bananas grow only in the tropics, they are so common in stores that they are quite affordable almost everywhere. Home-dried banana slices have a very strong banana flavor; they are not as sweet and crisp as purchased "banana chips," which have been sweetened and often deep-fried. Unless pretreated with a sulfite solution, home-dried banana slices are also fairly dark in the center and may be somewhat dreary looking, but they can still be rehydrated and mashed for banana bread.

Select firm, just-ripe bananas with yellow skins or those that are flecked very lightly with brown; overripe bananas that are heavily flecked with brown are not suitable for drying (but they can be mashed and dried into a tasty leather, as described in chapter 8). Peel bananas and slice crosswise ¼ inch thick. If you're drying in a dehydrator or oven, no pretreatment is necessary, although untreated bananas will be much darker in color than those that have been treated. For the best color with any drying method, pretreat the slices in sulfite solution; commercial fruit protector also does a good job and doesn't add sulfites to the dried bananas. You could also use acidulated water, pectin dip, or light honey dip; these lessen but do not prevent discoloration and lengthen drying time compared to untreated bananas. For a deliciously sweet, chewy dried banana confection, syrup-blanch slices for 3 minutes (simmer gently without boiling), then rinse briefly before spreading on trays; the finished banana slices are more candylike than other dried bananas and are great for snacking, but they can't be rehydrated to use in recipes. If you are drying bananas in the sun, always use one of the pretreatments recommended above.

If you prepare a lot of banana bread, you can mash enough ripe bananas to measure the amount needed for your recipe, then spread the mashed fruit ½ inch thick on a solid liner sheet and dry it the same as a leather (see chapter 8 for leather instructions). For an unusual treat that can't be bought at the supermarket, try candied bananas, which are even more candylike than the syrup-blanched bananas above; instructions are on page 120.

Recipes in this book featuring dried bananas:

- Double Banana Bread
- Dried Fruit Snack Mix
- Overnight Oatmeal with Fruit and Nuts

DEHYDRATOR/ CONVECTION OVEN

For mashed bananas, use a solid liner sheet or a baking sheet lined with kitchen parchment; coat trays, racks, and liner sheets with cooking spray before adding slices or mashed bananas. Banana slices or mashed banana generally take 7 to 12 hours at 135°F.

SUN-DRYING

Mashed bananas are not recommended for sun-drying. For slices, line drying trays with nylon fabric netting (or cheesecloth). Spread pre-treated slices in a single layer on trays. At the end of the day, turn slices by flipping the netting containing the fruit onto a clean piece. Banana slices will probably take 2 to 4 days to dry completely.

OVEN (NON-CONVECTION)

For mashed bananas, line a baking sheet with kitchen parchment; for slices, coat racks with cooking spray before adding slices. Rearrange and flip pieces once or twice during drying. At 135°F, banana slices may take as little as 6 hours to dry, or as long as 18 hours.

DONENESS TEST: Slices will be leathery and a bit flattened, particularly in the center. Dried bananas that have been treated with sulfite solution will be pale yellowish to golden with dark golden centers. Bananas that have been treated with acidulated water, pectin dip, or commercial fruit protector will be darker, with mottled brown centers. Untreated bananas will be fairly dark overall. Syrup-blanched bananas will be rich golden in color, with only a small amount of brown speckling in the center; they will be supple and may be slightly sticky when squeezed but should no longer be moist-sticky. Mashed bananas will dry as a flattened, leathery sheet; it should be flexible and no longer sticky.

YIELD: 1 pound of whole bananas yields about 1½ cups of dried slices. When rehydrated, 1 cup of dried banana rounds yields about 1¼ cups of slices, which can be mashed to produce about ¾ cup mashed bananas.

TO USE: Dried banana slices are great for a sweet snack; syrup-blanched bananas are particularly good for this, as they are delightfully chewy and flavorful, somewhat like toffee. All dried bananas work well in dried fruit mixes and are particularly good combined with apricots, peaches, or pineapple. For a different twist to fresh fruit salads, stir in some dried banana slices and let them rehydrate in the juices from the fresh fruits. You can also add dried banana slices (cut up if you like) to cake or cookie mixes, much in the way you'd add raisins or other dried fruit. To rehydrate plain dried bananas (not syrup-blanched), hot-soak for about 1 hour. Mash rehydrated bananas and use as you would use fresh, mashed bananas.

Blueberries and Huckleberries

When prepared from top-quality fruit and properly pretreated, dried blueberries and huckleberries are a nice addition to the pantry. They rehydrate well for use in baked goods, and berries that have been syrup-blanched before dehydrating are a delicious out of hand snack.

With blueberries, you'll get the best results if you grow your own, buy locally grown berries when they're in season, or pick them from the wild. Supermarket blueberries purchased in the off-season are often disappointing in flavor and cost so much that it is not worth buying them for dehydrating. For out-of-season dehydrating, buy frozen blueberries; these are picked and frozen at the height of the blueberry season, so the quality is good.

There are two types of fruits that are called huckleberries. Those that grow in the western United States belong to the same family as blueberries (*Vaccinium* spp.) and can be used in the same way, although "hucks" are generally smaller and a bit more spicy-tart. Eastern huckleberries are from a different family (*Gaylussacia* spp.). These are generally much less sweet and have numerous small, crunchy seeds that become annoying when the fruits are dehydrated; they are best used for jam.

Choose well-ripened but firm berries that are deeply colored; pick out and discard any that are soft or mushy. Wash the berries in cold water just before using; they may begin to spoil if washed in advance. These fruits can be a challenge to dehydrate because the skins have a natural waxy coating that must be *checked* (broken) before the fruit is dried. With other fruits, checking is accomplished by blanching in boiling water, but because blueberries and huckleberries are so tender and small, the fruit cooks quickly during blanching, breaking apart or becoming too soft to spread on the dehydrator trays. Special care must be taken to prepare these tender berries for dehydrating. Checking the skins is the key to success; if the skins remain whole, the berries will become bloated and soft and may take days to dry. (An option to checking is to cut each berry in half; this produces good results but is very time-consuming if you're processing a lot of berries.)

Brief syrup-blanching checks the fruit and also improves the taste and texture; blueberries and huckleberries that have been syrup-blanched before drying will be leathery-soft, chewy, and sweet and are similar to commercially dried blueberries. Large blueberries should be syrup-blanched by simmering (not boiling) for 3 minutes; huckleberries or small blueberries should be syrup-blanched for 2 minutes. Rinse the blanched berries briefly in cold water before spreading on trays.

Another method to check the skins is freezing, and this is the best option for dehydrating a quantity of berries. Wash the berries and pat lightly with paper towels to dry. Arrange them in a single layer on a waxed paper–lined baking sheet and freeze overnight. The next day, if you aren't ready to dehydrate the frozen berries, pack them into freezer containers and keep them frozen for up to two months. When you're ready to dehydrate, preheat the dehydrator and place screens on your trays. Working with a cup or two at a time, place the frozen berries in a wire-mesh strainer or colander set in the sink and rinse the berries for about 10 seconds with very hot tap water, shaking the strainer or colander the whole time. Working quickly, spread the berries — which will still be partially frozen — on the prepared trays and place immediately in the preheated dehydrator. This method works much better than thawing frozen berries completely before dehydrating, a process which causes them to lose too much of their flavorful juices; use the same method if you purchase frozen berries.

Water-blanching fresh berries can be used to check the skins, although the results may be frustratingly inconsistent unless you blanch in small batches. A large quantity of berries drops the temperature of the water well below boiling, so many of the berries will cook before the water heats up enough to split the skins. For best results, use a wire-mesh strainer and a pot large enough to allow the bottom of the strainer to be immersed in the water. Place about 1 cup of berries in the strainer; set aside. Heat the water to a full, rolling boil, then immerse the bottom of the strainer into the water so the berries are covered by an inch or so. Blanch for 30 seconds; the berries should all float, a sign that the skins have split. Immediately plunge the berries into a large bowl of ice water, and stir gently until the berries are cool; drain and spread on trays. Check the berries after several hours of dehydrating; if most of the berries look somewhat flattened but some look round and bloated, the still-round berries need to be pressed gently with a table knife until partially flattened to break the skins.

Blueberries and huckleberries need no pretreatment other than checking the skins; however, treating them to a pectin dip before drying produces dried berries that are a bit softer, chewier, and sweeter than those that have

Recipes in this book featuring dried blueberries and huckleberries:

- Berry-Cherry Trail Mix
- Berry Cobbler
- Best-Ever Fruitcake
- Frosty Fruit Cluster Mix in a Jar
- Fruit Smoothie
- Lemon-Blueberry Yogurt Muffins
- Overnight Oatmeal with Fruit and Nuts

simply been frozen or water-blanched (although they will not be as sweet and soft as syrup-blanched berries). After rinsing frozen berries or draining blanched, cooled berries, stir them gently into a bowl of pectin syrup. Drain and spread on trays, then place immediately in the dehydrator.

DRYING METHODS: BLUEBERRIES AND HUCKLEBERRIES

DEHYDRATOR/ CONVECTION OVEN

Use screens on trays or racks; coat with cooking spray if you're drying syrup-blanched or pectin-dipped berries. Huckleberries, small blueberries, and blueberries that have been cut in half generally take 8 to 12 hours at 135°F; large blueberries may take up to 24 hours. Syrup-blanched berries take longer to dry than those that have been frozen or water-blanched.

SUN-DRYING

Coat drying screens with cooking spray if you're drying syrup-blanched or pectin-dipped berries. Blueberries and huckleberries will probably take 2 to 4 days to dry completely; smaller berries dry more quickly than large berries.

OVEN (NON-CONVECTION)

Use screens on racks; coat with cooking spray if you're drying syrup-blanched or pectin-dipped berries. Stir and rearrange berries several times during drying. At 135°F, huckleberries and small blueberries may take as little as 7 hours to dry, or as long as 18 hours; large blueberries may take over 18 hours and are not recommended for oven-drying.

DONENESS TEST: Shrunken, dark, wrinkled, leathery to hard, with a dry texture. Pectin-dipped berries will be pliable and have a slight gloss but should not be sticky. Syrup-blanched berries will be pliable and slightly sticky but no longer moist inside; they may be more flattened than berries that have not been syrup-blanched.

YIELD: 1 pound fresh berries yields ¾ to 1 cup of dried berries, depending on the size of the berries. When rehydrated, 1 cup of dried berries yields 1⅓ to 1½ cups.

TO USE: Syrup-blanched dried blueberries and huckleberries make a good out-of-hand snack and work well in dried fruit blends and trail mixes. Plain dried blueberries and huckleberries (those that have not been syrup-blanched) may be somewhat hard and crumbly; plain dried huckleberries may also be too tart to enjoy as a snack. Use dried blueberries or huckleberries in any recipe calling for raisins or dried cranberries; the taste will be different but the recipe will work fine. To rehydrate, hot-soak for 2 to 3 hours or cold-soak overnight. The rehydrated berries may be puréed with the remaining soaking liquid, sweetened as needed, and used as a sauce. Use drained, rehydrated berries in pies, sauces, cobblers, or any other recipes in which the berries will be cooked.

Cantaloupe and Honeydew Melons

Dried melon pieces make a tasty snack that is quite different from more-familiar dried fruits. They don't rehydrate well, so are generally eaten in the dry state. Cut fully ripe melons in half, then use a spoon to scoop out the seeds and any stringy or pulpy portions. Peel generously, removing any trace of green (it becomes much darker during drying). Slice about ⅜ inch thick, then cut the slices into chunks that are about ½ inch across. The melon pieces need no pretreatment.

Recipes using dried cantaloupe or honeydew melons:

- Fruit Smoothie

DRYING METHODS: CANTALOUPE AND HONEYDEW MELONS

DEHYDRATOR/ CONVECTION OVEN

Cantaloupe pieces generally take 5 to 6 hours at 135°F; honeydew pieces may take a little longer.

SUN-DRYING

Cantaloupe or honeydew pieces will probably take 2 to 3 days to dry completely.

OVEN (NON-CONVECTION)

Rearrange pieces after about 2 hours. At 135°F, cantaloupe pieces may take as little as 5 hours to dry, or as long as 10 hours; honeydew pieces may take a little longer.

DONENESS TEST: Very thin, leathery, and pliable.

YIELD: One whole cantaloupe of average size yields about 1⅔ cups of dried pieces.

TO USE: Eat as an out of hand snack, or cut up and add to trail mixes for an unusual flavor accent.

Cherries

Many varieties of sweet cherries are available in supermarkets and farmers' markets. Colors range from yellow with a red tinge, to bright red, to deep burgundy. Look for locally grown sweet cherries from early through late summer, depending on variety and location. Out-of-season cherries will probably be too expensive to dehydrate in quantity, but it's fun to candy a small amount of cherries before the winter holiday fruitcake season. Sour cherries are much more difficult to find; look for them at farmers' markets and some self-pick farms in midsummer. Most sour cherries are bright red, but some are dark red.

Any cherry variety can be dried, as long as the fruits are meaty, with a good amount of flesh in proportion to the pits. (Wild black cherries, chokecherries, and pin cherries are mostly pit and don't work well for drying.) Choose fully ripe but firm cherries; light-colored or bright red varieties are usually somewhat translucent when ripe. Wash the cherries and pull off the stems. You'll also need to remove the pits before the cherries are dried. Some sweet cherries that are firm when ripe, including Bing cherries, are very reluctant to part with their pits, so try a few before buying in quantity for dehydrating. With most cherries, however, a plunger-style cherry pitter makes quick work of this tedious task and is well worth the small investment; look for this hand-held tool at cookware stores and old-fashioned hardware stores. Otherwise, cut the fruit in half and pry out the pit with your fingernail or a small tool. Small pitted cherries can be dried whole but will take a long time; you'll have better success if you cut cherries in half regardless of size. For softer, more richly colored dried cherries that have a slight gloss, treat the cherries with pectin dip; you may also syrup-blanch cherries for 5 minutes before drying.

Frozen and canned cherries also work well for drying but are usually not a very economical choice. Frozen cherries should be thawed and drained, then cut in half before drying; they may be syrup-blanched for 5 minutes or treated to a pectin dip if you like. Canned cherries should be drained, rinsed briefly, and drained again before drying. Cherry halves, whether fresh or frozen, are also excellent candied; see page 120.

DEHYDRATOR/ CONVECTION OVEN

Use screens on trays or racks; coat with cooking spray if you're drying pectin-dipped or syrup-blanched cherries. Small cherry halves generally take 10 to 15 hours at 135°F; large cherry halves generally take 14 to 20 hours. Whole cherries may take 24 hours or longer.

SUN-DRYING

Coat drying screens with cooking spray if you're drying pectin-dipped or syrup-blanched cherries. Cherry halves will probably take 1 to 2 days to dry completely; whole cherries may take as long as 5 days.

OVEN (NON-CONVECTION)

Large cherry halves and whole cherries may take 24 hours or longer and are not recommended for oven-drying. For small cherry halves, use screens on racks; coat with cooking spray if you're drying pectin-dipped or syrup-blanched cherries. Stir and rearrange cherries every 2 hours, separating any clumps. At 135°F, small cherry halves may take as little as 10 hours to dry, or as long as 22 hours.

DONENESS TEST: Flattened, wrinkled, leathery, and much darker in color than when fresh. Pectin-dipped cherries will be more brightly colored and a bit softer but not sticky; syrup-blanched cherries will be pliable and very slightly sticky but no longer moist inside.

YIELD: 1 pound fresh, whole cherries yields about ¾ to 1 cup of dried cherry halves, depending on variety and the size of the pits. When rehydrated, 1 cup dried cherry halves yields about 1¼ cups.

TO USE: Home-dried sweet cherries are a delightful snack and work well in dried fruit blends and trail mixes. Feel free to use dried sweet cherry halves in any recipe calling for raisins or dried cranberries; the taste will be different but the recipe will work fine. Dried sour cherries are a bit tart for eating out of hand but work well when rehydrated and used for pies, sauces, cobblers, and the like. To rehydrate dried sweet or sour cherries, hot-soak for about 30 minutes, or cold-soak overnight.

Cranberries

Cranberries are grown commercially in only a handful of states; Wisconsin produces about half of all cranberries sold in the United States, with Massachusetts coming in second. Luckily, cranberries ship well and are available fresh from late fall through midwinter in many supermarkets outside the growing region. They also freeze beautifully and are often found in supermarket freezer cases. Fresh and frozen cranberries both work well for dehydrating.

Cranberries have tough skins that prevent the interior from drying. Whole berries can be cut in half to expose the interior, but this is a tedious process and not feasible for more than a small amount. For larger quantities, blanch whole berries in water, steam, or syrup; this *checks* (breaks) the skin, so the fruits dry more quickly.

Because they are so tart, cranberries are best when syrup-blanched for 5 minutes, then rinsed briefly, before dehydrating. This makes the dried fruit softer and sweeter than cranberries that have been blanched in water; dried, syrup-blanched cranberries are very similar to purchased dried sweetened cranberries and can be used the same way. If you prefer unsweetened dried cranberries, blanch them in boiling water for 90 seconds, or steam-blanch for 2 minutes, to check the skins; you should hear the skins popping. If you're working with frozen cranberries, drop them, still frozen, into boiling water and blanch for 1 minute before draining. Dried cranberries that have not been syrup-blanched work fine for cranberry sauce and other cooked uses where the tartness is not a problem; they are too sour to eat out of hand or to use in recipes calling for commercially dried cranberries.

Recipes in this book featuring dried cranberries:

- Berry-Cherry Trail Mix
- Berry Cobbler
- Best-Ever Fruitcake
- Couscous with Fruit and Nuts
- Cranberry-Cherry Relish
- Frosty Fruit Cluster Mix in a Jar
- Overnight Oatmeal with Fruit and Nuts
- Squash or Pumpkin Bread

DRYING METHODS: CRANBERRIES

DEHYDRATOR/ CONVECTION OVEN

Use screens on trays or racks; coat with cooking spray if you're drying syrup-blanched cranberries. Cranberries generally take 14 to 25 hours at 135°F; halved cranberries dry more quickly.

SUN-DRYING

Coat drying screens with cooking spray if you're drying syrup-blanched cranberries. Stir berries several times each day. Cranberries will probably take 2 to 4 days to dry completely.

OVEN (NON-CONVECTION)

Cranberries will probably take longer than 24 hours and are not recommended.

DONENESS TEST: Flattened, wrinkled, leathery, and deep, bright red; syrup-blanched cranberries will be somewhat glossy. The dried fruits will be flexible and chewy, but there should be no trace of moisture in the centers. They should feel springy, not mushy or soft, when squeezed.

YIELD: 1 pound fresh, whole cranberries yields about 1½ cups of dried cranberries. When plumped and softened, 1 cup dried cranberries yields about 1½ cups.

TO USE: Syrup-blanched dried cranberries can be used just as you would use commercially dried, sweetened cranberries; they also work well in trail mixes and granolas. Like raisins, dried cranberries may be plumped and softened by soaking in boiling water or cooking briefly, but dried cranberries can't be returned to the fresh form. To plump and soften cranberries, hot-soak for 1 to 2 hours, or cold-soak overnight. Plumped, softened unsweetened cranberries can be used in sauces or other sweetened dishes or any other recipes in which the cranberries will be cooked; they may also be puréed with sweetener to taste for a smooth sauce.

Currants

First, let's clear up some confusion. The dried "currants" sold in the store are actually small raisins, made from a small grape called Zante (*Vitis vinifera*). These black grapes are about one-quarter the size of grapes used to make regular raisins; like all grapes, they grow on vines. True currants are small berries that grow on shrubs belonging to the *Ribes* genus, which also includes gooseberries. The distinction becomes more than a botanical curiosity when one considers studies reporting that compounds in black currants may help prevent Alzheimer's and other diseases — and the currants in question are true black currants, not the raisin imposter.

In the United States, three types of currants are cultivated commercially and grown in home gardens: white, red, and black. White currants are actually a variety of red currant; they are the sweetest, but much harder to find than red currants, which are deliciously sweet-tart. Both are popular for jam- and syrup-making, and are used for desserts including English summer pudding and Scandinavian fruit soup. Black currants have a stronger, almost musky flavor and are often used to make preserves, liqueurs, syrup, and the like. Currants of all colors are also used in savory dishes, where their sweet-tart flavor works with pork, lamb, beef, and venison. In addition to cultivated varieties, over a dozen types of currants grow in the wild in the northern and western United States; golden currants are common in the West and are delicious, but other varieties are worth seeking out as well.

Choose currants that are fully ripe, with taut, glossy skins. Rinse the clusters in cold water, then pick the berries off the stems. Blanch in boiling water for 30 to 60 seconds to *check* (break) the skins, then chill in ice water and drain before spreading on trays. No other pretreatment is needed.

DRYING METHODS: CURRANTS

DEHYDRATOR/ CONVECTION OVEN

Use screens on trays or racks. Currants generally take 12 to 18 hours at 135°F.

SUN-DRYING

Stir currants twice a day. Currants will probably take 2 to 3 days to dry completely.

OVEN (NON-CONVECTION)

Currants may take longer than 18 hours and are not recommended.

Recipes in this book featuring dried currants:

- Hot Breakfast Nuggets
- Overnight Oatmeal with Fruit and Nuts
- Swedish Fruit Soup Mix in a Jar
- Tropical Trail Mix

DONENESS TEST: Shriveled, leathery, and chewy, with no trace of moisture in the centers.

YIELD: ½ pound fresh, whole currants yields about ½ cup of dried currants.

TO USE: Dried true currants can be included as an ingredient in sauces, but they don't rehydrate well for use as fresh fruit and are generally used in the dried state. They work well as a substitute for commercially dried, sweetened cranberries; use about half of the amount of cranberries called for in the recipe. Dried true currants can also be used to replace commercial currants in baked goods and other recipes, although the flavor will be different. Some currant varieties are seedless, but most have small seeds that may be noticeable in the finished dish.

Figs

In the United States, figs are grown in warm, dry areas of the West Coast; if you live in a fig-growing area, you may enjoy drying some of this delicious, nutritious fruit. Ripe figs are very soft and don't ship well, so they are uncommon in other areas and too expensive to buy for dehydrating.

Choose fully ripened figs for dehydrating. Wash them gently and cut away any stem remnant. For faster drying, cut figs into ½- to ¾-inch pieces or quarter each fig vertically. Halved and whole figs can be home-dried but take much longer than smaller pieces. Whole figs should be steam-blanched or water-blanched for 30 seconds before drying to break the skins.

DRYING METHODS: FIGS

DEHYDRATOR/ CONVECTION OVEN

For pieces, use screens on trays or racks. Place quarters or halves on trays/racks with the cut side up; turn when the centers no longer feel sticky. Pieces take 6 to 10 hours at 135°F. Quarters take 20 to 30 hours; halves take 24 to 36 hours. Whole figs may take up to 48 hours.

SUN-DRYING

Place quarters or halves on drying screens with the cut side up; turn when the centers no longer feel sticky to the touch. Pieces generally take 1 to 2 days, quarters and halves may take up to 4 days, and whole figs may take 6 days or longer.

OVEN (NON-CONVECTION)

Whole, halved, and quartered figs take over 18 hours and are not recommended. For pieces, use screens on racks; stir and rearrange pieces every 2 hours. At 135°F, fig pieces may take as little as 5 hours to dry or as long as 15 hours.

DONENESS TEST: Chewy and pliable; cut portions should not be sticky, and the center should not be moist. Whole figs may collapse downward somewhat; the edges of halves and quarters will shrink inward slightly.

YIELD: 1 pound of fresh figs yields 1¼ to 2 cups when dried, depending on shape.

TO USE: Dried figs are a delicious snack; pieces work well in trail mixes or dried fruit blends. When cut into ¼-inch cubes and softened slightly, dried figs can be used in any recipe that calls for raisins; steam the cubes for 5 to 10 minutes, then cool before using. Stew cut-up dried figs in water to just cover until soft for a delicious addition to fruit compotes.

Recipes in the book featuring dried figs:

- Dried Fruit Bars

Gooseberries

Gooseberries are uncommon in commercial cultivation, but they may be found at farmers' markets and roadside stands. They are also fairly easy to pick in the wild and are a good choice for beginning foragers as they are easy to identify, easy to pick, and generally abundant. Unlike most other fruits, gooseberries are used at both the green and the fully ripened stages; green fruits are quite sour, but even fully ripe berries are usually somewhat tart. Some wild gooseberries are covered in small but sharp spines; these varieties aren't suitable for dehydrating.

Green gooseberries should be slightly translucent and should taste sour but pleasant; if they are astringent or hard, they are too underripe. Ripe berries are sweeter and range in color from red to purple to black; sweetness varies between varieties. No matter what color, the gooseberries should yield to pressure when squeezed gently. Wash the berries in cold water and pull or snip off the stems; gooseberries also have a tail-like flower remnant at the bottom that needs to be removed as well. Gooseberries have a natural waxy coating that prevents the insides from drying properly, so they need to be *checked* by steam-blanching for 1 minute or water-blanching for 30 seconds to break the skins. As an option,

DRYING METHODS: GOOSEBERRIES

DEHYDRATOR/ CONVECTION OVEN:

Use screens on trays or racks; coat with cooking spray if you're drying syrup-blanched gooseberries. Small gooseberries generally take 8 to 10 hours at 135°F; large gooseberries may take up to 24 hours.

SUN-DRYING:

Coat drying screens with cooking spray if you're drying syrup-blanched gooseberries. Small gooseberries will probably take 1 to 2 days to dry completely; larger gooseberries may take up to 4 days.

OVEN (NON-CONVECTION):

Large gooseberries may take over 18 hours and are not recommended. For small gooseberries, use screens on racks; coat with cooking spray if you're drying syrup-blanched gooseberries. Stir and rearrange gooseberries several times during drying. At 135°F, small gooseberries may take as little as 7 hours to dry or as long as 15 hours.

whole berries may be checked by syrup-blanching for 5 minutes then rinsing briefly; when dried, these berries will be softer, sweeter, and more vibrantly colored than those that have been checked in boiling water.

Freezing gooseberries before dehydrating also produces good results; follow the instructions given for blueberries on page 78.

Attempting to dehydrate gooseberries with no pretreatment isn't recommended. The fruits often become bloated and soft but fail to dry properly.

DONENESS TEST: Shrunken, slightly flattened, leathery, dark, and wrinkled; syrup-blanched gooseberries will be pliable and slightly sticky but no longer moist inside.

YIELD: 1 pound fresh gooseberries yields 1 to 1⅓ cups of dried berries. When rehydrated, 1 cup of dried berries yields about 1½ cups.

TO USE: Dried ripe gooseberries are a bit tart but may be eaten out of hand, especially if they have been syrup-blanched; their tartness is welcome in some dried fruit mixes and trail mixes. Feel free to use dried ripe gooseberries in any recipe calling for raisins or dried cranberries; the taste will be different but the recipe will work fine. Dried green gooseberries are generally best when rehydrated and used in sauces, pies, or cooked dishes; dried ripe gooseberries can be rehydrated and used in the same ways. To rehydrate, hot-soak for 1 to 2 hours, or cold-soak overnight.

Recipes in this book featuring dried gooseberries:

- Berry Cobbler
- Overnight Oatmeal with Fruit and Nuts

Grapes (Raisins)

First, a bit of advice: If you have to purchase grapes from the supermarket, it's probably not worth your time to dehydrate them. Raisins are available everywhere at a good price; your home-dried grapes are going to cost a lot more to produce and take a long time to dehydrate, and the taste is about the same. However, if you grow your own grapes, live in a grape-growing region, or pick wild grapes, then dehydrating them makes a lot more sense. You might also want to dry grapes, whether purchased or picked, to avoid the sulfites common in purchased raisins.

Leave the grapes on the stems until you're ready to work with them; they spoil quickly if the end is exposed. Discard any mushy or shriveled grapes or any with soft spots or signs of mold. We've become accustomed to seedless table grapes, but the grapes you dry may not be seedless; all wild grapes, for example, have seeds, and many home-grown varieties do, too. You'll need to remove the seeds before dehydrating the fruit. Cut each washed grape in half and pick out the seeds with the tip of a small knife; hold the grape half up to a strong light to check for seeds you might have missed. As you might imagine, it takes a long time to remove the seeds from a big batch of grapes! Grape halves need no further pretreatment; simply spread them on screens, starting with the cut side up.

If you're lucky enough to be working with seedless grapes, you can dry them whole, with no pretreatment other than washing and pulling them off the cluster, but they will take a long time to dry. To speed things along, steam-blanch or water-blanch small grapes for 60 seconds, 90 seconds for larger grapes. This *checks* (breaks) the skin so they will dry more quickly. Another alternative is to syrup-blanch them; blanch small grapes for 5 minutes, larger ones for 8 minutes. Syrup-blanched grapes dry more quickly than those that have been blanched with steam or water and have a sweeter flavor.

DRYING METHODS: GRAPES (RAISINS)

DEHYDRATOR/ CONVECTION OVEN

Use screens on trays or racks; coat with cooking spray if you're drying syrup-blanched grapes. Turn grapes over after about 6 hours. Drying time will generally be 12 hours to 20 hours at 135°F for whole small grapes or halves of larger grapes; whole large grapes may take 36 hours or longer.

SUN-DRYING

Coat drying screens with cooking spray if you're drying syrup-blanched grapes. Turn grapes over at the end of the first day. Take trays inside at night. Grapes will probably take 3 to 5 days to dry completely, depending on size.

OVEN

Because grapes take so long to dry, oven-drying is not recommended.

DONENESS TEST: Home-dried grapes resemble purchased raisins; depending on the variety, the dried grapes may be golden, purplish, or dark brown. They should feel springy, not mushy or soft, when squeezed. Syrup-blanched dried grapes will be very slightly sticky and may be a bit softer and more chewy than grapes that have not been syrup-blanched.

YIELD: 1 pound fresh grapes yields ¾ to 1 cup of raisins.

TO USE: Dried grapes are delicious when eaten as a snack and work well in dried fruit blends and trail mixes. Use them in any recipe calling for raisins. Like any raisins, they may be plumped by soaking in boiling water or cooking briefly, but dried grapes can't be returned to the fresh grape form.

Mangoes

Although some mangoes are grown commercially in California, Florida, Texas, and Hawaii, most mangoes that reach U.S. markets are from Mexico. Numerous varieties of mangoes are grown in equatorial zones, but in the United States, we generally see only a few types. The most common is the Tommy Atkins, a large fruit whose skin is primarily green with a red blush. Champagne mangoes, a smaller variety with yellowish skin, are sweeter but may be hard to find. Mangoes are best from early summer through early fall. A ripe mango yields slightly to gentle pressure; if the fruit is still hard, let it ripen on the countertop for a few days but don't let it get too soft or it will be stringy. Peeled mango chunks are increasingly easy to find in the supermarket freezer case, and these dehydrate well with no pretreatment other than cutting up any larger chunks. Dried mangoes make a tasty, sweet snack. Mango chunks are also excellent when candied; see page 121 for instructions.

Fresh mangoes have tender, juicy flesh with a large, flat, fibrous core. Wash and dry the mango, then set it on a cutting surface with the stem end up; the two plump, rounded sides (called "cheeks") should face sideways. Use a very sharp knife to slice off the cheeks, keeping the knife as close as possible to the core without cutting any of it off; the core is generally about ¾ inch thick on a large mango, and you'll be able to feel it with your knife as you slice alongside it. Now use your knife to cut off the narrow, fleshy strips attached to the core, following the core's rounded contour.

Place the cheeks on the cutting surface with the skin side down. Use a paring knife to cut the flesh into cubes roughly ⅜ inch in size, cutting down to but not through the skin. Use a large soup spoon to scoop the cubes out of the skin; if the mango is properly ripe, the flesh should come away from the skin easily. Use the spoon to separate the flesh from the skin on the two side strips, then cut into ⅜-inch cubes. (As an alternative to slicing the skin-on cheeks, you can simply peel the cheeks and strips, then cut the flesh into cubes, but the flesh is quite slippery so you need to be very careful.) The cubes are ready to dehydrate with no pretreatment.

preparing a mango

DRYING METHODS: MANGOES

DEHYDRATOR/ CONVECTION OVEN

Coat trays or racks with cooking spray. Mango chunks generally take 6 to 12 hours at 135°F.

SUN-DRYING

Coat drying screens with cooking spray. Turn pieces at the end of each day. Mango chunks will probably take 2 to 4 days to dry completely.

OVEN (NON-CONVECTION)

Coat racks with cooking spray. Rearrange pieces several times during drying. At 135°F, mango chunks may take as little as 5 hours to dry, or as long as 18 hours.

DONENESS TEST: Leathery and flexible, with a color like pale orange sherbet; pieces will be shrunken and flattened, especially in the center. Thicker pieces will yield to pressure when squeezed, and there should be no moisture in the thickest part. Frozen mango pieces may be slightly glossy when dried; fresh mango pieces have a dull surface when dried.

YIELD: A typical mango yields about ¾ cup of dried pieces, loosely packed. When rehydrated, 1 cup of dried mango pieces yields about 1½ cups.

TO USE: Dried mango pieces are a delicious out of hand snack. They can be snipped into smaller pieces to add to dried fruit mixes and trail mixes; scissors work better than a knife for cutting the pieces. To rehydrate, hot-soak for about an hour, or cold-soak overnight. The rehydrated mangoes may be puréed with the remaining soaking liquid, sweetened as needed, and used as a sauce.

Recipes in this book featuring dried mangoes:

- Best-Ever Fruitcake
- Frosty Fruit Cluster Mix in a Jar
- Fruit Smoothie
- Overnight Oatmeal with Fruit and Nuts
- Tropical Trail Mix

Oranges, Lemons, Limes, and Other Citrus

Whole dried citrus slices look really pretty; indeed, they are often featured in photos showing home-dried foods. Unfortunately, the whole slice contains a thick band of spongy white pith under the colored rind. The pith is very bitter, making the slices unpleasant to eat. Rather than drying the sliced fruit with the peel (that is, the rind and pith) attached, a better approach when drying citrus slices for eating is to remove the peel entirely and dry the fruit slices that way. There are two ways to do this: by peeling the whole fruit before slicing, or by cutting the peel off the fruit slices.

Choose fully ripe fruit, avoiding overripe fruit that has started to soften. Scrub the whole fruit thoroughly; a nylon bristle brush works well. If you're working with easy-to-peel citrus fruits such as Valencia oranges, clementines, and tangerines, you can simply peel the whole fruit with your fingers, then use a sharp knife to slice the peeled fruit crosswise, a bit thinner than ¼ inch; a serrated tomato knife works very well. The peeled slices are now ready to go into the dehydrator.

Most citrus isn't easy to peel, however, and for these it's better to slice the whole, unpeeled fruit, and then remove the peel from individual slices. Use a sharp knife (as noted above, a serrated tomato knife works well) to slice the whole fruit crosswise, a bit thinner than ¼ inch. Lay a slice flat on a cutting board, then cut straight down around the edges of the fleshy part of the fruit, making sure to include all the bitter white pith with the colored rind; each slice will require 7 to 10 cuts, but it goes very quickly. (Don't try to pick up the slice and cut away the peel in a continuous strip; it's inefficient and dangerous.) The peel-free slices are now ready to go into the dehydrator.

The colored part of the rind is called the *zest*. It contains aromatic oils that have a pleasant flavor and tang. If you plan to dry the zest — and you should, as it's a great seasoning and much more useful than the dried slices — you'll need a very sharp, thin-bladed knife. It's a bit tricky to cut the zest away from the curly peel pieces you'll have left if you peel the fruit before slicing. The easiest method is to lay a piece of peel flat on a cutting board with the pith facing down, then use the knife to shave the zest off in strips. Grasp the peel firmly with the fingertips of your non-knife hand. Hold the knife parallel to the cutting board with the sharp edge facing away from your body, then seesaw the knife slightly to cut away only the colored portion of the rind. Continue until you've cut away the zest from all the pieces of peel, discarding the pithy portions.

If you've cut the peel away from the fruit after slicing it, it's a quick job to remove the zest. Place a chunk of the cut-away peel upright (on its edge) on the cutting board and hold the pithy part with the fingertips of your left hand (if right-handed) so the colored rind is facing away from your finger-tips. Carefully cut away just the colored portion of the rind, keeping the knife as close as possible to the edge to avoid getting any of the white pith. You'll almost be shaving the zest off, although the piece won't be quite that thin. The strips of zest will be fairly small, roughly ½ to ¾ inch long and ¼ inch wide; continue until you've cut away the zest from all the pieces of peel, discarding the pithy portions.

Because dried zest is so useful as a seasoning, you might also want to remove the zest from whole citrus fruits that you're using in the fresh state. Use a very sharp paring knife and an abundance of caution to shave the colored zest off a whole washed orange or other citrus fruit; for safety, place the fruit on a work surface and cut away from yourself rather than holding the fruit in your hands. Dry the zest strips as directed and use the fresh fruit as you like.

DEHYDRATOR/ CONVECTION OVEN

If you're drying zest pieces, use screens on trays or racks; spread pieces out as evenly as possible, and stir after about an hour to separate. For slices, use screens if your trays or racks have gaps that are 1 inch or larger. Citrus slices generally take 9 to 13 hours at 135°F. Zest pieces generally take 3 to 8 hours, depending on thickness.

SUN-DRYING

Stir zest pieces after about 4 hours to separate. Turn slices over at the end of each day. Citrus slices will probably take 2 to 3 days to dry completely. Zest pieces will generally be completely dry in a day, less for very thin pieces.

OVEN (NON-CONVECTION)

If you're drying zest pieces, use screens on racks; spread pieces out as evenly as possible, and stir after about an hour to separate. For slices, use screens if your racks have gaps that are 1 inch or larger. At 135°F, citrus slices may take as little as 8 hours to dry, or as long as 19 hours. Zest pieces generally take 3 to 12 hours, depending on thickness.

DONENESS TEST: Slices will be flattened, flexible, leathery, and no longer sticky; they will appear translucent when held up to the light. If you dehydrate slices with the peels still attached, the rind will be darker in color and fairly brittle. Zest pieces will be lightweight, curled, and very brittle.

YIELD: 1 pound of whole fruit will yield 3 to 4 ounces of dried slices, which will generally take up about half of a 1-quart canning jar. Zest is very lightweight when dried; in general, the zest from two average oranges will yield about ½ cup of loosely packed, curly strips.

TO USE: Dried orange, lemon, or lime slices can be cut up and added to stewed fruit or other cooked-fruit dishes; if the peel is included, it will add a bitter note that may work well in some dishes, but for most uses, the peel

TO PEEL OR NOT TO PEEL?

Depending on how you'll be using them, you may not have to peel your citrus slices. Peel-on citrus slices, and strips of the peel that include the zest and a bit of the pith, are interesting when candied; see page 121. If you are using the dried slices for a simmering fragrance mix or crafts, leave the peel intact for appearance.

and pith should be removed. Some people enjoy eating them out of hand as an unusual snack, with or without the bitter rind. The dried zest strips should be stored in a glass bottle, then crumbled or chopped before adding to various dishes as a seasoning. Finely chopped dried zest works well as a replacement for minced fresh zest in recipes; use about half of the amount of fresh zest called for, then taste and adjust as necessary. If you prefer, use an electric coffee grinder/spice mill or blender to finely chop all the zest to a powdery consistency, then store the powder in a spice bottle; use a pinch of the powder in place of fresh minced zest in recipes. Orange, lemon, and lime slices that have been dried with the peel intact make lovely Christmas-tree ornaments.

Papayas

Recipes in this book featuring dried papayas:

- Frosty Fruit Cluster Mix in a Jar
- Fruit Smoothie
- Overnight Oatmeal with Fruit and Nuts
- Tropical Trail Mix

The sweet papaya discussed here has soft, sweet, reddish-orange flesh and a green skin (a different variety has firm greenish flesh that is not very sweet; it is popular in Thai and Vietnamese salads). Most sweet papayas found in the supermarkets are from Hawaii, although some are grown in southern California, Florida, and Mexico; they are generally available year-round. Dried papayas have a mild, somewhat musky flavor that is a bit reminiscent of fresh cantaloupe with perhaps a slight orange overtone; they are an unusual addition to dried fruit mixes or trail mixes but might not be worth the cost. Candied papaya chunks, however, are excellent; see page 122 for instructions.

Fresh papayas are pear-shaped; the most common red-fleshed varieties generally weigh ¾ to 1 pound, but some varieties may be up to 10 pounds. The center is filled with soft, round black seeds that are a good source of papain, an enzyme commonly used as a meat tenderizer. A ripe papaya is slightly soft and yields to gentle pressure; if the fruit is still hard, let it ripen on the countertop for a few days, but don't let it get too soft or it will spoil. Wash and dry the papaya, then cut it in half from top to bottom. Use a spoon to scoop out the seeds; if you wish to dry the seeds to use as a meat tenderizer, rinse them in a wire-mesh strainer, separating and discarding as much of the stringy orange flesh as possible, then spread them out on a solid liner sheet. For the flesh, use a paring knife to remove the skin from the halves, trimming deeply enough to remove the pale layer underneath. Cut each half vertically so the fruit is quartered, then slice crosswise about ¼ inch thick (for candied papaya, slice ½ inch thick; see page 122 for candying instructions). The slices are ready to dry with no pretreatment. For a sweeter, more chewy product that is great for snacking (but can't be rehydrated for use in recipes), syrup-blanch the slices for 4 minutes (simmer gently without boiling), then rinse briefly before spreading on trays.

DRYING METHODS: PAPAYAS

DEHYDRATOR/ CONVECTION OVEN

If drying syrup-blanched papaya slices, coat trays or racks with cooking spray. If drying the seeds, use a solid liner; stir seeds after about an hour to break them up. Papaya slices generally take 6 to 11 hours at 135°F. Seeds should be dry in 3½ to 4½ hours.

SUN-DRYING

If drying syrup-blanched papaya slices, coat drying screens with cooking spray. If drying the seeds, stir them every 4 hours; turn slices at the end of each day. Papaya slices will probably take 2 to 4 days to dry completely. Seeds take 1 to 2 days.

OVEN (NON-CONVECTION)

If drying syrup-blanched papaya slices, coat racks with cooking spray. If drying the seeds, use a baking sheet; stir seeds after about 2 hours. Rearrange slices every 2 to 3 hours during drying. At 135°F, papaya slices may take as little as 5 hours to dry, or as long as 16 hours. Seeds take 3 to 7 hours.

DONENESS TEST: Leathery and flexible, with a rich orange color; the slices will be shrunken and flattened, especially in the center. Thicker pieces will yield to pressure when squeezed, and there should be no moisture in the thickest part. Syrup-blanched slices will be reddish-orange and glossy; they may be slightly sticky when squeezed, but should no longer be moist-sticky. Seeds should be hard and brittle.

YIELD: A whole papaya of the common size yields about ⅔ cup of dried slices, loosely packed, and 2 to 3 tablespoons of dried seeds, which will yield about 2 tablespoons when ground or powdered. Dried papaya pieces don't return to their original shape when rehydrated; you'll end up with about the same amount of rehydrated papaya as the amount of dried papaya you started with.

TO USE: Dried papaya slices make an interesting out of hand nibble, especially if they've been syrup-blanched before drying. They can be snipped into smaller pieces to add to dried fruit mixes and trail mixes; scissors work better than a knife for cutting the pieces. Papaya slices that have not been syrup-blanched can be rehydrated for use in sauces or cooked dishes. To rehydrate, hot-soak for 15 minutes, or cold-soak overnight. The rehydrated mangoes may be puréed with the remaining soaking liquid, sweetened as needed, and used as a sauce. If you've dehydrated the seeds, powder them in an electric coffee grinder/spice mill or blender and store in a glass jar; sprinkle on meat before cooking to tenderize, similar to commercial meat tenderizers. The dried seeds have a peppery flavor, so the powder can also be used as an unusual seasoning. Note that some people are allergic to papaya, especially the enzyme found in the seeds.

Peaches and Nectarines

If you're lucky enough to live in an area where peaches or nectarines are grown, they are an excellent fruit to dehydrate. However, if you must purchase fruits that have been shipped in from afar, they may be prohibitively expensive; the quality might not be worth the investment, either, because peaches and nectarines destined for shipping long distances are not fully ripened and may never attain full sweetness.

Pick or buy peaches and nectarines when just ripe but not too soft. Any variety will work, as long as you choose fruits with bright color and sweet flesh; freestone varieties are easier to work with than clingstone varieties. Frozen (thawed) or canned peaches also dry well; they may not be an economical choice, though. Peach and nectarine slices and chunks may also be candied; see page 119.

Peaches have moderately thin skins and don't need to be peeled, although the finished dried fruit will be more tender if the skins have been removed; nectarine skins are a bit thicker, and peeling is recommended. To peel peaches or nectarines, drop them into a large pot of boiling water for 1 minute, then plunge into cold water for 1 minute; the skins will slip off easily.

Use a paring knife to cut the fruit in half, following the natural seam and cutting just until the knife encounters the pit. Hold the fruit in both hands and gently twist in opposite directions; if the fruits are freestone, one half should pop away from the pit (if it doesn't, you probably have a clingstone variety; see below for an alternative cutting method). Now remove the pit from the other half; if the pit doesn't come out easily, dig it out with a spoon or use the tip of your knife to carefully cut the flesh close to the pit until you can separate them (be careful if using a knife, as the peeled fruits are *very* slippery). Cut the halves into ⅜-inch slices or ½-inch chunks; for better appearance, cut away any dark red or brownish flesh from the area that had been next to the pit, as this darkens considerably during drying and may look unappealing.

Clingstone varieties are really difficult to pit cleanly; you'll usually end up mangling the fruit. It's easiest to ignore the pit and simply cut the fruit from top to bottom into ⅜-inch slices (½-inch slices if you want to dry the fruit in chunks), cutting parallel to the natural seam and skimming the knife along the edge of the pit when you get towards the center of the fruit. When you've sliced off the sides of the fruit, cut off the flesh around the pit in the center section that remains. Cut each ⅜-inch slice in half so you have two half-round pieces, or cut the ½-inch slices into ½-inch chunks if you prefer.

Drying untreated fresh peaches or nectarines is not recommended; they will become unappealingly dark and hard when dried. Pretreating the fruit with acidulated water, pectin dip, light honey dip, or commercial fruit protector will minimize this, but your home-dried fruits will still be darker and more chewy than purchased, sulfured dried peaches. A sulfite solution is the most effective pretreatment to prevent darkening and is a good choice unless you need to avoid sulfites. Another option is to syrup-blanch peach or nectarine slices or chunks for 5 minutes before drying; the dried fruit will be softer and more brightly colored than fruits pretreated with any of the options mentioned above. If you are drying

DRYING METHODS: PEACHES AND NECTARINES

DEHYDRATOR/ CONVECTION OVEN

Use a screen when drying chunks. Coat trays, racks, or screens with cooking spray. Slices and chunks generally take 6 to 12 hours.

SUN-DRYING

Coat drying screens with cooking spray. Turn pieces at the end of each day. Slices and chunks will probably take 2 to 4 days to dry completely.

OVEN (NON-CONVECTION)

Use a screen when drying chunks. Coat racks or screens with cooking spray. Rearrange pieces every few hours. At 135°F, slices and chunks may take as little as 5 hours to dry, or as long as 18 hours.

peaches or nectarines in the sun, always use one of the pretreatments recommended above.

Frozen peach slices need the same pretreatment as fresh peaches; if any of the slices are thicker than ½ inch, cut them into thinner slices. If you're drying canned peaches, simply drain them and pat them dry and cut into chunks if you like; home-dried canned peaches are soft and brightly colored and are very similar to commercially dried peaches.

DONENESS TEST: Slices will be leathery and may be somewhat crisp or brittle along the thinner edges. Chunks will be leathery and will yield slightly to pressure; there should be no moisture in the thickest part. Peaches and nectarines treated with sulfite solution will be bright yellowish-orange overall, even on the edges (unless the fruits were not peeled). Those that have been treated with acidulated water or commercial fruit dip will be darker, and the edges will generally be reddish even if the fruits were peeled. Canned peaches will be deep orange and flexible.

YIELD: The yield varies depending on the size of the fruit and ratio of pit. On average, 1 pound of fresh, whole peaches or nectarines will yield about 1 cup of dried slices or chunks. When rehydrated, 1 cup of dried slices or chunks yields about 1⅓ cups.

TO USE: Slices and chunks make a delicious snack, alone or in combination with other dried fruits. Add chopped pieces to fruitcakes or other recipes that call for dried peaches. Simmer slices or chunks over low heat in water just to cover for 30 to 45 minutes, then cool and serve in a fruit compote. To rehydrate slices or chunks, hot-soak for 45 minutes to 1¼ hours, or cold-soak overnight. The rehydrated fruit may be puréed with the remaining soaking liquid, sweetened as needed, and used as a sauce. Use drained, rehydrated peaches or nectarines in pies, sauces, cobblers, or any other recipes in which the fruit will be cooked.

Pears

Pears come in a wide array of varieties, from the tiny, somewhat rare Seckel to the larger, more common Bartlett, Bosc, d'Anjou, and others; colors range from green to yellow to brown to red. All can be successfully dehydrated, so use whatever you can purchase for a good price or pick yourself. Unlike most other fruits, pears are picked when mature but not fully ripe, then held in cold storage until needed; they are brought out of cold storage and ripened as needed. As a result, pears are available for an extended period, but they are at their best from late summer through midwinter.

Wash pears well. Peel or not, according to your preference; the peels will be tougher than the pear flesh after drying, but offer good fiber and extra nutrition. Cut away and discard any bruised or damaged portions. Cut pears in half from top to bottom, then use a melon baller or teaspoon to scoop out the seedy core. Use a paring knife to make a V-shaped notch along the central axis of each half, cutting away the narrow but tough line that runs through the middle (it looks like an extension of the stem); be careful with the knife as peeled or cut pears are *very* slippery. Slice the halves crosswise into ¼-inch-thick half-circles.

Home-dried pears that have not been pretreated are usually golden or tawny in color when first dried, but they will continue to darken in storage unless vacuum-packed or frozen. To reduce the slight darkening, pretreat slices with a light honey dip, acidulated water, or commercial fruit protector; for snow-white dried pears, use a sulfite solution. Sun-drying takes longer than drying in a dehydrator or oven, so all pears should be pretreated with one of the above methods to prevent excessive browning and possible spoilage; sulfite treatment produces the nicest-looking sun-dried pears. Candied pears are delicious; see page 119 for instructions.

Recipes in this book featuring dried pears:

- Hot Cereal with Fruit
- Overnight Oatmeal with Fruit and Nuts
- Stewed Pears

preparing a pear

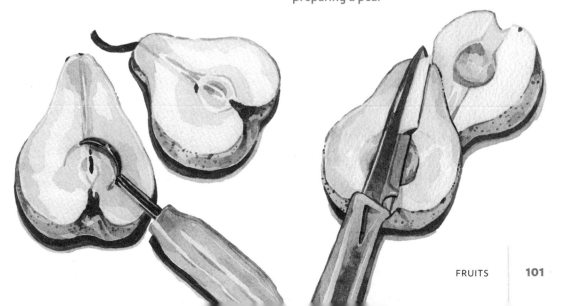

DEHYDRATOR/ CONVECTION OVEN

Coat trays or racks with cooking spray. Pear slices generally take 6 to 15 hours at 135°F.

SUN-DRYING

Coat drying screens with cooking spray. Turn and rearrange slices once or twice per day. Pear slices will probably take 2 to 3 days to dry completely.

OVEN (NON-CONVECTION)

Coat racks with cooking spray. During drying, rotate racks and rearrange pieces every 2 or 3 hours. At 135°F, pear slices may take as little as 5 hours to dry, or as long as 21 hours.

DONENESS TEST: Leathery and flexible, with a slightly grainy surface; there should be no moisture in the thickest part.

YIELD: 5 pounds of whole pears will yield about 3 quarts of dried slices. When rehydrated, 1 cup of dried pear slices yields about 1¼ cups.

TO USE: Dried pear slices are delicious as an out of hand snack. To rehydrate, hot-soak for 30 to 45 minutes or cold-soak overnight. Use drained, rehydrated pears in pies, sauces, cobblers, or any other recipes in which the fruit will be cooked.

Persimmons

Two types of commercially grown persimmons are often available at supermarkets and specialty shops from late fall through early winter. Hachiya persimmons are heart-shaped, with broad shoulders and a slightly pointed base; when ripe, they are reddish-orange with insides that are so soft they are jellylike. Underripe Hachiyas contain a large amount of extremely astringent tannins, so the fruits must be perfectly ripe for eating fresh. The squat, flattened-looking Fuyu is often referred to as a non-astringent persimmon because it can be eaten while still firm enough to slice; it is yellowish-orange when ripe, and the flesh is soft but not jellylike. A third type of persimmon, the native American persimmon (*Diospyros virginiana*), grows in the wild in the southeastern quarter of the United States; some people in that region also grow them in home orchards. American persimmons are astringent like Hachiyas and must be jelly-soft before eating fresh.

Recipes in this book featuring dried persimmons:

- Dried Fruit Bars
- Fruit Smoothie

Interestingly, drying mellows or eliminates the tannins, so it's possible to dehydrate persimmons — even Hachiyas and American persimmons — that are still firm enough to slice. Jelly-soft persimmons make delicious fruit leathers; see page 268.

For dehydrating, choose persimmons that are similar in texture to a ripe slicing tomato. Wash them well just before you are ready to work with them. Persimmons have a large, flat cap, rather like that found on a strawberry but much thicker and harder. Cut around the cap with your knife angled slightly downward, removing a pointed piece from the top of the fruit. Slice the unpeeled persimmons crosswise ¼ inch thick and pick out any seeds you find (the seeds are large and flat, but not all persimmons have them). Cut the circular slices into halves or quarters, or leave whole if you prefer; dried persimmon rounds are pretty but rather large. Persimmons need no pretreatment before drying.

DRYING METHODS: PERSIMMONS

DEHYDRATOR/ CONVECTION OVEN

Coat trays or racks with cooking spray. Persimmon slices generally take 9 to 14 hours at 135°F.

SUN-DRYING

Coat drying screens with cooking spray. Turn and rearrange slices once or twice per day. Persimmon slices will probably take 3 to 5 days to dry completely.

OVEN (NON-CONVECTION)

Coat racks with cooking spray. During drying, rotate racks every hour, and rearrange pieces every 2 or 3 hours. At 135°F, persimmon slices may take as little as 8 hours to dry, or as long as 21 hours.

DONENESS TEST: Leathery, flexible, and slightly translucent, with no moisture in the thickest part. Persimmons that have been dried in a dehydrator or convection oven are deep orange, while those that have been sun-dried or dried in a non-convection oven may be brownish-orange.

YIELD: 1 pound of whole persimmons (typically 3 Fuyu or Hachiya) will yield about 2 cups of dried slices, loosely packed. When rehydrated, they plump up but also pack into the measuring cup more closely, so you'll end up with about the same amount of rehydrated persimmons as the amount of loosely packed dried persimmon slices you started with.

TO USE: Dried persimmons are delicious as an out of hand snack; they have a rich, datelike flavor, and can be chopped to use in recipes that call for chopped dates. They can also be rehydrated and used in recipes that call for fresh persimmons. The centers rehydrate very quickly, but the peels remain somewhat tough, so they are best used in dishes where they'll be chopped or will get additional cooking. To rehydrate, hot-soak for 30 minutes, or cold-soak overnight. If persimmon slices are dried until crisp and brittle, they may be very finely chopped in a blender to produce persimmon sugar — delicious on hot cereal or other places where you'd use brown sugar as a garnish.

Pineapples

Fresh pineapples are widely available and are delicious whether dried plain or candied (see page 123 for candying instructions). Choose a pineapple that has a sweet fragrance, especially at the base; the central leaves on top should pull out with a fairly gentle tug when the fruit is ripe. Dark, wet spots on the sides or a mushy bottom indicate an overripe pineapple, which should not be used for dehydrating. Large supermarkets offer fresh pineapples that have been peeled and cored; this saves a lot of tedious prep time but adds significantly to the cost. Canned pineapple may also be dehydrated; all it needs is a quick rinse and cutting to size desired.

To clean a fresh pineapple, use a large, heavy knife to slice off the base and the leaves at the top. Pineapples have numerous eyes that are arranged in diagonal rows over the entire fruit; they're tough when the pineapple is fresh and become even tougher and harder when the fruit is dried. The eyes are deeply recessed below the surface of the thick rind, and if you cut away enough rind to remove the eyes, you'll be throwing away a lot of the delicious flesh. Instead, stand the trimmed fruit on its base and use your knife to cut down along the sides of the pineapple, cutting away just enough to remove the hard brown rind; when all rind has been removed, the eyes will look like small dark pockets all over the golden flesh. Now lay the pineapple on its side and begin to cut the eyes away in narrow, V-shaped channels just deep enough to remove the eyes. For the best results, cut the V-shaped channels on a diagonal, rotating the fruit as needed.

When you're done removing the eyes, stand the pineapple up on its base; the fruit will have rows of narrow V-shaped channels spiraling around it. Cut the sides of the fruit away from the core, which is visible

Recipes in this book featuring dried pineapple:

- Dried Fruit Snack Mix

- Frosty Fruit Cluster Mix in a Jar

- Tropical Trail Mix

as a pale circle at the top of the fruit; the core is very fibrous and should be discarded. Finally, cut the cleaned pineapple pieces lengthwise into batons that are about ¾ inch wide at the widest part, then cut these crosswise into ½-inch slices.

If you've purchased pineapples that have been mechanically peeled and cored, the fruit will look like a thick tube with a hole in the center where the core was removed. Slice the fruit crosswise into ¼-inch-thick

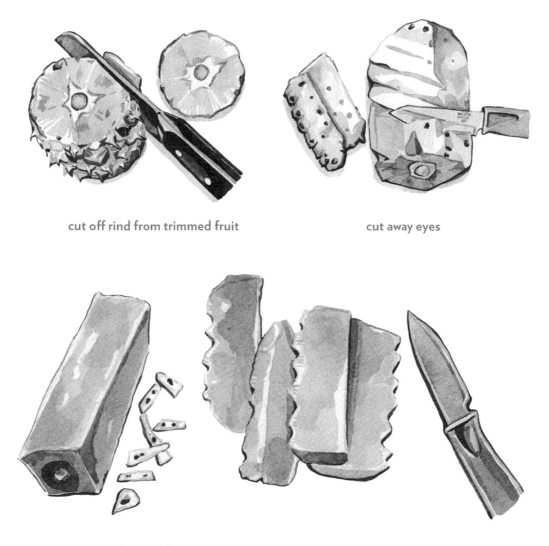

cut off rind from trimmed fruit   cut away eyes

core (inedible)   cleaned pineapple pieces

rings, then cut the rings into wedges that are ¾ inch at the wider outside edge; if you prefer diced dried pineapple (often called "bits"), cut the wedges into quarters. The pineapple pieces can be dried with no pretreatment; for softer, sweeter dried pineapple, syrup-blanch chunks for 5 minutes before placing on dehydrating trays. Pineapple chunks are also excellent when candied; see page 123.

DRYING METHODS: PINEAPPLES

DEHYDRATOR/ CONVECTION OVEN

Use a screen when drying bits. Coat trays, racks, or screens with cooking spray if drying canned or syrup-blanched pineapple. Pineapple chunks generally take 8 to 14 hours at 135°F; bits dry more quickly.

SUN-DRYING

Coat drying screens with cooking spray if drying canned or syrup-blanched pineapple. Turn and rearrange pieces once or twice per day. Pineapple chunks will probably take 2 to 5 days to dry completely, depending on shape and size.

OVEN (NON-CONVECTION)

Use a screen when drying bits. Coat racks or screens with cooking spray if drying canned or syrup-blanched pineapple. During drying, rotate racks and rearrange pieces every 2 or 3 hours. At 135°F, pineapple chunks may take as little as 7 hours to dry, or as long as 21 hours.

DONENESS TEST: Straw-colored, puckered, and fairly shrunken. The pieces will yield slightly when squeezed, but there should be no moisture in the thickest part.

YIELD: 1 fresh whole pineapple (about 4 cups of cleaned, cut-up fruit) will yield about 1½ cups of dried chunks. When rehydrated, 1 cup of dried pineapple chunks yields about 1½ cups.

TO USE: Dried pineapple chunks are delicious as an out-of-hand snack and work really well in dried fruit mixes. Bits work well in cookies and other baked goods, as a substitute for raisins or dried sweetened cranberries. Dried pineapple can also be rehydrated and used in recipes that call for fresh pineapple pieces. To rehydrate chunks, hot-soak for 1½ to 2½ hours, or cold-soak overnight. The rehydrated pineapple may be puréed with the remaining soaking liquid, sweetened as needed, and used as a sauce.

Plums

Plums of some variety grow throughout the continental United States, both in commercial production and in the wild. Generally, trees bear heavily, so fresh plums are readily available in most areas. Most plum varieties can be dehydrated. Purchased prunes are made from so-called "prune-plums," which are purplish to blue-black in color. Other plum varieties produce dried plums that look quite different from prunes; red-skinned plums, for example, produce dried plums with rich, deep reddish skin and golden-orange flesh. Plums are delicious when cut into slices or chunks and candied; see page 123.

For dehydrating, choose taut-skinned plums that are just ripe and yield slightly to pressure; if the plums are too soft, it is really difficult to remove the pits. Prune-plums are generally freestone, meaning that the flesh pulls away easily from the pit. Other varieties may be clingstone, which are much more difficult to pit. While plums can be dehydrated whole, you'll get better results if you pit the fruit and cut it in half or into quarters. If you do choose to dry whole plums, you must *check* (break) the skins by boiling whole fruits for 1½ minutes, then plunging into ice water.

To prepare plums, wash them well and remove any stem remnants. Use a paring knife or sharp, serrated tomato knife to cut the plum in half, following the natural seam and cutting just until the knife encounters the pit. Hold the plum in both hands and twist gently in opposite directions; if the fruits are freestone, one half should pop away from the pit (if it doesn't, you probably have a clingstone variety; see the next paragraph for an alternative cutting method). Now remove the pit from the other half; if the pit doesn't come out easily, use the tip of your knife to carefully cut the flesh close to the pit until you can separate them. Dry the halves as they are, or cut each pitted half vertically to quarter the fruit, if you like. For faster drying (or if your plums are large), cut each half into 4 pieces, or chop into ½- to ¾-inch chunks.

Clingstone plum varieties are really difficult to pit cleanly; you'll usually end up mangling the fruit. If your plums are small (as is usually the case with wild plums), it's best to simply check the whole fruits as described above and dry them with the pits in. Larger plums are best cut into slices or chunks. Simply cut the fruit from top to bottom into ⅜-inch slices (½-inch slices if you want to dry the fruit in chunks), cutting parallel to the natural seam and skimming the knife along the edge of the pit when you get towards the center of the fruit. When you've sliced off the

Recipes in this book featuring dried plums:

- Carrot-Oat Cookies
- Chocolate-Dipped Fruit Treats
- Dried Fruit Snack Mix
- Fruit Smoothie
- Hot Cereal with Fruit
- Overnight Oatmeal with Fruit and Nuts
- Quick Bread with Dried Fruits
- Squash or Pumpkin Bread
- Swedish Fruit Soup Mix in a Jar

sides of the fruit, cut off the flesh around the pit in the center section that remains. Cut each ⅜-inch slice in half so you have two half-round pieces, or cut the ½-inch slices into chunks that are ½ to ¾ inch wide.

Plums need no pretreatment. When drying halves, it's best to "pop" the fruit before putting it on the trays; this exposes more of the flesh and speeds drying. Hold a half in your fingers, cut-side up, and push the skin side upward with your thumbs to turn it inside out.

DRYING METHODS: PLUMS

DEHYDRATOR/ CONVECTION OVEN

Use a screen when drying chunks. When drying halves, position them on trays/racks with the cut side up; when the cut side no longer looks wet, turn halves over and continue drying. Plum quarters, slices, or chunks generally take 8 to 12 hours at 135°F; halves generally take 12 to 18 hours, and whole plums may take up to 36 hours, depending on size.

SUN-DRYING

When drying halves, position them on drying screens with the cut side up. At the start of the second day, or when the cut side no longer looks wet, turn halves over and continue drying. Plum quarters, slices, or chunks will probably take 2 to 3 days to dry completely; halves generally take 3 to 4 days, and whole plums may take up to 5 days, depending on size.

OVEN (NON-CONVECTION)

Plum halves and whole plums take longer than 18 hours and are not recommended. Use a screen when drying chunks. Rearrange pieces every few hours. At 135°F, plum quarters, slices, or chunks may take as little as 8 hours to dry, or as long as 18 hours.

DONENESS TEST: Flexible and somewhat springy, with no moisture in the thickest part; if pieces feel mushy rather than springy, they are not dry enough. The skins and flesh will be darker than those of the fresh fruits; color will depend on the type of plum used.

YIELD: Yield varies depending on size; 4 pounds of fresh, whole plums generally yield a bit more than a quart of dried slices or chunks. When rehydrated, 1 cup of dried plum chunks (without pits) yields about 1¾ cups.

TO USE: Dried plums have a delicious sweet-tart flavor and chewy texture; they are excellent eaten as a snack. Home-dried plums may be used in any recipe calling for prunes; if you've dried your plums whole, be sure to remove the pit before using! When coarsely chopped, dried plums may be used in place of raisins in cookies and quickbreads. Dried plums may also be plumped by steaming over boiling water until tender, generally 3 to 5 minutes. To rehydrate pieces, hot-soak in water to cover by an inch for 1½ to 2½ hours, or cold-soak in water to cover by an inch overnight. Halves, slices, or chopped plums also may be puréed in the blender after soaking or cooking for a delicious sauce. Dried prune-plums are sometimes puréed and used to replace some of the fat in baked goods; prune purée pairs particularly nicely with chocolate.

Raspberries

Like blueberries, fresh raspberries are now available in supermarkets year-round, but prices are high and quality is generally substandard when they have been shipped in from afar during fall, winter, and spring. For best results, dry raspberries only when they are in season, generally midsummer. (Note: These instructions may also be used for other compound berries including boysenberries, blackberries, dewberries, loganberries, marionberries, and youngberries; however, these berries all have lots of hard seeds that make the dehydrated fruit crunchy, which some people find unpleasant.)

Raspberries that are firm-ripe rather than juicy-soft or crumbly retain their shape surprisingly well after dehydrating. Softer raspberries may collapse on themselves and usually take longer to dry. Don't wash raspberries until you're ready to dehydrate because they'll spoil quickly once wet. When you're ready, rinse them in cold water and shake gently to remove excess water, then place on absorbent towels for a few minutes to dry them. No pretreatment is necessary (however, note that if you're dehydrating large blackberries or large specimens of the other berries listed above, you should cut them in half vertically to speed drying). When raspberries are abundant, you can use them to make a tasty leather; see page 268.

Recipes in this book featuring dried raspberries:

- Berry Cobbler
- Fruit Smoothie
- Raspberry Cake Topping
- Raspberry or Blackberry Tapioca

DEHYDRATOR/ CONVECTION OVEN

Use a screen when drying small raspberries. Firm-ripe raspberries generally take 12 to 20 hours at 135°F; softer raspberries usually take longer.

SUN-DRYING

Gently stir and turn berries at the start of the second day. Raspberries will probably take 2 to 4 days to dry completely.

OVEN (NON-CONVECTION)

Raspberries will probably take longer than 18 hours and are not recommended.

DONENESS TEST: Raspberries that were firm-ripe retain their shape fairly well after drying; they will be lightweight and somewhat puffy-feeling, with hollow centers like the fresh fruit. Raspberries that have collapsed on themselves will be more chewy when dried; they should have no moisture in the center.

YIELD: 1 pound of fresh raspberries yields 1½ to 2½ cups of dried berries, depending on whether the berries retained their shape or collapsed. When rehydrated, 1 cup of dried raspberries yields about 1¼ cups.

TO USE: Dried raspberries make an unusual snack. If the raspberries were firm-ripe, they will look like fresh raspberries when dried, but have a light and dry texture; when eaten, the fruits feel almost crispy on the outside, but the centers are pleasantly chewy and flavorful. Softer raspberries are more flattened and chewy and may have a better flavor. Dried raspberries make an interesting addition to dried fruit blends or trail mixes and may also be added in the dried state to muffin or cake batter; they are also delicious when added to green salads. Raspberries become pale and mushy when rehydrated; rather than rehydrating them separately, it's best to use them where they are rehydrated as part of the recipe, as in the ones listed below. For a quick raspberry sauce, add water to just cover and soak for 2 to 3 hours, or overnight in the refrigerator; purée the soaked berries with the remaining soaking liquid and sweeten as needed.

Rhubarb

Also called the "pie plant," rhubarb is technically a vegetable, but is included in this chapter since it is most often used as a fruit. Anyone who has a decent rhubarb patch will probably have more rhubarb than can be used fresh, and dehydrating is a great way to preserve some for later use. When dehydrated, rhubarb loses most of its bulk, so it takes up very little room in the pantry. When rehydrated it can be used just like fresh rhubarb for sauces, baked dishes, and many other recipes. Rhubarb also can be used in combination with other fruits to make tasty leathers; see page 268.

Choose fresh, firm rhubarb that is crisp and tender; avoid any gigantic stalks that may be lurking in the center of the patch, or any that feel limp or have started to soften. As you pick the rhubarb, cut off the leaves and a bit of the stalk at the base of each leaf; the leaves are somewhat toxic, so it's a good idea to trim generously when removing them. Also trim off the curved, wide base portion, and add the leaves and trimmings to the compost pile. (It's a lot easier to get rid of the leaves, in particular, before you bring the rhubarb in the house!) Rinse the rhubarb well in cold water. If some of the stalks are thicker than others, split them vertically so the pieces are more equal in thickness. Slice the stalks crosswise about ½ inch thick. If you'll be using the rhubarb to make sauces, pies, or other cooked dishes, no pretreatment is necessary; simply spread the rhubarb on the trays and start dehydrating. If you'd like to eat the dried rhubarb as a snack or add it to trail mixes, syrup-blanch the cut pieces for 5 minutes (simmer gently without boiling), then rinse briefly before spreading on trays. Frozen rhubarb works well for dehydrating; simply spread the still-frozen

Recipes in this book featuring dried rhubarb:

- Overnight Oatmeal with Fruit and Nuts
- Rhubarb and Apple Crisp

DRYING METHODS: RHUBARB

DEHYDRATOR/CONVECTION OVEN

Line trays or racks with screens. Coat with cooking spray if drying syrup-blanched rhubarb, and spread out pieces as best you can; after about 2 hours of drying, use clean fingers to separate any clumps. Rhubarb generally takes 6 to 10 hours at 135°F; syrup-blanched pieces may take up to 15 hours.

OVEN (NON-CONVECTION)

Line racks with screens. Coat with cooking spray if drying syrup-blanched rhubarb, and spread out pieces as best you can (they may clump together); after about 2 hours of drying, use clean fingers to separate any clumps. At 135°F, rhubarb may take as little as 5 hours to dry, or as long as 15 hours.

Rhubarb, which is actually a vegetable, is not recommended for sun-drying (see page 42)

pieces on the trays and put in the dehydrator. If any pieces are stuck together, you can separate them after about an hour of drying.

Note that rhubarb shrinks considerably during dehydrating, so even if it looks like your trays have small enough gaps to prevent it from falling through, always use screens on your trays or racks.

DONENESS TEST: Rhubarb dried with no pretreatment will be shriveled and shrunken, with a leathery to hard texture. Syrup-blanched rhubarb dries into flattened, lumpy clumps that are glossy and flexible; its texture is nicely chewy.

YIELD: 3 pounds of fresh rhubarb (about 3 quarts when cut up) yields about 2 cups of dried pieces. When rehydrated, 1 cup of dried rhubarb pieces yields about 2 cups.

TO USE: Syrup-blanched dried rhubarb makes a nice snack and also works well when cut up and added to dried fruit combinations or trail mixes. Rhubarb dried with no pretreatment is too tart to eat as is. To rehydrate it for use in sauces, pies, or other cooked dishes, pour boiling water in a ratio of 1½-to-1 (1½ cups water to 1 cup dried rhubarb pieces) over dried rhubarb pieces, let cool, then cover and refrigerate overnight. For quicker results, simmer rhubarb in water to cover generously until tender, generally 30 to 45 minutes; add additional water during simmering if necessary.

Strawberries

Modern fruit-growing practices have not done any favors for strawberry lovers. Sure, the fruits are available fresh throughout the year, and they are huge, plump, and impressive to look at; but anyone who's enjoyed a home-grown strawberry right off the plant knows that modern "super strawberries" are mostly about looks, not flavor. Whether you're dehydrating strawberries, using fresh ones to make pies or other dishes, or eating them *au naturel*, there simply is no substitute for locally grown, in-season strawberries — period. That said, it's worth noting that dehydrating intensifies the fruity flavor, making the supermarket behemoths taste more like, well, strawberries. Self-pick strawberry farms are a great place to get field-fresh berries bursting with flavor — and it's a fun outing for the family, too.

Choose just-ripe strawberries for dehydrating; overly soft berries are hard to work with. The best strawberries are richly red outside, with

Recipes in this book featuring dried strawberries:

- Dried Fruit Snack Mix
- Fruit Smoothie
- Strawberry Sherbet

flesh that's red all the way through; however, you can dehydrate strawberries that are pale inside — they just won't be as flavorful. Rinse gently in cold water, and then remove the leafy cap and any hard, white flesh at the crown. Slice large berries ⅜ to ½ inch thick, or quarter them vertically. Smaller berries that are less than an inch at the widest can be cut in half vertically rather than sliced; the smallest berries can be dried whole. Frozen strawberries also work for dehydrating; thaw, cut any large pieces in half, and spread in a single layer on trays. No pretreatment is necessary for either fresh or frozen berries, although a quick treatment with pectin dip produces slightly glossy dried fruit that is more colorful and somewhat chewier in texture. For a delightful treat, try candied strawberries; instructions are on page 124. Strawberries also work very well in fruit leathers; see page 268. For a special treat, also see the section on sun-style jams in chapter 9 (page 301).

DRYING METHODS: STRAWBERRIES

DEHYDRATOR/ CONVECTION OVEN

Line trays or racks with screens; coat lightly with cooking spray. The fruit may drip (especially previously frozen or pectin-dipped strawberries), so it's a good idea to place an empty tray with a solid liner (or an empty baking sheet, if drying in a convection oven) underneath the trays of strawberries. Slices or quarters generally take 7 to 11 hours at 135°F; whole strawberries may take up to 14 hours.

SUN-DRYING

For best results, coat drying screens lightly with cooking spray. Slices or quarters will probably take 1 to 2 days to dry completely; whole strawberries may take up to 3 days.

OVEN (NON-CONVECTION)

Whole strawberries may take longer than 18 hours and are not recommended. Slices and quarters may be oven-dried; line racks with screens, and coat lightly with cooking spray. The fruit may drip (especially previously frozen or pectin-dipped strawberries), so it's a good idea to place an empty baking sheet underneath the trays of strawberries. Rearrange pieces and rotate trays every 2 hours. At 135°F, strawberry slices or quarters may take as little as 6 hours to dry, or as long as 17 hours.

DONENESS TEST: Leathery to crisp; thicker areas will feel spongy, not soft or mushy, when squeezed. Previously frozen strawberries will be flattened and leathery.

YIELD: Depending on how they were cut up, 1 pound of fresh, whole strawberries yields 1½ to 2 cups of dried strawberries, loosely packed. Strawberries don't increase in volume when rehydrated, so you'll end up with about the same amount you started with.

TO USE: Dried strawberries make a nice snack and can be added while still dry to dried fruit blends and trail mixes; they are also delicious when added to green salads. Strawberries rehydrate very quickly and may be added while still dry to juicy fruit salads; once the mixture stands for 15 minutes, the strawberries will be soft enough to enjoy. Strawberries become mushy when rehydrated; rather than rehydrating them separately, it's best to use them where they are rehydrated as part of the recipe. For a quick strawberry sauce, add water to just cover and soak for 2 to 3 hours or overnight in the refrigerator; purée the soaked berries with the remaining soaking liquid and sweeten as needed.

Watermelon

Dried watermelon pieces resemble taffy in texture and make an unusual but delicious snack with a sweet, fruity, somewhat musky flavor. They should be enjoyed in the dry state as they don't rehydrate well. Slice the melon about ½ inch thick. Cut away the rind, removing all traces of white. Cut the fruit into strips that are about an inch wide, then cut the strips into 2-inch lengths; if you're preparing a seedless watermelon, the pieces are ready to arrange on the trays. If the watermelon is not seedless,

DRYING METHODS: WATERMELON

DEHYDRATOR/ CONVECTION OVEN	SUN-DRYING	OVEN (NON-CONVECTION)
Watermelon pieces generally take 10 to 15 hours at 135°F.	Turn pieces at the end of each day. Watermelon pieces will probably take 2 to 4 days to dry completely.	Watermelon pieces will probably take longer than 18 hours and are not recommended.

pick out the large dark seeds; the soft, tiny white seeds may be left in. Watermelon pieces need no pretreatment.

DONENESS TEST: Deep rosy red, puckered, shrunken, and flexible; pieces will yield to pressure when squeezed, and there should be no moisture in the thickest part.

YIELD: 1 pound of prepared watermelon pieces yields about 1⅓ cups of dried pieces.

TO USE: Eat as an out of hand snack. Dried watermelon pieces do not rehydrate well.

Recipes in this book featuring dried watermelon:

- Fruit Smoothie

Preparing Candied Fruit

HOME-CANDIED FRUIT is a delicious out-of-hand treat and works well when combined with other dried fruits as a snack. It may also be used in recipes calling for purchased candied or glacéed fruits.

The candying process used here is similar to syrup-blanching, but the candying syrup is more concentrated and the fruit is simmered for a longer time before going into the dehydrator. During simmering, the fruit becomes translucent and absorbs quite a bit of sugar. When dried, the fruit is typically shiny and jewel-like, with a sweet, fruity flavor and chewy texture. Home-candied fruit is also free of dyes and preservatives commonly used in the preparation of commercially candied fruits.

The predrying process recommended here is much simpler than some others, which require treatment that stretches over the course of several days (or even longer). Fruits treated with this quicker method — which takes less than an hour to prep for the dehydrator — may have a lower sugar content than fruits prepared with the longer treatment, but are still plenty sweet and candied enough for most uses.

Many fruits may be candied. The instructions below provide information on a variety of different fruits, but you can try candying other fruits by following the basic steps here and using the simmering times below as a guideline. Kumquats, for example, are delicious when halved, seeded, and candied; for a special treat, fill the hollow centers of the candied kumquats with melted white or dark chocolate, then chill until firm.

A dehydrator — purchased or home-built — works the best for drying candied fruit, which takes a fairly long time to dry. Sun-drying is an acceptable method if you can be assured of several days of hot, sunny weather with low humidity. If your oven has a convection fan and features a dehydrator setting, it will work for drying candied fruit, although it will have to run for a long time and may not be an economical choice. Because home-dried candied fruit takes a long time to dry, a non-convection oven is not recommended.

When you've candied all the fruit you're working with that day, strain the syrup through cheesecloth and pour into a clean jar; let it cool, then

Recipes in this book featuring candied fruit:

- Chocolate-Dipped Fruit Treats
- Dried Fruit Snack Mix
- Dried Fruit Bars
- Holiday Oatmeal Drops
- Best-Ever Fruitcake

Home-Dried Candied Fruit

Step 1.

Assemble your tools. In addition to a dehydrator (or convection oven) and appropriate racks and screens, you will need a heavy-bottomed stainless steel saucepan, a large slotted metal spoon, a candy thermometer or quick-read thermometer, a wire-mesh strainer, a large heatproof bowl that the strainer rests on comfortably, and nonstick cooking spray. If you live in an area where sun-drying is an option, you'll need screens as described on pages 50–51.

Step 2.

Select firm, ripe but not over-soft fruit. Wash and prepare as directed below for each type of fruit. If you are preparing more than one type of fruit on one day, prepare the lightest-color fruit first. Have the first batch of fruit completely prepped before you start making the syrup.

Step 3.

To make the candying syrup, measure 1 cup of honey in a 2-cup measure. Add 1 cup of water, and then stir until the honey is incorporated into the water. Pour into the saucepan. Add an additional ½ cup water to the measuring cup, stirring to get any clinging honey remnants, then add to the saucepan. Add 1 cup white sugar to the saucepan. Cook over medium-high heat, stirring constantly, until the sugar dissolves. Continue to

cook *without stirring* until the mixture boils, then cook without stirring until the mixture reaches 235°F on a candy thermometer or quick-read thermometer; this usually takes 15 to 20 minutes. Keep a close eye on the syrup as it cooks, and if it threatens to boil over, remove the pan from the heat immediately, then reduce the heat a bit and return the pan to the heat. Be careful not to spill or splatter any of the syrup on your hands; the boiling syrup is far hotter than boiling water and also sticks to your skin, so it can produce serious burns.

Step 4.

As soon as the syrup reaches 235°F, add a batch of the prepared fruit, adding no more than will fit comfortably with all pieces at least partially submerged (typically 2 to 3 cups of fruit). Stir to combine. Reduce the heat to medium and cook until the mixture is simmering (not boiling). Start timing, and cook for the amount of time indicated below for the specific fruit, adjusting heat so mixture continues to simmer without boiling and gently stirring occasionally. While the fruit is simmering, place the wire-mesh strainer over the large bowl, and have it close to the stove.

Step 5.

When the fruit has simmered for the proper amount of time, remove the pan from the heat. Use the slotted spoon to transfer the fruit to the wire-mesh strainer. Let the fruit drain for a few minutes; meanwhile, coat a dehydrator tray or rack with cooking spray (if the instructions for the specific fruit indicate that a screen is necessary, position that on the tray/rack, then coat that with cooking spray rather than spraying the tray/rack).

Step 6.

Gently spread the drained fruit on the prepared tray/rack or screen in a single layer, avoiding overlaps; use a spoon to move the fruit around, because it will be too hot to touch with your fingers. If the fruit is soft and clumps together, gently separate the pieces as best you can but don't worry too much if they are somewhat overlapping or touching. Place the filled tray/rack into the dehydrator and adjust it for 145°F; if sun-drying, cover the screen with cheesecloth and position outside in the sun, as directed on pages 41–46.

Step 7.

You may use the same syrup for another batch or two of fruit; use smaller amounts of fruit for these batches, since the quantity of the syrup will have been reduced when the first batch was cooked. After simmering a total of two or three batches, add an additional 1 cup honey, 1½ cups water, and 1 cup white sugar to the syrup and cook to 235°F as you did for the first batch; this second batch will cook a bit more quickly than the first batch. (If you don't have very much fruit left to prepare, use half of the amounts listed above: ½ cup honey, ¾ cup water, and ½ cup white sugar.)

Step 8.

Dry the fruit until it is no longer sticky and there is no moisture in the thickest parts, rotating trays/racks as needed and separating fruit if indicated. Turn the pieces of fruit after 4 to 5 hours of drying, or as indicated; this ensures more even drying and also makes it easier to remove the finished fruit from the trays/racks. Approximate drying times for specific fruits are given below; these times are for a dehydrator or convection oven at 145°F. Sun-drying will generally take two to three times as long; turn the fruit after a day of drying, and take the screens inside at night.

Step 9.

Store the candied fruit as directed below; before storing sun-dried fruit, place it in the oven set at 125°F for 30 minutes, or freeze at 0°F or below for several days.

refrigerate it for up to a month. You'll have a lovely fruit-flavored syrup that is great to top pancakes, pour over ice cream, or use in any way that you would use fruit-flavored syrup.

Candied fruit can be stored in sealed containers or plastic bags at room temperature, but may become sticky. Refrigerate the fruit if it seems too sticky, but bring it back to room temperature before eating as a snack; it's so chewy-hard and sticky when cold that it could pull out a filling.

APPLES OR PEARS (CANDIED): Slices, rings, and chunks all work well for candying. Slices and rings make a particularly lovely confection when coated halfway with chocolate; see instructions on page 127. Have a bowl of acidulated water ready before you start cutting up the fruit (do not use sulfite on fruit to be candied). Prepare fruits as directed on pages 71 (apples) and 100 (pears), peeling if you like and removing the cores; note that the peels get tougher during candying. Cut the fruit into ½-inch rings or slices; for chunks, slice the fruit crosswise ½ inch thick, then cut into chunks that are ½ to ¾ inch wide at the widest part. As you cut up the fruit, transfer it to the acidulated water to prevent browning before the fruit is added to the syrup, then drain the pieces just before adding to the syrup. Simmer in candying syrup for 20 to 25 minutes; the fruit should be golden and somewhat translucent. *Timing:* After about 5 hours in a dehydrator or convection oven, turn slices or rings; for chunks, use a wooden spoon or clean fingertips to separate individual pieces that may be clumped together. Candied slices and rings generally take 10 to 18 hours at 145°F; chunks may take somewhat longer.

DONENESS TEST: Translucent, shiny, and a rich, deep golden color; they will be brittle but flexible. Slices and rings will look like opaque stained glass with a slightly rough surface; chunks will be somewhat shriveled or puckered-looking.

YIELD: 1 pound of whole fruit will yield about 1½ cups candied slices or chunks.

APRICOTS, PEACHES, OR NECTARINES (CANDIED): These stone fruits are all excellent when candied, with a sweet, very fruity flavor; candied apricots are tangy-sweet. Slices and chunks both work well for candying. Prepare fruits as directed on pages 73 (apricots) and 98 (peaches and nectarines), skinning if you like and removing the pits. Slice fruits ⅜ to ½ inch thick; for chunks, slice fruit crosswise ½ inch thick, then cut into chunks that are ½ to ¾ inch wide at the widest part. Prepare no more than 3 cups at a time (or whatever will fit into your syrup), and be ready to put it into the candying syrup immediately; if the cut-up fruit is allowed to sit for very long, it will start to brown. Simmer in the candying syrup for 15 to 20 minutes; the fruit should be darker in color and somewhat translucent. *Timing:* After about 5 hours in a dehydrator or convection oven, turn slices; for chunks, use a wooden spoon or clean fingertips to separate individual pieces that may be clumped together. Candied slices generally take 9 to 16 hours at 145°F; chunks may take somewhat longer.

DONENESS TEST: Flexible, with a rich, deep orange color and a somewhat wrinkled, glossy surface.

YIELD: 1 pound of whole fruit will generally yield 1½ to 2 cups of candied slices or chunks.

BANANAS (CANDIED): These unusual treats are delightfully chewy, with a rich banana taste; they make a wonderful addition to a plate of sweet snacks and nuts at holiday time. Peel bananas and slice crosswise ½ inch thick. Simmer in candying syrup for 5 to 10 minutes; pick out individual pieces as they become puffy and somewhat translucent, transferring to prepared trays. Note that the candying syrup will become cloudy with particles from the bananas and is probably not worth saving for use as a pancake syrup. *Timing:* Candied banana slices generally take 12 to 15 hours at 145°F.

DONENESS TEST: Candied banana slices are puffy and somewhat swollen. They are golden to tan in color, with a burnished finish. When sliced or bitten, the bananas will be dry and chewy in the center, not moist; slices should be flexible and should yield to pressure when squeezed.

YIELD: 1 pound of fresh bananas will yield about 2¼ cups of candied slices.

CHERRIES (CANDIED): Sweet or tart cherries work equally well for candying. Fresh cherries look the prettiest when candied; thawed frozen cherries are acceptable but may look a little more ragged due to the mechanical pitting method used. Pit and halve cherries as directed on page 82. Simmer pitted halves in candying syrup for 25 minutes; the fruit should be somewhat translucent, although this may be difficult to judge if you're working with dark cherries. Previously frozen cherries may clump together when you put them on the screens, so you should break up any clumps as best you can. *Timing:* For previously frozen cherries, dry for about 5 hours, then use a wooden spoon or clean fingertips to separate individual pieces that may be clumped together. (For sun-drying, separate pieces after a day of drying.) Candied fresh cherry halves generally take 18 to 22 hours at 145°F; previously frozen cherries may take longer.

DONENESS TEST: Candied cherries are very shiny and somewhat wrinkled but still plump; they are flexible and will yield somewhat when squeezed. Previously frozen cherries will be flatter than fresh cherries. Depending on the variety used, the candied cherries may be bright translucent red or a deeper reddish-black that will not look as translucent.

YIELD: 1 pound of whole cherries will yield about 2 cups of candied cherry halves.

MANGOES (CANDIED): Fresh or frozen mangoes work equally well. Prepare fruit as directed on page 91, cutting into chunks as close to ½ inch as possible. Simmer in candying syrup for 20 minutes; the chunks should be somewhat translucent. *Timing:* Candied mango chunks generally take 20 to 25 hours at 145°F.

DONENESS TEST: Candied mango chunks are jewel-like, fairly translucent, and somewhat glossy, with a bright, deep golden color and very chewy texture. The chunks are generally somewhat lumpy and irregular in shape; they are flexible and will yield somewhat when squeezed. Candied mangoes are a bright, deep golden color.

YIELD: 1 pound of mango chunks (cleaned weight) will yield about 2¼ cups of candied chunks.

ORANGE, LEMON, OR LIME SLICES (CANDIED): Citrus fruits have bitter white pith under the colored zest, but candying mellows the pith quite a bit, making candied slices a tasty snack with a slightly bitter tang that many people enjoy. Scrub citrus fruits very well before drying or candying. Slice unpeeled fruit crosswise ⅜ inch thick and pick out seeds. Cut slices into halves or quarters. Simmer in candying syrup for 15 minutes; the rinds will be darker and may appear somewhat translucent, and the centers will be quite soft. Separate slices as much as possible when arranging on trays. *Timing:* Candied citrus slices generally take 12 to 15 hours at 145°F.

DONENESS TEST: Candied citrus slices look like stained glass, with a translucent center and dark, shiny rind. There should be no moisture in the fleshy part; bite into a piece to check.

YIELD: 1 pound of whole oranges, lemons, or limes will yield 2½ to 3 cups of candied slices, loosely packed.

ORANGE, LEMON, OR LIME PEELS (CANDIED): Candied citrus peels work well when cut up finely and added to baked goods; some people enjoy snacking on them as is. When candied, citrus peels are quite different from the dried citrus zest on page 94. It isn't necessary to remove every trace of the white pith, as you must do when drying plain zest strips, because the pith loses much of its bitterness during the candying process. It doesn't have the nice citrus flavor of the zest, though, so the layer of pith should be fairly thin. Cut small strips of peel from fruit slices as described on page 93, or simply use a sharp knife to carefully pare away a thin layer of peel from whole fruit; a sharp, serrated tomato knife works well on citrus rinds. Simmer the thin peels in candying syrup for 15 minutes. Spread out as evenly as possible on trays or racks that have been covered with screens; it is nearly impossible to separate the thin, sticky pieces at this point, but do the best you can. *Timing:* After 3 to 4 hours in a dehydrator or convection oven, use clean fingers to separate the peel pieces; it will be much easier at this point. (For sun-drying, check after about 6 hours and separate pieces if possible; otherwise, separate at the end of the day.) Candied citrus peels generally take 10 to 12 hours at 145°F.

DONENESS TEST: The peels will be very glossy and deeply colored; they are crunchy, brittle, and candylike.

YIELD: The candied peels will take up more room than the fresh peels did because they can't be packed together closely. In general, the zest from two average oranges will yield about 1 cup of candied peels, loosely packed.

PAPAYAS (CANDIED): Prepare fruit as directed on page 96, cutting into ½-inch chunks. Simmer in candying syrup for 20 minutes; the chunks should be somewhat translucent. *Timing:* Candied papaya chunks generally take 12 to 18 hours at 145°F.

DONENESS TEST: Candied papaya chunks are glossy and fairly translucent, with a very chewy texture. They are jewel-like in appearance, with a bright, deep reddish-orange color. Candied papayas are generally somewhat lumpy and irregular in shape. They are flexible and will yield somewhat when squeezed.

YIELD: 1 average papaya will yield about ¾ cup of candied chunks.

PINEAPPLE (CANDIED): Candied pineapple chunks have an intense, sweet pineapple flavor, with no trace of the acidity that some people object to in fresh pineapple; they're nicely chewy and make a delicious snack. Use fresh pineapple chunks for candying; canned pineapples are already fairly saturated with sugar and should simply be drained and dried with no further treatment according to the instructions on page 104. For fresh pineapple, clean and cut into chunks as directed on page 105. Simmer in candying syrup for 25 minutes; the chunks should be translucent around the edges. *Timing:* Candied pineapple chunks generally take 15 to 20 hours at 145°F.

DONENESS TEST: Candied pineapple chunks are slightly translucent and moderately glossy, with a bright, deep golden color; they are generally somewhat lumpy and irregular in shape. They are leathery to the touch and will yield somewhat when squeezed.

YIELD: 1 fresh whole pineapple (about 3½ cups of fresh chunks) will yield about 2 cups of candied chunks.

PLUMS (CANDIED): Candied plums are quite different from dried plums; they make an outstanding snack eaten as is and are excellent in fruitcakes or other recipes calling for candied fruit. Slices and chunks both work well for candying. Prepare fruits as directed on page 107. Slice quartered or halved fruits ¼ to ⅜ inch thick; for chunks, slice fruit crosswise ½ inch thick, then cut into chunks that are ½ to ¾ inch wide at the widest part. Simmer in candying syrup for 15 to 20 minutes; the fruit should be somewhat translucent. The skins may slip off the pieces after the fruit has been simmered; simply pick them out and discard them as you spread the fruit on the trays. *Timing:* After 5 to 6 hours in a dehydrator or convection oven, turn slices; for chunks, use a wooden spoon or clean fingertips to separate individual pieces that may be clumped together. (For sun-drying, turn slices and separate chunks after a day of drying.) Candied slices generally take 9 to 15 hours at 145°F; chunks may take somewhat longer.

DONENESS TEST: Candied plums are translucent, shiny, and jewel-like; their color varies depending on the type of plum used. Slices will be flexible; chunks will yield to pressure but there should be no moisture in the thickest parts.

YIELD: 1 pound of whole fruit will yield about 1½ cups of candied slices or chunks.

STRAWBERRIES (CANDIED): Candied strawberries aren't as pretty as some other candied fruits, but they have a wonderful flavor and are delightfully chewy. Start with fresh, just-ripe strawberries; frozen or over-ripe berries fall completely apart during candying. Wash and hull fresh strawberries as described on page 113. If the hulled fruits are small — ½ inch across or less at the top — they should be candied whole; larger fruits should be cut into halves, or quarters if very large. Simmer in candying syrup for 15 to 18 minutes; they will get very soft, so near the end of simmering it's best to swirl the pan rather than stir the fruit and risk breaking it up. Drain in a wire-mesh strainer for a few minutes, then gently transfer to prepared trays. Use a wooden spoon and a gentle touch to spread the pieces out, separating them as much as possible. *Timing:* For a dehydrator or convection oven, let dry for 3 to 4 hours, then use a wooden spoon or clean fingertips to separate individual pieces that may be clumped together. (For sun-drying, check after about 6 hours and separate pieces if possible; otherwise, separate at the end of the day.) Candied strawberries generally take 9 to 12 hours at 145°F.

   DONENESS TEST: Candied strawberries are flattened or somewhat lumpy, with a leathery texture and a dull, deep red color.

   YIELD: 1 pound of fresh, whole strawberries will yield about 1 cup of candied strawberries.

Recipes Using Dried Fruits

THE RECIPES ARE listed alphabetically by the type of fruit used (apples, apricots, bananas, and so on). Dried ingredients from this book are highlighted in **bold type**. Recipes that are especially written to highlight candied fruits are at the end of this section.

Fruit Smoothie

Make smoothies with one favorite type of fruit, or mix fruits to suit your taste and mood (see below).

Makes 2 servings (about 1 cup each)

⅓–½	cup **dried fruit slices, diced dried fruit, or dried berries**
1¾	cups milk (dairy milk, soy milk, or almond milk)
½	fresh banana
½	cup plain yogurt
1–1½	tablespoons honey
⅛	teaspoon vanilla extract

1. Combine the fruit and milk in a medium mixing bowl, stirring well. Cover and refrigerate overnight.

2. Pour the fruit mixture into a blender. Pulse a few times, then blend until the fruit is fairly well chopped.

3. Add the banana, yogurt, honey, and vanilla. Pulse a few times, then process on high until the mixture is smooth. If the mixture is thicker than you like, add a little more milk and process briefly. Divide between 2 glasses and serve immediately.

Use all one type, or a mix: apples, apricots, blackberries, blueberries, cantaloupe, cherries (sweet), honeydew melon, huckleberries, mangoes, nectarines, papayas, peaches, persimmons, plums, raspberries, strawberries, **or** watermelon

Overnight Oatmeal with Fruit and Nuts

Makes 6 servings (about ¾ cup each)

This is the easiest way to make hot, hearty, fruit-and-nut-enriched oatmeal. The mixture is cooked briefly and then soaked at room temperature overnight. In the morning, the oatmeal is tender; all it needs is a quick heating, and it's ready to serve. As a bonus, you won't have a sticky pan to clean.

3	cups water
¼	teaspoon salt
1¼	cups steel-cut oats
½	cup **dried fruit** (see below)
¼	cup chopped pecans or walnuts
	Milk, syrup, and butter (or other preference)

1. Combine water and salt in a nonreactive saucepan and heat to boiling over medium-high heat. Add the oats, dried fruit, and pecans; stir well. Return to boiling, then cover tightly and remove from the heat. Let stand at room temperature overnight.

2. The next morning, when you're ready to serve, spoon individual servings into microwave-safe bowls and heat at 70 percent power until hot. You may also heat the oatmeal on the stovetop over medium heat; you'll probably have to add a little water and stir to keep it from scorching. Serve with milk, syrup, and butter, or whatever you like.

3. If you don't eat all of the oatmeal in the morning, simply transfer the leftovers to a food storage container and refrigerate until needed; it will keep for several days.

Use all one type or a mix: cut-up apples, diced apricots, banana slices, blueberries, huckleberries, cherries, cranberries, currants, gooseberries, grapes, cut-up mangoes, cut-up papaya, cut-up pears, diced peaches, diced plums, **or** diced rhubarb

Chocolate-Dipped Fruit Treats

Yield varies

This easy technique is tailor-made for home-dried candied fruits of any type. It also works great with any dried fruit that is naturally sweet, such as apricots, sweet cherries, or plums; syrup-blanched fruit is particularly good.

> Chocolate chips (semi-sweet, white, or dark chocolate)
> **Candied fruit** or **sweet dried fruit chunks** (see headnote)

1. Set up your work area. Place a cake-cooling rack over a baking sheet or a piece of waxed paper; the rack will hold the dipped fruit, so you need something underneath it to catch drips. Also have a table knife, a rubber spatula, and a selection of spoons and forks ready. Position the candied or dried fruit next to the rack.

2. Work with no more than ¾ cup (4 ounces) chocolate chips at one time; this amount will coat about 1½ cups of fruit. Place the chocolate chips in a *completely dry* microwave-safe bowl. Microwave on 70 percent power for 45 seconds, then stir with a spoon. Some chips will be melted, but most will still be firm. Microwave on 70 percent power for another 15 seconds, stirring again afterwards; repeat until the chocolate can be stirred smooth. (Alternatively, melt the chocolate in the top half of a double boiler set over simmering water, stirring frequently until smooth.)

3. Place the bowl of melted chocolate next to the rack. Drop in a batch of fruit; try about ⅓ cup of fruit at a time until you get used to the process. Stir with a spoon to coat the fruit. Use a fork to lift a piece of fruit out of the chocolate, letting the excess chocolate drip back into the bowl; if the fruit is too heavily coated, roll the fruit between two forks, or against the sides of the bowl, to lessen the amount of chocolate adhering to the fruit. Place the chocolate-coated fruit on the rack; continue until all of the fruit in the bowl has been coated and placed on the rack.

4. Scrape the sides of the bowl with the rubber spatula, then add another batch of fruit and continue as above. If the chocolate becomes too stiff to work with, rewarm it in the microwave at 70 percent power, in 15-second intervals, until it is smooth again. If you need more chocolate, add fresh chocolate chips to the bowl and melt in the same manner.

Crumb-Topped Dried Apple Pie

Makes 1 pie

The filling in this pie is not high and full like pies made from fresh apples, but the flavor is outstanding — many people find it far superior to fresh apple pie. Try it and see what you think.

	Pastry for one 9-inch piecrust
2½	cups (packed) **dried apple slices** (a little over 3 ounces)
2	cups apple juice or cider
¼	cup white sugar
1	tablespoon cornstarch
½	teaspoon ground cinnamon
¼	teaspoon ground nutmeg
1½	teaspoons butter

CRUMB TOPPING

¾	cup all-purpose flour
⅓	cup light brown sugar, packed
¼	cup white sugar
½	teaspoon salt
6	tablespoons butter, slightly softened, cut into 6 pieces

1. Fit the pastry into a standard 9-inch pie plate (not deep-dish), decoratively fluting the edges. Refrigerate until needed. Position an oven rack at the bottom of the oven; preheat to 375°F.

2. Combine the apple slices and juice in a nonreactive saucepan, and heat to boiling over medium heat, stirring occasionally. Reduce the heat to medium-low and cover the saucepan. Simmer for 20 minutes, stirring occasionally. Stir in the sugar, cornstarch, cinnamon, and nutmeg. Simmer, uncovered, until thickened, about 5 minutes, stirring constantly. Remove from the heat and set aside, uncovered.

3. Prepare the crumb topping: Stir together the flour, brown sugar, white sugar, and salt in a mixing bowl. Add the 6 tablespoons butter and rub together with your fingers until the mixture is crumbly, with a mix of large and small clumps.

4. Scrape the apple filling into the prepared piecrust, spreading evenly. Dot with 1½ teaspoons butter, breaking into small pieces as you scatter over the filling. Sprinkle the crumb topping over the filling. Bake on the bottom rack for 35 to 45 minutes; the filling should be bubbling and the crust should be richly browned. Cool at least an hour before serving.

DRIED FRUIT SNACK MIX

These combinations aren't really recipes, just dried fruit combinations that I find appealing as snack mixes. Fruits should be dried separately, and then chopped as needed and combined. Serve as a finger snack, top with yogurt, or fold into whipped cream and serve in pudding cups.

Some good dried fruit combinations are:
Chopped apples, sweet cherries, and coconut
Strawberry slices, banana slices, and pineapple chunks
Chopped apricots and banana slices
Peach or nectarine slices, chopped candied orange zest, and banana slices
Peach or nectarine slices, pineapple chunks, banana slices, and coconut
Chopped plums, banana slices, and nuts

Cooked Applesauce

Makes about 1½ cups

1   cup water
1   cup **dried apple slices**
¼   teaspoon ground cinnamon, optional

1. Heat the water to boiling in a nonreactive saucepan over medium-high heat. Stir in the dried apple slices and cinnamon.

2. Reduce the heat and cover; simmer for 30 minutes, stirring occasionally, until the apples have softened and broken up. Cool before serving. The applesauce is ready to serve, or can be refrigerated until needed.

Quick Bread with Dried Fruits

Makes 1 loaf

1	cup **dried apple slices**
1	cup water
2	teaspoons baking soda
1	cup sugar
½	cup vegetable shortening
1	egg
2	cups all-purpose flour
1	teaspoon ground cinnamon
¼	teaspoon ground cloves
¼	teaspoon salt
1	cup chopped walnuts
¾	cup chopped **dried plums**
¼	cup **dried seedless grapes** (halved if large)

1. Preheat the oven to 350°F. Grease a 9- by 5-inch loaf pan; set aside.

2. Combine the dried apple slices and water in a blender and purée until smooth. Add the baking soda; pulse to blend and set aside.

3. Combine the sugar and shortening in a large mixing bowl; beat with an electric mixer until smooth. Add the egg and beat well. Sift together the flour, cinnamon, cloves, and salt into another mixing bowl. Add about ⅔ cup of the flour mixture to the shortening mixture and stir just until moistened. Add half of the apple purée and stir to blend. Stir in another ½ cup of the flour mixture, then the remaining purée; add the remaining flour mixture and stir until moistened. Stir in the walnuts, plums, and grapes. Scrape into the prepared loaf pan.

4. Bake for 40 to 45 minutes, or until a tester inserted in the center comes out clean. Cool before serving.

Double Banana Bread

Makes 1 loaf

1	cup (slightly packed) **dried banana slices**
⅔	cup boiling water
1	cup sugar
½	cup (1 stick) butter, softened
2	eggs
1	teaspoon vanilla extract
1½	cups all-purpose flour
1	teaspoon baking powder
¼	teaspoon baking soda
½	teaspoon salt
¼	teaspoon ground nutmeg
½	cup chopped walnuts or pecans, optional

1. Place ¾ cup banana slices in a heatproof bowl. Add the boiling water. Set aside until just soft, about 45 minutes.

2. Preheat the oven to 350°F. Grease and flour a 9- by 5-inch loaf pan.

3. Mash the soaked bananas well with a potato masher. Combine the remaining ¼ cup dried banana slices with ¼ cup of the sugar in a blender; pulse until the bananas are coarsely chopped. Add to the mashed bananas; stir well.

4. In a mixing bowl, beat the butter with an electric mixer until fluffy. Add the remaining ¾ cup sugar and beat well. Add the eggs one at a time, beating well after each. Add the banana mixture and vanilla; stir with a wooden spoon until well mixed.

5. Sift together the flour, baking powder, baking soda, salt, and nutmeg into another mixing bowl. Add the flour mixture to the banana mixture, and then stir with a wooden spoon until just moistened. Stir in the walnuts, if using. Scrape the mixture into the prepared loaf pan, spreading evenly.

6. Bake for 1 hour, or until a tester inserted in the center comes out clean. Cool on a wire rack for 15 minutes, and then turn the loaf out onto the rack to cool completely before slicing.

Lemon-Blueberry Yogurt Muffins

Makes 12 muffins

- 1 cup **dried blueberries**
- 1 cup lemon yogurt
- 2 teaspoons lemon juice
- 2 cups all-purpose flour
- 1 teaspoon baking soda
- 1 teaspoon baking powder
- ½ cup sugar
- 4 tablespoons butter, melted and cooled slightly
- 2 tablespoons honey
- ½ teaspoon salt
- 2 eggs, lightly beaten

1. Preheat the oven to 375°F. Grease a 12-cup muffin tin, or line with paper liners.

2. Stir together the dried blueberries, yogurt, and lemon juice in a large mixing bowl; set aside to rest for 15 minutes.

3. Meanwhile, sift together the flour, baking soda, and baking powder into a medium mixing bowl; set aside.

4. When the blueberry-yogurt mixture has rested for 15 minutes, add the sugar, butter, honey, salt, and eggs; stir well with a wooden spoon. Add the flour mixture and stir just until moistened; do not overmix or the muffins will be tough.

5. Spoon the batter into the prepared muffin tin and bake for 15 to 20 minutes, or until golden brown. Cool on a wire rack for 15 minutes, and then turn the muffins out onto the rack to cool completely.

Berry-Cherry Trail Mix

Makes about 3 cups

This basic trail mix can be altered to suit your taste. Keep the ratio of fruit to nuts about the same, but feel free to substitute any dried fruits you have in your pantry. You may also substitute peanuts or other nuts for one of the types listed. Use raw or roasted nuts, salted or unsalted as you prefer.

¾   cup whole unsalted almonds, skin-on or skinless (blanched)

½   cup **dried blueberries or huckleberries**

½   cup **dried sweet cherry halves**

½   cup **dried syrup-blanched cranberries**

½   cup walnut pieces

½   cup unsalted cashews

Combine the almonds, blueberries, cherries, cranberries, walnuts, and cashews in a large jar or other storage container; mix well. Store at room temperature, tightly sealed, for up to 1 month.

Berry Cobbler

Makes 6–8 servings

FILLING

2	cups **dried blueberries, raspberries, gooseberries, or huckleberries** (all one kind of fruit or a mix; if using a mix of fruits, you may include up to ½ cup **dried cranberries**)
2	cups boiling water
1–1½	cups sugar (depending on the sweetness of the berries)
2	tablespoons instant tapioca
1	tablespoon butter, optional

BATTER

4	tablespoons butter, softened
½	cup sugar
1	egg
1½	cups all-purpose flour
2	teaspoons baking powder
½	teaspoon salt
½	cup milk (2 percent fat or whole)

1. Begin preparing the filling: Place the dried berries in a heatproof bowl. Stir in the boiling water and let soak for 1 to 2 hours.

2. At the end of the soaking time, preheat the oven to 375°F. Coat a 9-inch square glass baking dish with cooking spray; set aside.

3. Drain the berries, reserving the soaking liquid. Add the soaking liquid and ½ cup of the soaked, drained berries to a blender. Process to a fine purée. Add sugar, to taste, and the tapioca to the purée, and blend.

4. Arrange the remaining berries in the prepared baking dish. Pour the purée over the berries in the baking dish. Dot with butter, if using. Set aside.

5. Prepare the batter: In a mixing bowl, beat the butter with an electric mixer until light and fluffy. Add the sugar and beat until smooth. Add the egg and beat well. Sift together the flour, baking powder, and salt into a medium bowl. Add about ½ cup of the flour mixture to the butter mixture

and stir with a wooden spoon just until moistened. Add half of the milk and stir to blend. Stir in another ½ cup of the flour mixture, then the remaining milk; add the remaining flour mixture and stir until moistened.

6. Spoon the batter over the berries in small clumps, distributing to cover the berries; the top of the batter will be uneven. Bake for 25 to 30 minutes, or until the filling is bubbling and the topping is nicely browned. Serve warm, with cream or whipped cream if you like.

Cranberry-Cherry Relish

Makes about 2 cups

- 1¼ cups water
- 1 cup **dried cranberries** (plain or syrup-blanched)
- 1 cup **dried cherries** (pitted if whole)
- ⅔ cup sugar
- ½ cup orange juice
- 1 tablespoon finely chopped **dried orange zest**, or 2 tablespoons grated fresh

1. Combine the water, cranberries, cherries, sugar, orange juice, and zest in a nonreactive saucepan. Heat to boiling over medium-high heat, and then adjust the heat so the mixture is bubbling very gently and cook, stirring occasionally, until the fruit has softened and most of the liquid has been absorbed, about 35 minutes.

2. Use a potato masher to partially mash the berries to the consistency you prefer. Let cool, then transfer to a storage container and refrigerate until well chilled. Serve cold.

Cherry Dumplings

Makes 4 servings

3½	cups boiling water
1	cup **dried tart cherries**
¾	cup sugar
4	tablespoons butter
½	teaspoon almond extract, optional
1	cup all-purpose flour
1½	teaspoons baking powder
¼	teaspoon salt
½	cup milk
½	teaspoon vanilla extract

1. Prepare the sauce: Combine the boiling water, cherries, ½ cup of the sugar, 2 tablespoons of the butter, and the almond extract in a heavy skillet or electric frying pan. Bring the mixture to a boil, reduce the heat, and simmer for 20 to 30 minutes, or until the cherries are tender.

2. When the cherries are almost tender, prepare the dumplings: Stir together the flour, the remaining ¼ cup sugar, the baking powder, and salt in a mixing bowl. Cut in the remaining 2 tablespoons butter with two knives or a pastry blender until the mixture is crumbly. Add the milk and vanilla, and stir just until the flour is moistened.

3. Drop the dumplings by tablespoons into the boiling sauce. Simmer over low heat, uncovered, for 5 minutes, then cover and steam gently for 15 minutes longer. Serve warm, spooning the sauce over the dumplings in individual bowls.

Tropical Trail Mix

Makes about 3 cups

- 1 cup roasted unsalted cashews
- ½ cup roasted macadamia nuts
- ½ cup white chocolate chips
- ¼ cup **dried red or white currants**
- ¼ cup **dried pineapple bits**
- ¼ cup (scant) **dried mango or papaya pieces,** cut in 1-inch lengths before measuring
- ¼ cup (scant) flaked dried coconut

Combine the cashews, macadamia nuts, chocolate chips, currants, pineapple, mango, and coconut in a large bowl; mix well. Store in a tightly sealed jar at room temperature for up to 1 month.

Tangy Grape Sauce

Served as a meat sauce, this is especially good with ham.

Makes about 2 cups

- 1 cup brown sugar, packed
- ½ cup boiling water
- 1 cup **dried seedless grapes**
- ¼ cup white vinegar
- 2 tablespoons butter
- 1½ teaspoons Worcestershire sauce
- ½ teaspoon salt
- ¼ teaspoon ground cloves

Combine the sugar and water in a saucepan. Simmer for 5 minutes, stirring until the sugar dissolves. Add the grapes, vinegar, butter, Worcestershire, salt, and cloves. Cook over low heat for 10 minutes, and serve warm as an accompaniment to meat. Refrigerate leftover sauce.

Couscous with Fruit and Nuts

Serve this easy recipe as a side dish with roast poultry; it also goes well with broiled or grilled fish or pork.

Makes 5 servings

- 1¾ cups chicken broth, low-sodium or regular
- 3 tablespoons diced **dried peaches, nectarines, or apricots**, cut into ¼-inch dice before measuring
- 3 tablespoons **dried grapes** or purchased raisins
- 2 tablespoons **dried cranberries**
- 2 teaspoons butter or olive oil
- ¼ cup slivered almonds
- ¾ teaspoon **dried herb blend** of your choice
- 1 cup couscous

1. Combine the broth, peaches, grapes, and cranberries in a medium saucepan. Heat over medium heat until boiling gently; cook for 5 minutes. Remove from the heat and let stand for 10 minutes.

2. Place a small strainer over a heatproof measuring cup. Strain the broth and fruit mixture. Set the strainer with the fruit in a bowl and set aside. Add water to the broth if needed to equal 1½ cups; set aside. Rinse and dry the saucepan.

3. Melt the butter or heat the oil in the cleaned saucepan over medium heat. Add the almonds and cook, stirring frequently, until golden brown; be careful not to burn the almonds. As soon as the almonds are nicely colored, add the broth and herbs. Heat to boiling, then stir in the drained fruit. Return to boiling, then add the couscous and stir well. Cover and reduce the heat so the mixture is simmering. Cook the couscous for 2 minutes, or until the liquid has been absorbed. Remove from the heat and set aside for 5 minutes. Fluff before serving.

Peachy Rice Pudding

Makes 6 servings

- 1 quart milk (2 percent fat or whole)
- 1 cup finely chopped **dried peaches or nectarines**
- ½ cup uncooked white rice
- ½ cup sugar
- ¼ teaspoon ground ginger
- ¼ teaspoon salt

1. Preheat the oven to 325°F. Lightly grease a 2-quart casserole dish.

2. Combine the milk, peaches, rice, sugar, ginger, and salt in the casserole; stir well. Bake, uncovered, for 2½ hours, or until the rice is tender, stirring occasionally. Cool before serving. The pudding will thicken and become creamy as it cools.

Stewed Pears

Makes 4 servings

- 2 cups water
- 1 cup **dried pear slices**
- 3 tablespoons sugar
- 1 teaspoon finely chopped **dried lemon zest**
- 3 whole cloves

Heat the water to boiling in a medium saucepan. Stir in the pears, sugar, lemon zest, and cloves. Cover and simmer over low heat for 20 to 30 minutes, or until the pears are tender. Serve warm or chilled.

Dried Fruit Bars

Makes 27 bars

1 cup **dried persimmon slices**

½ cup **dried apricot slices**

½ cup **dried fig pieces**

½ cup **dried candied cherry halves**

1 cup chopped walnuts or pecans

⅔ cup all-purpose flour

1 teaspoon baking powder

¼ teaspoon salt

½ cup (1 stick) butter, softened

1 cup sugar

2 eggs

1 teaspoon vanilla extract

Confectioners' sugar

1. Preheat the oven to 350°F. Grease a 9-inch square baking pan; set aside.

2. Cut the dried persimmons, apricots, and figs into small pieces; kitchen scissors may work better than a knife for this. Combine in a medium bowl with the cherries, walnuts, flour, baking powder, and salt; stir to coat the fruit with the flour. Set aside.

3. Combine the butter and sugar in a large mixing bowl; beat with an electric mixer until smooth. Add the eggs and vanilla, and beat well. Add the fruit-flour mixture, 1 cup at a time, beating with a spoon after each addition. Spread the batter in the prepared baking pan.

4. Bake for 45 minutes. Cool completely in the pan before cutting into 1- by 3-inch bars. Roll each bar in confectioners' sugar.

Raspberry or Blackberry Tapioca

Makes 4 servings

2	cups water
½	cup **dried raspberries or blackberries**
½	cup sugar
¼	cup quick-cooking tapioca
⅛	teaspoon salt
1	teaspoon finely chopped **dried lemon zest**
	Whipped cream, for serving

1. Heat the water to boiling in a medium saucepan. Stir in the raspberries. Cover the saucepan and let soak for 2 to 3 hours, or refrigerate overnight.

2. When you're ready to continue, add the sugar, tapioca, and salt to the berry mixture in the saucepan. Cook over medium heat for 10 to 12 minutes, stirring constantly, until the tapioca is cooked and the mixture has thickened. Remove from the heat and stir in the lemon zest. Scrape into a serving bowl and set aside until the mixture cools. Cover the bowl and refrigerate until well chilled. Serve with whipped cream.

Raspberry Cake Topping

Makes 12 servings

⅓ cup **dried raspberries**

⅓ cup boiling water

2 egg whites*

1⅓ cups sugar

1 teaspoon finely chopped **dried lemon zest**

1 white, yellow or angel food cake, baked in an 8- by 12-inch pan

1. Place the raspberries in a heatproof bowl. Stir in the boiling water and let soak for 2 to 3 hours, or refrigerate overnight.

2. Combine the egg whites and sugar in a large deep mixing bowl; beat with an electric mixer until light and stiff enough to stand in peaks. Fold in the raspberry mixture and lemon zest. Spread over the top of the cooled cake. Serve immediately.

* Use commercially pasteurized egg whites (available in the dairy case) if concerned about salmonella.

Rhubarb and Apple Crisp

Makes 6 servings

¾ cup **dried rhubarb**

1¼ cups boiling water

2 medium Braeburn apples or other apples suitable for pie

⅔ cup white sugar

1 tablespoon cornstarch

½ teaspoon ground cinnamon

½ teaspoon vanilla extract

1 cup old-fashioned rolled oats

½ cup granola

⅓ cup all-purpose flour

⅓ cup golden brown sugar, packed

½ cup (1 stick) butter, softened

1. Place the rhubarb in a heatproof bowl and stir in the boiling water. Set aside until cool, then cover and refrigerate overnight.

2. When you're ready to bake, preheat the oven to 350°F. Lightly grease a 9-inch square baking dish. Drain the rhubarb thoroughly, discarding the soaking water. Place the rhubarb in a mixing bowl. Peel, core, and slice the apples, then cut each slice into 3 pieces. Add to the rhubarb. Add the white sugar, cornstarch, cinnamon, and vanilla to the rhubarb; stir well and scrape into the prepared baking dish.

3. Stir together the oats, granola, flour, and brown sugar in a clean mixing bowl. Cut the butter into 8 chunks, adding them to the oat mixture one by one. Use your fingers to rub the oat mixture and the butter together, forming clumps ranging from ¼ to ½ inch in size. Scatter the clumps evenly over the rhubarb mixture.

4. Bake for 45 to 50 minutes, or until the fruit is bubbling and the topping is lightly browned. Cool for at least 1 hour before serving.

Strawberry Sherbet

Makes 4 servings

This is a great summer snack.

¾ cup water

¾ cup **dried strawberries**

10 ounces sweetened condensed milk

2 tablespoons lemon juice

2 egg whites*

1. Heat the water to boiling in a small saucepan over medium heat. Stir in the strawberries. Cover and simmer over low heat for 20 to 30 minutes, or until the strawberries are soft.

2. Press the strawberries and cooking liquid through a wire-mesh strainer into a bowl, discarding the seedy material in strainer. Stir the condensed milk and lemon juice into the strained strawberries in the bowl. Cover and refrigerate until cold.

3. In a clean mixing bowl, beat the egg whites with a whisk or electric mixer until stiff peaks form. Fold into the strawberry mixture. Transfer to a flat, rimmed container, such as an undivided ice cube tray; freeze until firm.

* Use commercially pasteurized egg whites (available in the dairy case) if concerned about salmonella.

Holiday Oatmeal Drops

Makes about 4 dozen cookies

¾ cup brown sugar, packed

⅔ cup (1 stick plus just under 3 tablespoons) butter, softened

1 egg

1 teaspoon vanilla extract

2 cups all-purpose flour

1 cup old-fashioned rolled oats

1 cup **mixed dried candied fruit**, cut into small pieces before measuring

½ cup shredded coconut

2 teaspoons baking powder

½ teaspoon salt

¼ cup milk

1 cup pecan halves, approximate

1. Preheat the oven to 350°F. Lightly grease several baking sheets; set aside.

2. Combine the sugar and butter in a large mixing bowl; beat with an electric mixer until smooth. Add the egg and vanilla, and beat well. In another bowl, stir together the flour, oats, candied fruit, coconut, baking powder, and salt. Add, a little at a time alternately with the milk, to the butter mixture, stirring well with a spoon after each addition.

3. Drop the dough by heaping teaspoons onto the prepared baking sheets. Press a pecan half into the top of each cookie. Bake for 10 to 12 minutes. Cool on baking sheets for 5 minutes, then transfer the cookies to a cooling rack and allow to cool completely.

Best-Ever Fruitcake

Makes 2 medium loaves

Feel free to substitute other types of candied or dried fruits for the ones listed. If you don't have enough home-prepared fruit, purchased fruit can be used to fill in, but this fruitcake is best with your own candied and dried fruits. If you prefer, substitute dark rum for the brandy.

FRUIT MIXTURE

½   cup **dried candied cherry halves**

½   cup **diced dried apricots***

½   cup **dried grapes** or purchased raisins, cut in halves or thirds if large

⅓   cup **dried candied mango chunks***

⅓   cup **dried candied pineapple chunks***

¼   cup **dried blueberries or huckleberries**

¼   cup **dried cranberries**, preferably syrup-blanched

¼   teaspoon finely chopped **dried orange zest**

½   cup brandy

½   cup apricot nectar

CAKE MIXTURE

1¼   cups all-purpose flour

½   teaspoon ground nutmeg

½   teaspoon salt

¼   teaspoon ground cinnamon

¼   teaspoon ground allspice

¼   teaspoon ground cardamom

¼   teaspoon baking soda

½   cup (1 stick) unsalted butter, softened

½   cup brown sugar, packed

3   eggs, room temperature

1½   teaspoons vanilla extract

1¼   cups chopped pecans

* Cut the fruits into ½-inch dice before measuring. Kitchen scissors work better than a knife when cutting dried or candied fruits.

1. Prepare the fruit mixture the day before you plan to bake: In a large glass mixing bowl, combine the cherries, apricots, grapes, mangoes, pineapple, blueberries, cranberries, orange zest, brandy, and apricot nectar. Stir well; cover and let stand at room temperature overnight.

2. Preheat the oven to 275°F. Grease two medium loaf pans (8½ by 4¼ by 2½ inches deep; 9- by 4- by 3½-inch foil pans will also work) and line with kitchen parchment; set aside.

3. Sift together the flour, nutmeg, salt, cinnamon, allspice, cardamom, and baking soda into a bowl; set aside. In a large mixing bowl, beat the butter with an electric mixer until light and fluffy. Add the sugar and beat until smooth. Add the eggs one at a time, beating well after each. Beat in the vanilla. Add the flour mixture, and then stir with a sturdy wooden spoon until well mixed. Add the pecans and the soaked fruit, including any unab-sorbed liquid; stir with the wooden spoon until combined. Spoon into the prepared pans, dividing evenly. Use a rubber spatula to smooth the tops.

4. Place the pans in the center of the oven and bake until a tester inserted into the center of one of the cakes comes out clean, 1 hour 30 minutes to 1 hour 45 minutes. Set the pans on a cooling rack and allow the loaves to cool completely.

5. Turn the cooled loaves out of the pans. Wrap tightly in plastic wrap, then wrap again with foil, sealing edges tightly. The loaves keep well at room temperature for a week or longer and may be frozen after wrapping for long-term storage.

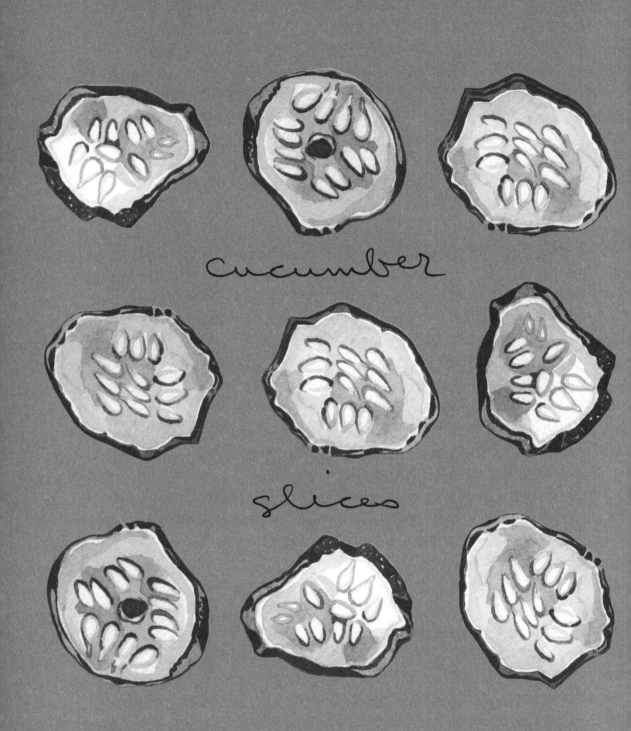

cucumber

slices

CHAPTER 5

Vegetables

VEGETABLES are often the mainstay of the dried-foods pantry because they can be used in so many ways. Rehydrated beets, corn, cauliflower, and winter squash, for example, look just like fresh-cooked vegetables and can be served by themselves to bring the taste of the harvest to any meal, any time of year. Other dried vegetables work best when used in hearty soups, stews, casseroles, or other dishes. Dried vegetables are easy to store and take up less room than canned or frozen vegetables.

Some dried vegetables can be enjoyed in the dried state; dried cauliflower chunks, thinly sliced parsnips, and radish slices make unusual out of hand snacks, and dried cucumber slices are wonderful when crumbled to top green salads. Powder made from dried vegetables can be used to make broth or to enrich soups and other liquids; vegetable powder can also be added to meatloaf and casseroles. Most dried vegetables, however, are rehydrated before use.

Depending on how you want to use them once they're dry, most vegetables should be sliced, chopped, or shredded before dehydrating. Some vegetables are best when blanched in steam or boiling water before dehydrating; this slows down enzymatic activity that would otherwise cause the dried vegetables to lose quality during storage. Like apples and some other fruits, potatoes, parsnips, and salsify benefit from pretreatment to minimize darkening. Pretreatments including blanching are optional; the pretreatments recommended in the listings of individual vegetables below will ensure the highest quality, particularly during storage, but it's up to you.

Compared to fruits, vegetables are naturally low in both acid and sugar, which means that they're more prone to spoilage and attack by harmful organisms. (This is also why vegetables can't be canned in a water-bath canner unless they are pickled.) As mentioned in the section on sun-drying in chapter 3, modern food science dictates that sun-drying should not be used for vegetables, due to risk of increased bacterial growth. Tomatoes and tomatillos are exempt from this caution because they are actually fruits, with enough acid to prevent problems. Shell beans, black-eyed peas, and crowder peas may also be dried in the sun if they are left on the vines until partially dry; see page 155 for information. Small hot chile peppers can also be sun-dried; see page 185 for details. Instructions are not given in this book for sun-drying other vegetables; should you choose to do so, the basic techniques are the same as those used for fruits.

Drying temperatures for vegetables should be a bit lower than those used for fruits. Too much heat may cause the cut surfaces of vegetables to harden prematurely. This "case hardening" traps moisture in the center of the piece (this isn't an issue with fruits because they contain more moisture and sugar, both of which help prevent case hardening). To avoid this, a target temperature of 125°F is recommended for most vegetables, although some cooks dehydrate vegetables at 135°F.

Some dried vegetables rehydrate very quickly and can be added directly to soups and stews while still in the dry form. These include leafy vegetables such as spinach and kale and small or thin pieces such as diced onions, shredded carrots, and sliced mushrooms. More substantial vegetables such as green beans, sliced carrots, and diced turnips rehydrate more slowly and are best when rehydrated as described below before cooking, whether you're serving them on their own or adding them to other dishes.

Vegetables that have been dried until very crisp or brittle can be powdered and then used to flavor soups, stews, casseroles, and other dishes. A blender works better than a food processor, because in a blender there's less room for the dried food to fly around and away from the blades. A small electric coffee mill/spice grinder is an even better choice; you may want to have one of these dedicated strictly to food so that coffee oils or strong spices don't end up flavoring your vegetable powders. Store vegetable powders in small, tightly sealed glass jars. Chapter 8 also explains how to make homemade baby foods from fresh vegetables, a process that's very similar to making powders.

Here you'll find specific instructions for more than 40 types of vegetables, including recommendations for pretreatment where appropriate. Vegetables are listed in alphabetical order, with a few exceptions. Parsnips, rutabagas, and turnips are discussed together because both dehydrating information and uses are the same; similarly, pimientos are combined with bell peppers, and pumpkin is included with winter squash. Approximate drying times are given for a dehydrator using a target temperature of 125°F (135 to 145°F for tomatoes and tomatillos). If you dehydrate at a higher or lower temperature, your times will change accordingly; variables such as humidity and the total amount of food in your dehydrator will also affect drying time, sometimes dramatically, so use the times given as a general guideline.

Each listing also includes suggestions for using the dried vegetable, including a list of recipes in this book that use the vegetable. Check the index to locate the specific recipe.

REHYDRATION REMINDER

To hot-soak, place the dried fruit in a *heatproof* bowl and add boiling water or fruit juice to just cover or as directed. Stir and let stand at room temperature until softened.

To cold-soak, place the dried fruit in a mixing bowl and add room-temperature or cold water, or fruit juice, to just cover or as directed. Stir. Cover the bowl and refrigerate overnight.

Drying Vegetables: From Asparagus to Zucchini

Asparagus

This spring vegetable is at its best when locally grown and processed shortly after picking. It's available in supermarkets throughout the year, however, and it holds up fairly well to shipping (although it gets quite expensive). Asparagus spears snap off easily at ground level when ready to pick. If buying asparagus, look for stalks that are firm, plump, and crisp, with tightly closed tips. If the stalk is beginning to wither, if the tips have started to open, or if the bottom half of the stem is woody, the asparagus is past prime and shouldn't be used for dehydrating.

Asparagus seems like two different vegetables, especially when it's been dehydrated. The tips are much more tender than the stalks; they dry more quickly and also rehydrate more quickly. The stalks have tough skins that act as a barrier, hindering both drying and rehydrating; even small asparagus suffers from this effect. The very best way to prepare asparagus for dehydrating is to cut off the tips at the point where the buds end, and then peel the stalks completely or split them vertically before cutting them into shorter lengths. The peeled or split stalks take about the same amount of time to dry, and to rehydrate, as do the tips; they also are a lovely bright green when rehydrated and cooked. If the stalks are dried without peeling or splitting, they take up to twice as long to dry, and they don't plump up very well during rehydrating; they're also a drab, dull color when rehydrated and cooked. Peeling or splitting the stalks is extra work and you can skip this step, but your results will be better if you take the time to do it.

Wash and drain the asparagus, then cut or snap off any dried ends. For best results, separate the tips as described above, then peel or split the stalks; for very thin stalks, it's sufficient to simply peel off a strip on two sides of the stalk. Cut asparagus spears — peeled, split, or unpeeled, as you prefer — into 1- to 2-inch lengths; stalk portions that are thicker than ½ inch should be split lengthwise whether they're peeled or unpeeled.

Recipes in this book featuring dried asparagus:

- Scalloped Asparagus

DEHYDRATOR/CONVECTION OVEN

Asparagus tips, and stalks that have been peeled or split before cutting into pieces, generally take 6 to 12 hours at 125°F; stalk pieces that have not been peeled may take up to 18 hours.

OVEN (NON-CONVECTION)

Stir pieces several times during drying. At 125°F, asparagus tips, and stalks that have been peeled or split, may take as little as 6 hours to dry, or as long as 18 hours. Stalk pieces that have not been split may take over 24 hours.

Vegetables are not recommended for sun-drying (see page 42)

Steam-blanch for 2 to 3 minutes or blanch in boiling water for 1½ to 2 minutes. Chill in ice water, then drain and pat dry.

DONENESS TEST: Withered, brittle, and stiff; if the asparagus can be bent, it isn't dry enough.

YIELD: 1 pound of fresh asparagus cut into pieces yields about ⅔ cup dried. When rehydrated, 1 cup of dried asparagus pieces yields 1½ to 2 cups.

TO USE: To rehydrate, hot-soak for 30 minutes to 1 hour, or cold-soak overnight. Add rehydrated asparagus to soups or stews for additional cooking, or simmer in the soaking water until tender for use as a plain vegetable. For additional appeal, serve cooked asparagus in a cheese sauce or cream sauce. Dried asparagus may also be powdered for use in soups or casseroles.

Beans and Peas: A General Discussion

Beans and peas are both *legumes*, plants that produce a long pod containing large seeds. Some legumes have tender pods that are eaten before the seeds mature; these include green beans, sugar-snap peas, and snow peas. Other legumes, including shell beans (pintos, black beans, navy beans, and the like) and fresh green (English) peas, have tough pods, so the seeds are the part that is eaten. To further complicate the matter, the edible seeds of shell beans and many other legumes are far more common in the dried form as the familiar dried beans, dried lentils, or dried split peas.

These distinctions are important to avoid confusion in the dehydrating instructions for each type of legume. For clarity, the tender-podded legumes are discussed separately from the tough-podded legumes; see Green Beans and Yellow Wax Beans on pages 157–158, and Snow Peas and Sugar-Snap Peas on pages 181–182. Shell beans, black-eyed peas, and crowder peas that are commonly dried for storage are listed together, under Shell Beans, Black-Eyed Peas, and Crowder Peas (Fresh) below. These are not grown in the home garden as frequently as, say, green beans or sugar-snap peas, but farm gardens may have enough space to grow a crop large enough to dry; you may also find fresh shell beans, in the pods, at farmers' markets or farm stands in late summer. Green (English) peas have their own listing (page 180), since they have inedible pods, but the seeds — the peas — are eaten fresh.

Finally, instructions are also given for drying cooked (or canned) shell beans, whether the beans were picked fresh and cooked or were cooked from the dried state. Drying cooked shell beans may seem like you're repeating a process, but there's a big distinction: dried beans that were cooked before drying rehydrate very quickly and are used in dried-food mixes like "soup jars" and prepackaged meal mixes such as those used for camping. Regular dried shell beans can't be substituted for dried cooked beans in these mixes, because they require lengthy soaking and cooking times. Instructions for drying cooked or canned beans are listed under Shell Beans, Black-Eyed Peas, and Crowder Peas (Cooked or Canned) on page 156.

Shell Beans, Black-Eyed Peas, and Crowder Peas (Fresh)

Although most common in the dried form at the supermarket, shell beans, black-eyed peas, and crowder peas can be grown in the home garden, and are also found in the fresh form at farmers' markets and roadside stands in late summer or early fall. Although they are similar to the familiar green bean that we eat as a whole pod, shell beans, black-eyed peas, and crowder peas have inedible pods and are grown specifically for their mature seeds — the "beans." Bean varieties include black beans, butter beans, cannellini beans, edamame, great northern beans, kidney beans, lima beans, navy beans, pinto beans, soybeans, and a host of others too numerous to mention. Black-eyed peas (also called cowpeas) and crowder peas are technically peas, but have the same characteristics as shell beans so are included here. Please read Beans and Peas: A General Discussion on page 153 for information about shell beans and peas.

Although "wet" beans and peas, freshly shelled from green pods and boiled, are a delicious harvest-time treat, they are difficult to dehydrate satisfactorily and should not be attempted by the beginner. Leave the pods on the vine in the garden until the beans or peas inside rattle. When the vines and pods are dry and shriveled, pick and shell the beans or peas; however, if the crop is threatened by rain or frost before the pods are dry enough, pull the plants by the roots and hang by the stems in a barn or shed until dry enough to shell. Once the beans or peas are shelled, no pretreatment is necessary. The shelled beans or peas are simply dehydrated or sun-dried to remove the final traces of moisture, preventing spoilage during storage. After drying, pasteurize by freezing at 0°F or below for 48 hours or baking at 125°F for 30 minutes to kill any insect eggs; see page 28 for more information on pasteurization.

DRYING METHODS: FRESH SHELL BEANS

DEHYDRATOR/ CONVECTION OVEN

Use screens on trays or racks. Spread partially dried, shelled beans or peas in a single layer. Dry at 120°F, stirring every few hours, until the beans or peas are so dry they will split when tapped with a hammer. Depending on the size and type of bean or pea, and how dry they were, this may take 6 to 12 hours.

SUN-DRYING

Spread partially dried, shelled beans or peas in a thin layer over drying screens or trays and place in a well-ventilated location in hot sun. Dry for 1 to 2 days or until dry enough to split when tapped with a hammer. Stir occasionally and take trays inside at night.

OVEN (NON-CONVECTION)

Use screens on racks. Spread partially dried, shelled beans or peas in a single layer. Dry at 120°F, stirring every few hours, until the beans or peas are so dry they will split when tapped with a hammer. Depending on the size and type of bean or pea and the efficiency of your oven setup, this may take anywhere from 6 to 18 hours.

TO USE: Beans and peas dried in this way are used exactly like store-bought dried beans and peas.

Shell Beans, Black-Eyed Peas, and Crowder Peas (Cooked or Canned)

Dried uncooked beans are the most familiar form of shell beans. These are found in bags on every supermarket shelf; most common are black beans, great northern beans, kidney beans, lima beans, navy beans, and pinto beans, but a number of heirloom varieties such as cranberry beans and borlotti beans are showing up at co-ops and high-end supermarkets. Black-eyed peas (also called cowpeas) and crowder peas are technically peas, but have the same characteristics as shell beans so are included here. Please read Beans and Peas: A General Discussion on page 153 for information about shell beans and peas.

Dried uncooked shell beans and peas (other than lentils and split peas, which cook very quickly) can't be combined in dried-food mixes with other dehydrated vegetables because the beans take so much longer to cook that everything else would turn to mush by the time the beans are done. The solution is to cook shell beans before dehydrating; the dried cooked beans rehydrate very quickly and are a boon to campers and anyone who wants to pack dried-food mixes. Canned shell beans, while not an economical choice, may be dehydrated in the same manner as those you cook yourself. If you grow shell beans (or can find them at farmers' markets before they have been dried), you may shell them when they are ripe but not yet dried, then cook and dehydrate them; you can also cook frozen edamame and other beans for dehydrating. Please read Beans and Peas: A General Discussion on page 153 for information about shell beans and peas.

Home-cooked shell beans are ready to dehydrate as soon as they have been cooked and drained. If you're using canned shell beans, drain them in a wire-mesh strainer and rinse them very well, then let them drain for several minutes. Spread the cooked or canned beans in a single layer on screens. Beans tend to shower small pieces onto whatever is below them, so it's a good idea to put an empty tray with a solid liner sheet underneath the trays holding the beans.

DEHYDRATOR/CONVECTION OVEN
Use screens on trays or racks. Cooked or canned shell beans generally take 4 to 7 hours at 125°F.

OVEN (NON-CONVECTION)
Use screens on racks. Stir beans several times during drying. At 125°F, cooked or canned shell beans may take as little as 3½ hours to dry, or as long as 11 hours.

Vegetables are not recommended for sun-drying (see page 42)

DONENESS TEST: Lightweight and brittle; many of the beans will "pop" like popcorn.

YIELD: 1 cup of cooked or canned shell beans yields about ¾ cup dried. When rehydrated, 1 cup of dried cooked or canned shell beans yields about 1 cup.

TO USE: Dried cooked or canned shell beans are usually used in dried-food mixes but also work fine for soups, stews, and casseroles being cooked in the normal fashion. They rehydrate quickly and may be added without rehydrating to soups and stews that will cook for at least 30 minutes longer. To rehydrate for use in recipes, cover with boiling or hot water and soak until no longer hard; most shell beans take 10 to 20 minutes, but larger beans such as lima beans and chickpeas may take an hour.

Recipes in this book featuring dried cooked or canned shell beans:

- Minestrone Soup Mix in a Jar

Green Beans and Yellow Wax Beans

Green beans are also called string beans or pole beans; they're certainly one of the most common vegetables in home gardens as well as at the supermarket. Yellow wax beans are very similar but are yellow when ripe. Please read Beans and Peas: A General Discussion on page 153 for information about green beans and other legumes.

Pick green or wax beans while still young, before the seeds swell inside the pods. Beans with large seeds will be tough when cooked. Wash well and trim off both ends. Cut into 1- to 2-inch pieces or leave whole if you prefer; for a nice variation that dries and rehydrates more quickly, slice the beans lengthwise, also known as French-cut (for the easiest method, lay the beans flat in a food processor feed tube and slice with the medium blade). Blanch the beans until they are brightly colored but still crisp; whole beans or shorter pieces take about 3½ minutes in steam or 2 minutes in boiling water, and French-cut beans require about half the time. Chill in ice water, then drain and pat dry. As a variation, freeze the blanched beans for about 45 minutes after draining and drying; beans that have been frozen will be more tender when rehydrated.

DRYING METHODS: GREEN BEANS AND YELLOW WAX BEANS

DEHYDRATOR/CONVECTION OVEN

For French-cut beans, use solid liner sheets or baking sheets lined with kitchen parchment; this prevents the dried beans from tangling in the racks or screens. For whole beans or shorter pieces, use screens on trays or racks. Stir pieces once or twice during drying; this is especially important with French-cut beans, which may clump together. Whole beans and shorter pieces generally take 8 to 12 hours at 125°F; French-cut beans generally take 6 to 9 hours.

OVEN (NON-CONVECTION)

For whole beans or shorter pieces, use screens on racks. Place French-cut beans on a baking sheet to prevent them from tangling in the screens. Stir pieces several times during drying. At 125°F, whole beans or shorter pieces may take as little as 8 hours to dry, or as long as 18 hours; French-cut beans dry more quickly.

Vegetables are not recommended for sun-drying (see page 42)

DONENESS TEST: Hard, dark, shriveled, and twisted; there should be no moisture inside. French-cut beans will be brittle and may be curly.

Recipes in this book featuring dried green or wax beans:

- Green Bean Casserole
- Homesteader's Meat and Vegetable Stew
- String Beans with Tarragon

YIELD: 1 pound of fresh beans that have been cut into shorter pieces yields about 1 cup dried; French-cut beans take up more room because they don't pack together tightly. When rehydrated, 1 cup of dried beans that have been cut into shorter pieces yields about 2½ cups.

TO USE: To rehydrate whole beans or shorter pieces, cover with twice the amount of boiling water (2 cups water to 1 cup beans) and soak until no longer hard, generally about an hour. Add rehydrated whole or cut-up beans to soups or stews for additional cooking, or simmer in the soaking water until tender for use as a plain vegetable or for use in recipes. French-cut beans rehydrate in about 30 minutes; they also may be added without rehydrating to soups and stews that will cook for at least 20 to 30 minutes longer.

Beets

In addition to the familiar deep-purple variety, beets of other colors are now found at large supermarkets and farmers' markets. Golden beets are fairly common; Italian Chioggia beets are more difficult to find but are quite attractive because they have alternating rings of purple and ivory. All work well for dehydrating. Smaller beets, 2 inches across or less, are the most flavorful and tender.

Wash whole beets and cut off the leaf stems, leaving 1-inch stubs (if the greens are in good shape, they may be dried; see Greens on page 172). Cook in boiling water to cover until they are barely fork-tender, typically 30 to 40 minutes. Drop cooked beets into cold water. Cut off the tops and roots and slip off the skins. Slice crosswise ⅛ to ¼ inch thick; for an attractive variation that also is quicker for both drying and rehydrating, cut ⅛-inch slices crosswise into ⅛-inch sticks (referred to as *julienne*). If you prefer diced beets, cut the whole beets into slices that are ⅜ inch thick, then cut each slice into ⅜-inch cubes. Until they have dried a bit, beets may drip dark juices during dehydrating, so the trays should be put on the bottom of the dehydrator for the first hour or so.

Beets may also be sliced very thinly, seasoned, and dried at low temperatures to make beet chips — a delicious snack that fits into raw-food and living-food diets. For instructions, see page 287.

Recipes in this book featuring dried beets:

- Borscht (Beet Soup)
- Harvard Beets

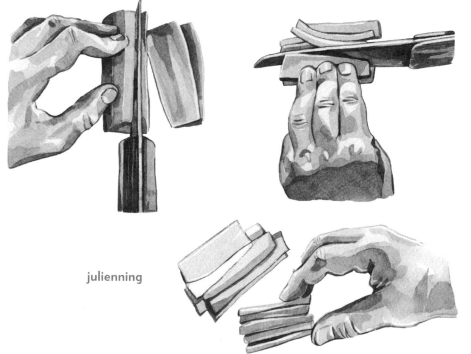

julienning

DEHYDRATOR/CONVECTION OVEN

For julienned or diced beets, use screens on trays or racks. Julienned beets generally take 4 to 6 hours at 125°F; slices or diced beets may take up to 12 hours, depending on thickness.

OVEN (NON-CONVECTION)

For julienned or diced beets, use screens on racks. Stir and rearrange pieces several times during drying. At 125°F, beets may take as little as 4 hours to dry, or as long as 18 hours; julienned beets dry more quickly than diced or sliced beets.

Vegetables are not recommended for sun-drying (see page 42)

DONENESS TEST: Leathery and dark, with no moisture in the center; julienned beets usually twist and curl up a bit.

YIELD: 1 pound of diced fresh beets yields about ¾ cup dried; slices and julienned pieces will measure about 1½ cups when dried. When rehydrated, 1 cup of dried beets yields about 1¾ cups.

TO USE: To rehydrate, cover with boiling water and soak until no longer hard. Julienned beets rehydrate very quickly, generally in about 15 minutes; slices or diced beets take 30 to 45 minutes. To use as a plain vegetable, simply heat the rehydrated beets in the soaking water for a few minutes, then drain and add a pat or two of butter, and salt and pepper to taste. Crisply dried beets may also be powdered for use in soups where their color is appropriate.

Broccoli

Broccoli becomes rather homely when dried and rehydrated, so don't plan on serving it by itself when you're looking for a bright green vegetable side dish. For best results, serve it with a sauce that makes it more attractive, or chop the rehydrated broccoli and add it to other dishes.

Pick or buy young, crisp, dark green broccoli with small, tightly closed buds. Heads that have woody or hollow stems are too old and should not be dehydrated; if the buds have begun to open, the broccoli is also past its prime and not suitable. Also pass by any specimens that feel limp or flabby.

Wash thoroughly and soak in salt water (1 teaspoon salt to 1 quart water) for 10 minutes to remove any insects or insect eggs, then rinse again. Cut the crown of florets away from the base, then cut the crown into serving-size pieces; florets may be up to an inch across, with stems no thicker than ½ inch. Cut the base lengthwise into stem pieces about ¾ inch thick, then slice the stems ½ inch thick on a diagonal. Steam-blanch for 3½ minutes or blanch in boiling water for 2 minutes, then chill in ice water; the broccoli should be bright green and the stems should still be crisp. Drain and pat as dry as possible before spreading loosely on trays. Broccoli often showers small floret pieces onto whatever is on the tray below it, so it's a good idea to put an empty tray with a solid liner sheet underneath the trays holding the broccoli.

DRYING METHODS: BROCCOLI

DEHYDRATOR/CONVECTION OVEN
Use screens on trays or racks. Broccoli generally takes 9 to 15 hours at 125°F.

OVEN (NON-CONVECTION)
Use screens on racks. Stir and rearrange pieces several times during drying. At 125°F, broccoli may take as little as 9 hours to dry, or as long as 21 hours.

Vegetables are not recommended for sun-drying (see page 42)

DONENESS TEST: Brittle and dark. The stalks will be shriveled and stiff, and the florets should feel crisp.

YIELD: Dried broccoli takes up a lot of room because it can't be packed tightly without breaking. When dried, 1 pound of fresh broccoli in serving-size pieces will generally fill a 1-quart jar, loosely packed. Broccoli doubles in volume when rehydrated.

TO USE: To rehydrate, cover generously with boiling water and soak until the stems are no longer hard, 1 to 2 hours; you may also cold-soak overnight. Simmer the rehydrated broccoli in the soaking water until tender, and then dress it up with cheese sauce or cream sauce. Rehydrated broccoli works well when chopped to add to soups, casseroles, soufflés, or quiche. Dried broccoli may also be powdered for use in soups or casseroles.

Recipes in this book featuring dried broccoli:

- Dried Vegetable Trio

Brussels Sprouts

Recipes in this book featuring dried Brussels sprouts:

• Baked Brussels Sprouts with Crumb Topping

Brussels sprouts are a late-fall vegetable that is best picked after the first frost, when it will be sweeter and milder. They grow as individual "sprouts" (like miniature cabbages, actually) attached to a tall, inedible central stalk. For the freshest Brussels sprouts, cut individual sprouts off the stalk just before use; you can sometimes find the stalks with sprouts still attached at farmers' markets.

To prepare Brussels sprouts for dehydrating, pull any tough or damaged outer leaves off the individual sprouts, cut off the base if it's dried out (as is often the case if you buy them already cut away from the central stalk), then cut the Brussels sprouts in half. Steam-blanch for 5 to 6 minutes or blanch in boiling water for 4 to 5 minutes. Chill in ice water, then drain and pat dry. Spread on trays with the cut side up. Brussels sprouts have a strong smell during dehydrating, so it's best not to dry fruits or delicate vegetables in the same load.

DRYING METHODS: BRUSSELS SPROUTS

DEHYDRATOR/CONVECTION OVEN
Turn halves over after 6 to 7 hours of drying. Brussels sprouts generally take 12 to 18 hours at 125°F.

OVEN (NON-CONVECTION)
Brussels sprouts will probably take longer than 18 hours and are not recommended.

Vegetables are not recommended for sun-drying (see page 42)

DONENESS TEST: Dry and brittle, with slightly fanned-out leaves; the centers should have no moisture inside when cut open.

YIELD: 1 pound of fresh Brussels sprouts yields about 1½ to 2 cups dried. When rehydrated, 1 cup of dried Brussels sprouts yields about 2 cups.

TO USE: To rehydrate, hot-soak for 30 minutes to 1 hour. Simmer in the soaking water until tender for use as a plain vegetable. For additional appeal, serve cooked Brussels sprouts in a cheese sauce or cream sauce.

Cabbage

Red, green (white), or Napa (Chinese) cabbage all work fine for dehydrating; cabbage stores and ships well and is available year-round. Select firm cabbage heads that feel heavy for their size. Remove any tough or wilted outer leaves, and cut the head into quarters. Core each quarter and shred the cored quarters by cutting crosswise into ¼-inch strips. Steam-blanch for 2 to 3 minutes or until the cabbage is bright in color and tender-crisp; to preserve the color of red cabbage, sprinkle it with a little vinegar before blanching. Chill blanched cabbage in ice water, then drain and pat dry. Cabbage has quite a strong smell during dehydrating, so it's best not to dry fruits or delicate vegetables in the same load.

As a side note: If you have a bumper crop of iceberg or Romaine lettuce, you can dehydrate it and use it in the same ways you'd use cabbage. Cut the lettuce head into quarters vertically, then cut out the hard core. Slice the quarters crosswise about ½ inch thick. Steam-blanch for 2 minutes if you like, then chill in ice water, drain, and pat dry. Proceed as directed for cabbage.

Recipes in this book featuring dried cabbage:

- Sweet and Tangy Cabbage with Apples

DRYING METHODS: CABBAGE

DEHYDRATOR/CONVECTION OVEN

Use screens on trays or racks. Dehydrate at 150°F for an hour, then reduce the heat to 135–140°F for the remainder of dehydrating. Stir every 2 hours, separating any shreds that have stuck together. Cabbage generally takes 6 to 10 hours at the temperatures above; the thinner pieces from the top of the head will dry more quickly than the thicker slices from the core area, so you'll need to pick through the cabbage after a few hours to remove pieces that dry more quickly.

OVEN (NON-CONVECTION)

Use screens on racks. Dehydrate at 150°F for 1 hour, then reduce the heat to 135–140°F for the remainder of dehydrating. Rotate racks and stir the cabbage every 2 hours, separating any shreds that have stuck together. At the temperatures above, cabbage may take as little as 5 hours to dry, or as long as 15 hours; the thinner pieces from the top of the head will dry more quickly than the thicker slices from the core area, so you'll need to pick through the cabbage after a few hours to remove pieces that dry more quickly.

Vegetables are not recommended for sun-drying (see page 42)

DONENESS TEST: Lightweight and very crisp, with no moisture in the thicker rib areas; if the cabbage is still pliable or rubbery, it isn't dry enough.

YIELD: Cabbage heads vary quite a bit in weight, so yields are given by the cup rather than by the head. 2 cups of tightly packed fresh cabbage shreds yield about ⅔ cup of loosely packed dried shreds. When rehydrated, 1 cup of dried cabbage shreds yields about 1½ cups.

TO USE: Dried cabbage shreds rehydrate fairly quickly and can be added without rehydrating to soups or stews that will cook for at least 40 minutes longer. To rehydrate for other uses, cover with boiling or hot water that has a little lemon juice added and soak until no longer hard, 30 minutes to 1 hour or until tender, then drain and use for cold salads or simmer in the soaking water until hot.

Carrots

Carrots are so common in the supermarket that we tend to take them for granted. However, if you've ever had the pleasure of eating a just-pulled carrot, still warm from the sun, you understand that freshness counts with carrots. And although they may look tempting, know that most "baby-cut" carrots in the market are simply larger carrots that have been cut to appear like small specimens; they are often woody or less sweet than fresh, full-size carrots.

Select young, tender carrots with no hint of softness, darkening, or wet areas on the surface. Scrub with a stiff vegetable brush and cut off the tops; for more tender (but less nutritious) dried carrots, peel thinly with a swivel-bladed vegetable peeler. Slice crosswise into ⅛-inch circles, or dice into ¼-inch cubes. For an attractive variation that also is quicker for both drying and rehydrating, cut carrots into 2-inch chunks, then slice lengthwise into ⅛-inch-thick planks; slice these lengthwise into ⅛-inch sticks (referred to as *julienne*; see illustrations on page 159). You can also buy julienned carrots in small bags in the produce department, and these work fine for dehydrating. Dried shredded carrots work well in salads, soups, and even baked goods; thicker shreds are better for drying than thin, wispy shreds. Blanch sliced, diced, or julienned carrots until they are bright, deep orange and just beginning to soften on the outsides; the insides should still be crisp. Julienned carrots will take about 1½ minutes

Recipes in this book featuring dried carrots:

- Borscht (Beet Soup)

- Carrot-Oat Cookies

- Curried Winter Squash Soup Mix in a Jar

- Dried Vegetable Trio

- Homesteader's Meat and Vegetable Stew

- Minestrone Soup Mix in a Jar

- Mock Chicken Broth Powder

- Mushroom-Barley Soup Mix in a Jar

- Shepherd's Pie

- Slow-Cooker Pork Chops with Root Vegetables

- Vegetable and Herb Dip Mix in a Jar

- Vegetable Flakes

DEHYDRATOR/CONVECTION OVEN

For diced or julienned carrots, use screens on trays or racks; use solid sheets for shreds. Stir pieces after 2 to 3 hours. Julienned or shredded carrots generally take 3 to 6 hours at 125°F; slices or diced carrots may take up to 9 hours.

OVEN (NON-CONVECTION)

For diced or julienned carrots, use screens on racks; use baking sheets for shreds. Stir pieces several times during drying. At 125°F, carrots may take as little as 2½ hours to dry, or as long as 12 hours; julienned and shredded carrots dry more quickly than slices or diced carrots.

Vegetables are not recommended for sun-drying (see page 42)

in steam or 1 minute in boiling water; slices and diced carrots will take 3 to 4 minutes in steam or 2 to 3 minutes in boiling water. Chill in ice water, then drain and pat dry. Shredded carrots should not be blanched.

DONENESS TEST: Leathery, shrunken, and deep orange, with no moisture in the center; julienned and shredded carrots usually twist and curl up a bit. Slices may be slightly flexible.

YIELD: 1 pound of fresh carrots yields about 1 cup dried. When rehydrated, 1 cup of dried carrots yields about 1½ cups.

TO USE: Julienned and shredded carrots may be added without rehydrating to soups and stews that will cook for at least 30 minutes longer. To rehydrate carrots, cover with boiling water and soak until no longer hard. Julienned and shredded carrots rehydrate fairly quickly, generally in about 30 minutes; slices or diced carrots take about an hour. Add rehydrated carrots to soups or stews for additional cooking, or simmer in the soaking water until tender for use as a plain vegetable or for use in recipes. Crisply dried carrots may be powdered for use in soups.

Cauliflower

While white cauliflower is still what most people visualize when thinking about cauliflower, these days you can also buy — or grow — colorful varieties including orange, purple, and green. Each has its own distinct flavor, so try them all. Regardless of the color, always look for heads with tight,

■ Dried
  Vegetable Trio

well-formed florets that are firm rather than flabby; gray spots indicate a cauliflower that is past its prime.

Trim off and discard the leaves and any protruding stem remnants, then cut the head lengthwise into quarters. Stand a quarter upright, then cut away the solid core as shown on the following page. Pull the florets apart in large clusters. Wash everything thoroughly and soak in salt water (1 teaspoon salt to 1 quart water) for 10 minutes to remove any insects or insect eggs. Rinse again. Cut or break the large clusters into serving-size florets; if any pieces are thicker than 1 inch, cut them into thinner pieces so none are more than ½ inch at the thickest. The core can be sliced about ½ inch thick, then into serving-size pieces, although some people discard it. Steam-blanch all cauliflower pieces for 3 to 4 minutes or blanch in boiling water for about 2 minutes. Chill in ice water, then drain and pat dry. Cauliflower has quite a strong smell during dehydrating, so it's best not to dry fruits or delicate vegetables in the same load. Cauliflower also tends to shower small pieces onto whatever is on the tray below it, so it's a good idea to put an empty tray with a solid liner sheet underneath the trays holding the cauliflower.

DRYING METHODS: CAULIFLOWER

DEHYDRATOR/CONVECTION OVEN
Use screens on trays or racks. Stir pieces after 3 or 4 hours. Cauliflower generally takes 6 to 10 hours at 125°F.

OVEN (NON-CONVECTION)
Use screens on racks. Stir and rearrange pieces several times during drying. At 125°F, cauliflower may take as little as 7 hours to dry, or as long as 15 hours.

Vegetables are not recommended for sun-drying (see page 42)

DONENESS TEST: Brittle or crisp, with no moisture in the thickest parts; the color will be darker than when fresh.

YIELD: 1 pound of fresh cauliflower yields about 1½ cups of loosely packed dried cauliflower. When rehydrated, 1 cup of dried cauliflower yields about 1½ cups.

TO USE: To rehydrate, hot-soak for 30 to 45 minutes, or cold-soak overnight. Add rehydrated cauliflower to soups or stews for additional cooking,

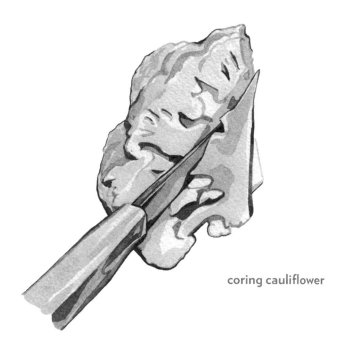

coring cauliflower

or simmer in the soaking water until tender for use as a plain vegetable. Dried cauliflower — particularly orange cauliflower, which is as lovely as it is tasty — is also surprisingly delicious in its dried form as a crunchy snack; for a seasoned variation, see the recipe for Cauliflower Popcorn on page 289.

Celery

This everyday vegetable is seldom grown in home gardens, but is widely available year-round at even small food stores. Choose celery that is crisp and bright green, with fresh-looking leaves; celery that is limp or beginning to lose its color should not be dehydrated. Celery's flavor intensifies during drying and it also loses its appealing crunch, so it is best used as an accent vegetable in soups, stews, casseroles, and other cooked dishes.

Wash and trim celery stalks. Cut off the leaves and dry them for use as seasoning according to the instructions on page 172. Dehydrated celery is slow to rehydrate. If you're planning to combine the celery in dried-food mixes with other vegetables that rehydrate fairly quickly, de-string the celery before dehydrating; it will rehydrate in half the time of celery that hasn't been de-stringed. To de-string, snap a rib near one end so the stalk is just held together with the strings, then peel the strings away from the rest of the stalk. De-stringing reduces the yield per pound.

DEHYDRATOR/CONVECTION OVEN
Use screens on trays or racks. Stir pieces every 2 hours. Celery generally takes 7 to 12 hours at 125°F; de-stringed celery dries a bit more quickly.

OVEN (NON-CONVECTION)
Use screens on racks. Stir pieces every 1 or 2 hours during drying. At 125°F, celery may take as little as 6 hours to dry, or as long as 18 hours; de-stringed celery dries a bit more quickly.

Vegetables are not recommended for sun-drying (see page 42)

Recipes in this book featuring dried celery:

- **Homesteader's Meat and Vegetable Stew**
- **Minestrone Soup Mix in a Jar**
- **Mock Chicken Broth Powder**
- **Salsify and Celery Chowder**
- **Shepherd's Pie**
- **Stovetop Chicken and Noodle Casserole**
- **Vegetable and Herb Dip Mix in a Jar**
- **Vegetable Broth Powder**
- **Vegetable Flakes**

Cut celery — de-stringed or not — into ¼-inch slices. It can be dehydrated with no pretreatment, but its color will be better and it will rehydrate more quickly if the pieces are steam-blanched until bright green, about 2 minutes.

DONENESS TEST: Very shrunken and shriveled, somewhat dark; pieces will be very hard or brittle. Dried celery is especially susceptible to mold unless it is perfectly dry in the center.

YIELD: Celery shrinks tremendously during dehydrating. 1 pound of fresh celery (one average bunch, which is about 4 cups after slicing) yields about ½ cup of dried slices. When rehydrated, celery doubles or triples in volume.

TO USE: De-stringed celery pieces may be added without rehydrating to soups and stews that will cook for at least 45 minutes longer. To rehydrate celery, cover with boiling water and soak until no longer hard; de-stringed celery will take about 1 hour, and celery which has not been de-stringed will take 2 to 3 hours. Add rehydrated celery to soups or stews for additional cooking, or simmer in the soaking water until tender for use in salads and other recipes that won't be cooked further. Dried celery that has been powdered is excellent in vegetable broth powder, or added to soups or casseroles; a small electric coffee grinder/spice grinder is highly recommended, as a blender probably will not do a good job with the tiny, hard pieces.

Corn

Fresh sweet corn is best when cooked immediately after picking — and your dehydrated corn will be best if processed promptly after picking as well. The natural sugar in corn begins turning to starch soon after picking, making the kernels tough and reducing the sweetness. Modern super-sweet varieties offer a little more flexibility as they remain sweet for a longer time after picking. Purchased frozen corn is generally frozen the same day it's picked, so it works well for dehydrating; if you're packing meals for camping or other dried-food mixes, you'll be better off buying frozen corn than out-of-season fresh corn or that which has been languishing at the supermarket for days. Frozen corn needs no pretreatment; simply dump it onto the trays and start dehydrating (it will thaw quickly).

If you're buying or picking fresh corn, press the ears through the husks; the cob should be evenly filled with plump kernels, and if you peel the husk back a bit and press on a kernel with your thumbnail, it should squirt milky juice. The silks should be moist and slightly sticky, the husks should be bright green and tightly wrapped, and the bottom of the stem should look fresh rather than brown and withered. Older corn, with starchy kernels, is tough when fresh and becomes even tougher after dehydrating; don't bother trying to dehydrate it.

To prepare fresh corn for dehydrating, pull off the husks and silk. Steam- or water-blanch until the kernels are no longer milky, 1½ to 3 minutes. Immediately transfer the ears to a basin of very cold water to stop the cooking. Drain the ears, and then cut the kernels from the cob. Spread the corn in a single layer on trays that have been lined with screens. It's a good idea to place an empty tray with a solid liner sheet underneath the trays holding the corn, because small, hard pieces will fall through the screens, showering whatever is beneath them with tiny bits of corn.

Recipes in this book featuring dried corn:

- Camper's Corn Chowder
- Scalloped Corn

DRYING METHODS: CORN

DEHYDRATOR/CONVECTION OVEN

Use screens on trays or racks. Stir the corn after about 2 hours of drying. Corn generally takes 6 to 12 hours at 125°F; fresh corn may take a bit longer than frozen corn.

OVEN (NON-CONVECTION)

Use screens on racks. Stir the corn several times during drying. At 125°F, corn may take as little as 6 hours to dry, or as long as 18 hours; fresh corn may take a bit longer than frozen corn.

Vegetables are not recommended for sun-drying (see page 42)

DONENESS TEST: Deep golden brown, hard, and wrinkled.

YIELD: 1 quart of corn kernels (from 5 or 6 typical ears) yields about 1½ cups dried. When rehydrated, 1 cup of dried corn yields about 2 cups.

TO USE: To rehydrate, cover with twice the amount of boiling water (2 cups water to 1 cup corn) and soak until no longer hard, generally 1 to 2 hours. Add rehydrated corn to soups or stews for additional cooking, or simmer in the soaking water until tender for use as a plain vegetable or for use in recipes. If you have a grain mill, you can grind your dried corn to make homemade cornmeal.

Cucumbers

Dried cucumbers are eaten as a snack; they can't be rehydrated back to the fresh state. If you're using regular slicing cucumbers, try to get them before the seeds have developed; slender, firm cukes with thin skins are more likely to have small seeds than large, fat, thick-skinned specimens. Japanese and English cucumbers are seedless or nearly so, and any seeds they do have are small and tender. Both can be cultivated in the home garden and can also be bought — for a hefty price — at high-end grocery stores or up-to-date farmers' markets.

Wash all cucumbers well, especially those that have been waxed. Slice crosswise, without peeling, ¼ inch thick. Spread in a single layer on trays without overlapping.

DRYING METHODS: CUCUMBERS

DEHYDRATOR/CONVECTION OVEN
Cucumbers generally take 4 to 6 hours at 125°F.

OVEN (NON-CONVECTION)
Rearrange slices every hour during drying to prevent scorching the ones on the outside edges of the rack. At 125°F, cucumbers may take as little as 3½ hours to dry, or as long as 9 hours.

Vegetables are not recommended for sun-drying (see page 42)

DONENESS TEST: Very lightweight and crispy; slices may curl or become wavy.

YIELD: 1 typical fresh cucumber yields ¾ to 1 cup of loosely packed dried slices.

TO USE: Dried cucumbers are used like crackers and can be eaten plain or served with dip; they are particularly good with hummus. Add them to tossed salads, either as whole slices or broken into pieces. They may also be chopped into small flakes for use as a sprinkle-on seasoning. Note that dried cucumber slices don't keep well, so don't plan on them for long-term storage.

Recipes in this book featuring dried cucumbers:

- Vegetable and Herb Dip Mix in a Jar

Eggplant

Here's a vegetable that is actually improved by dehydrating: when rehydrated and pan-fried or used in casseroles, previously dried eggplant has a slightly firm texture rather than the cotton-soft texture it has when it's cooked from fresh. Whether you grow eggplants or buy them, you'll have at least a half-dozen varieties to choose from. All can be successfully dehydrated; specimens that are on the small side for the variety work best because the seeds, which are often bitter, will be smaller. Peel whole eggplant and slice crosswise ¼ inch thick. Leave slices whole, quarter them if large, or cut into ¼-inch strips or 1 inch squares. Some cooks steam-blanch eggplant pieces for 2 to 3 minutes to remove some of the bitter flavor, but the blanched pieces darken considerably during dehydrating.

DRYING METHODS: EGGPLANT

DEHYDRATOR/CONVECTION OVEN
Eggplant generally takes 8 to 10 hours at 125°F.

OVEN (NON-CONVECTION)
Rearrange and turn pieces once or twice during drying. At 125°F, eggplant may take as little as 7 hours to dry, or as long as 15 hours.

Vegetables are not recommended for sun-drying (see page 42)

Recipes in this book featuring dried eggplant:

- Eggplant and Tomato Casserole

DONENESS TEST: Lightweight, shrunken, and leathery; the centers should have no moisture inside. Pieces that have been dehydrated without blanching will be light brown; those that were blanched are typically blotched with dark brown.

YIELD: 1 pound of fresh eggplant yields about 2 cups of loosely packed dried pieces. When rehydrated, 1 cup of dried eggplant yields about 1¼ cups.

TO USE: Eggplant rehydrates fairly quickly, and may be added without rehydrating to soups or stews that will cook for at least 30 minutes longer. To rehydrate, hot-soak for about an hour, or cold-soak overnight. Prepare rehydrated eggplant as you would fresh eggplant by frying or using in casseroles.

Greens

Beet greens, collards, dandelion greens, kale, mustard greens, spinach, Swiss or rainbow chard, and turnip greens can all be dried to give you a supply of fresh-tasting greens all year long. Cut or tear large leaves into manageable-size pieces, pulling away any thick ribs (save the ribs to add to a pot of stock; chard ribs are also delicious when cooked on their own as a vegetable). Wash the greens very thoroughly, lifting them out of the water so any grit stays behind. Spin the greens dry in a salad spinner.

Blanching is optional. Greens that have been steam-blanched for 1 minute before drying will have a much deeper, brighter color than those that have not been blanched; give them another spin in the salad spinner after blanching. Thin-leaved greens such as spinach and dandelion greens, however, are easiest to spread on the trays when they haven't been blanched. Pile the greens loosely on the trays. Curly kale takes up a lot of room, so if you're using a box-style or home-built dehydrator, take out alternating trays to make enough room; if you have a stackable dehydrator, you will have to cut curly kale into smaller pieces to fit between the trays. As you turn the greens during drying, they may shower small pieces onto whatever's beneath them, so put them on the bottom of the dehydrator or put an empty tray with a solid liner beneath them. Store dried greens in jars rather than plastic bags to avoid crumbling and smashing them.

DEHYDRATOR/CONVECTION OVEN
Use screens on trays or racks. Turn and
separate greens after the first hour of drying
and again after the second. Greens generally
take 3 to 5 hours at 125°F.

OVEN (NON-CONVECTION)
Use screens on racks. Turn and separate
greens every hour during drying. At 125°F,
greens may take as little as 3 hours to dry,
or as long as 7 hours.

Vegetables are not recommended for sun-drying (see page 42)

DONENESS TEST: Crisp, brittle, and crumbly.

YIELD: Because greens vary so much in thickness and texture, it's impossible to accurately predict yield as a group. In general, expect dried greens to take up about two-thirds the amount of space as the fresh, chopped greens did; for example, 6 cups of cut-up curly kale will probably just fit in a quart jar when dried. When rehydrated, 3 cups of dried greens, loosely packed, generally yield about 1½ cups of cooked greens.

TO USE: Dried greens rehydrate quickly and may be added without rehydrating to soups and stews that will cook for at least 20 to 30 minutes longer. To rehydrate for use as a cooked vegetable or for use in recipes, pour 1½ cups of boiling water over 3 cups of dried greens, adding a little lemon juice if you like for better color; cover and cook for 15 minutes over low heat. Dried greens are very easy to powder; the powder adds delicious flavor and valuable nutrients to broth and other soups.

Recipes in this
book featuring
dried greens:

- Creamed
  Greens Soup

- Minestrone
  Soup Mix in
  a Jar

Kohlrabi

This member of the cabbage family tastes like cabbage mixed with radishes and turnips. The large bulb is the edible portion; for dehydrating, choose medium-sized bulbs rather than huge ones, which may have a strong flavor. Trim off and discard the leaves and stalks. Peel bulbs and slice ¼ inch thick, then cut the slices into strips, squares, or quarters as you prefer. Steam-blanch for 3 to 4 minutes or blanch in boiling water for 2 to 3 minutes. Chill in ice water, then drain and pat dry.

DEHYDRATOR/CONVECTION OVEN
Use screens on trays or racks. Kohlrabi generally takes 12 to 18 hours at 125°F.

OVEN (NON-CONVECTION)
Kohlrabi may take longer than 18 hours and is not recommended.

Vegetables are not recommended for sun-drying (see page 42)

DONENESS TEST: Crisp, brittle, and darker in color; thicker areas will have no moisture inside.

YIELD: 1 pound of fresh kohlrabi yields ¼ cup to ½ cup of dried pieces. When rehydrated, 1 cup of dried kohlrabi yields about 1½ cups.

TO USE: To rehydrate, hot-soak for 1 to 2 hours, or cold-soak overnight. Add rehydrated kohlrabi to soups or stews for additional cooking. It's also delicious when simmered in the soaking water until tender, then seasoned with butter, salt, and pepper; for a special touch, garnish with broiled mushrooms or grated nuts. Dried kohlrabi may also be powdered for use in soups or casseroles.

Leeks

This member of the onion family looks like a huge scallion (green onion), with stiff leaves that flare out into a fan at the top. The leaves are tough and can't be eaten as a vegetable (however, they can be saved to add flavor to stock). The white base is the edible part; when trimming a leek, cut the leaves away from the base at the point where the white is just changing to

DEHYDRATOR/CONVECTION OVEN
Use screens on trays or racks. Stir pieces after 1 or 2 hours to separate any slices that have stuck together. Leeks generally take 5 to 8 hours at 125°F.

OVEN (NON-CONVECTION)
Use screens on racks. Stir pieces after 1 or 2 hours to separate any slices that have stuck together, then stir once or twice more during drying. At 125°F, leeks may take as little as 4 hours to dry, or as long as 12 hours.

Vegetables are not recommended for sun-drying (see page 42)

pale green. Trim and discard the wiry roots from the base as well. Split the trimmed base vertically, then hold under cold running water to wash away any dirt between the layers. Slice the halves into ¼-inch-thick half-circles; no pretreatment is needed.

DONENESS TEST: Crisp and lightweight.

YIELD: 1 cup of fresh sliced leeks yields about ½ cup dried. When rehydrated, 1 cup of dried leeks yields about 1½ cups.

TO USE: Dried leeks rehydrate quickly and may be added without rehydrating to soups and stews that will cook for at least 20 minutes longer. To rehydrate for use in other recipes, cover with boiling or hot water and soak for about 15 minutes. Dried leeks are very easy to powder; the powder adds delicious flavor to broth and other soups.

Mushrooms

Select only commercially grown varieties or those that you know beyond any doubt are nontoxic. The toxins of poisonous mushrooms are not destroyed by the drying or cooking processes. When working with morels, always cut the mushrooms in half, both to clean out any dirt or debris that is trapped inside and to confirm the mushroom's identity (true morels are *completely hollow inside*). Also, all mushrooms picked from the wild should be cooked before eating, so keep that in mind when using your dried mushrooms.

Wash mushrooms very briefly in cold water without soaking or peeling; a soft mushroom brush is helpful when cleaning morels, chanterelles, or other mushrooms that have crevices or folds. Trim off the stem end if it looks tough or dry. Solid mushrooms such as commercial button or cremini mushrooms should be cut into quarters or sliced about ¼ inch thick. For shiitake mushrooms, remove and discard the stems (or use them to add flavor to stock), then slice the cap into ¼-inch strips. For oyster mushrooms, break apart the cluster; small individual oysters can be dried whole, while larger ones should be cut vertically through the stem into strips about 1 inch wide. For large portobellos, pull out and discard the stem, then scrape out the black gills; rinse the cap, pat it dry, slice ¼ inch thick, then cut the longer slices into 2 or 3 shorter pieces. The mushrooms listed here need no pretreatment and should never be blanched.

Recipes in this book featuring dried mushrooms:

- Green Bean Casserole
- Mock Chicken Broth Powder
- Mushroom-Barley Soup Mix in a Jar
- Stovetop Chicken and Noodle Casserole
- Vegetable Broth Powder

Because of wide variation in the sizes, shapes, and water content of mushrooms, dehydrating times below are based on sliced button mushrooms, which are a good starting point. Thinner mushrooms such as small morel halves will probably dry more quickly; thicker pieces such as those from portobello caps will take longer. Dried mushrooms should be stored in tightly sealed glass jars, both to prevent crushing and to keep them from absorbing moisture from the air.

DRYING METHODS: MUSHROOMS

DEHYDRATOR/CONVECTION OVEN
Use screens on trays or racks. Button mushroom slices generally take 3 to 6 hours at 125°F.

OVEN (NON-CONVECTION)
Use screens on racks. Stir pieces several times during drying. At 125°F, button mushroom slices may take as little as 2½ hours to dry, or as long as 9 hours.

Vegetables are not recommended for sun-drying (see page 42)

Vegetables are not recommended for sun-drying (see page 42)

DONENESS TEST: Lightweight and leathery to crisp depending on variety; thicker areas will have no moisture inside. Some mushroom pieces curl up when dried.

YIELD: 1 pound of fresh mushrooms generally yields 2 to 4 cups of dried slices or pieces, depending on the variety, how they were cut, and if they curled up during drying. When rehydrated, 1 cup of dried mushrooms yields 1¼ to 2 cups, depending on variety.

TO USE: Dried mushrooms rehydrate quickly and may be added without rehydrating to soups and stews that will cook for at least 30 minutes longer. To rehydrate for use as a cooked vegetable or for use in recipes, cover with boiling or hot water and soak until no longer hard, 15 minutes to 1 hour. Dried mushrooms are very easy to powder; the powder adds delicious flavor and valuable nutrients to broth and other soups.

Okra

Okra is a thin, many-sided green pod that is famous for its ability to thicken soups and stews — most notably, Creole gumbo. (Some cooks, however, use roux to thicken their gumbo, while others use filé powder;

DEHYDRATOR/CONVECTION OVEN

Use screens on trays or racks. Stir pieces after about 2 hours of drying. Okra generally takes 7 to 10 hours at 125°F.

OVEN (NON-CONVECTION)

Use screens on racks. Stir and rearrange pieces several times during drying. At 125°F, okra may take as little as 7 hours to dry, or as long as 15 hours.

Vegetables are not recommended for sun-drying (see page 42)

see page 233 for information on dehydrating sassafras leaves.) It is also fried whole as a vegetable, and fresh pods can be pickled.

Select young, tender, 2- to 4-inch okra pods that snap easily, a sign of freshness. Avoid pods that are tough, pale, or limp, or those with black edges or tips; they are past prime and won't work well for dehydrating. Wash okra well and cut off the stem ends. Slice crosswise ¼ inch thick. No pretreatment is necessary.

DONENESS TEST: Shrunken and leathery to crisp; when squeezed, there should be no moisture in the center.

YIELD: 1 pound of fresh okra yields about ½ cup dried. When rehydrated, 1 cup of dried okra yields about 1½ cups.

TO USE: To rehydrate, cover with double the amount of boiling water (2 cups of water to 1 cup of okra) and soak until no longer hard, generally about an hour. Add rehydrated okra to soups, stews, or casseroles that will cook for at least 20 minutes longer; it's particularly good with those containing tomatoes. It's delicious when dredged in seasoned cornmeal and deep-fried or pan-fried.

Recipes in this book featuring dried okra:

- Green Tomatoes and Okra
- Stewed Okra and Rice

Onions

Although globe onions keep well for several months when air-cured for 2 to 3 weeks after harvest, chopped, dried onions are a convenience to keep on the kitchen shelf or at the vacation cabin. Dried onions also are a must for campers or anyone who wants to pack dried-food mixes. In the spring, when winter-stored onions threaten to sprout, they may be saved by slicing or chopping and drying for later use.

DEHYDRATOR/CONVECTION OVEN

For sliced onions, use screens on trays or racks; for chopped onions, use solid liner sheets or baking sheets lined with kitchen parchment. Separate slices when they begin to dry, generally about 4 hours, and once or twice after that; stir chopped onions every 2 hours. Onions generally take 6 to 10 hours at 125°F.

OVEN (NON-CONVECTION)

For sliced onions, use screens on racks; for chopped onions, use baking sheets lined with kitchen parchment. Separate and rearrange slices after 2 hours of drying, and every 2 hours after that; stir chopped onions every 2 hours. At 125°F, onions may take as little as 4½ hours to dry, or as long as 15 hours.

Vegetables are not recommended for sun-drying (see page 42)

Recipes in this book featuring dried onions:

- Borscht (Beet Soup)
- Camper's Corn Chowder
- Chili-Spiced Ground-Meat Jerky Seasoning
- Curried Butternut Squash Soup in a Jar
- Flax and Parmesan Crackers
- Green Bean Casserole
- Green Tomatoes and Okra
- Harvard Beets
- Homesteader's Meat and Vegetable Stew

Any type or color of globe onion may be dehydrated. Peel the onions and cut off the ends. Cut vertically into halves or quarters, then slice crosswise ⅛ to ¼ inch thick. For chopped onions, cut across the slices at ¼ to ⅜-inch intervals; the onions will shrink considerably when dried, so you don't want them too fine to start. You may also use a food processor to chop onions, but unless you're very careful, it's easy to end up with onions that are too finely chopped or that are chopped unevenly. No pretreatment is needed. Separate the slices and pile in a loose, somewhat shallow heap when loading trays, or spread the chopped onions in a thin layer. As you might expect, onions have a strong smell during dehydrating, so it's best not to dry fruits or delicate vegetables in the same load.

DONENESS TEST: Dry, crisp, and thin; slices will be leathery or papery.

YIELD: 1 pound of fresh onions yields about 2 cups of packed dried slices, or 1 cup of chopped dried onions. When rehydrated, 1 cup of packed dried onion slices yields about 1½ cups; chopped onions almost double in volume when rehydrated.

TO USE: To make **onion flakes**, pulse dried onions in a blender until the consistency is flaky; for **onion powder**, continue processing until very fine. Dried onions rehydrate quickly and may be added without rehydrating to soups and stews that will cook for at least 20 minutes longer; simply measure one-half as much dried onion as the fresh onion called for in the recipe. To rehydrate for use as an ingredient, cover with boiling or hot water and soak until no longer hard, 15 to 30 minutes. Dried onions readily absorb moisture from the air, so they are best stored in tightly sealed glass jars. If you plan to powder onions, it's best to do so just before using to prevent the powder from clumping during storage.

Parsnips, Rutabagas, and Turnips

These sturdy root vegetables are all dehydrated in the same manner. They are sweetest when harvested after the first hard frost and store well, so if you're buying them, look for them in fall and winter. Choose small to medium specimens; larger ones are apt to be woody in the middle.

To prepare for dehydrating, trim off the tops and root ends (if the greens are in good shape, they may be dried; see Greens on page 172). Peel the tough skins. Cut rutabagas into quarters. For dehydrated parsnips, rutabagas, or turnips that will be used as a cooked vegetable, slice crosswise ¼ inch thick, or dice into ⅜-inch cubes (when working with parsnips, drop them into a bowl of acidulated water as you cut each piece to prevent darkening). Steam-blanch for 4 minutes, or blanch in boiling water for 3 minutes. Chill in ice water, then drain and pat dry.

You may also enjoy trying crisps made from parsnips, rutabagas, or turnips. To make plain crisps, slice the peeled vegetables as thinly as possible; a mandoline or food processor with a very thin blade will produce slices of even thickness, but you can do it by hand as well (as noted above, drop parsnip slices into acidulated water as you work, but don't leave them in the water more than 5 minutes). The thin slices don't need to be blanched. For a seasoned variation, see the recipe for Sliced Vegetable Crisps on page 290.

More recipes in this book featuring dried onions:

- Minestrone Soup Mix in a Jar
- Mock Chicken Broth Powder
- Mushroom-Barley Soup Mix in a Jar
- Onion and Bacon Pie
- Red-Hot Marinade for Meat
- Shepherd's Pie
- Simple Ground-Meat Jerky Seasoning
- Southwestern Jerky Stew
- Stewed Okra and Rice

DRYING METHODS: PARSNIPS, RUTABAGAS, AND TURNIPS

DEHYDRATOR/CONVECTION OVEN

Cubes and thicker slices generally take 5 to 12 hours at 125°F. Thin crisps will be dry in 4 to 6 hours at 125°F.

OVEN (NON-CONVECTION)

Stir and rearrange pieces several times during drying. At 125°F, cubes and thicker slices may take as little as 5 hours to dry, or as long as 18 hours; thin crisps take from 4 to 9 hours.

Vegetables are not recommended for sun-drying (see page 42)

DONENESS TEST: Cubes and thicker slices will be brittle, wrinkled around the edges, and somewhat shrunken; the color will be deeper, and thicker areas will have no moisture inside. Thin crisps will be papery and crisp and wavy or curled up.

YIELD: 1 pound of fresh parsnips, rutabagas, or turnips that have been cut into cubes or thicker slices yields about 1 cup dried; thin crisps will measure 2 to 3 cups, depending on how curled they are. When rehydrated, 1 cup of dried cubes or thicker slices yields about 1½ cups.

TO USE: To rehydrate cubes or thicker slices, hot-soak for 45 minutes to 1 hour, or cold-soak overnight. Add rehydrated parsnips, rutabagas, or turnips to soups or stews for additional cooking, or simmer in the soaking water until tender for use as a plain vegetable. Rehydrated, cooked rutabaga is excellent when mashed (add a cooked potato if you like) and garnished with crisp diced bacon. The thin crisps are eaten as a snack in the dried form and are good with cheese dip, hummus, or other dips; thin crisps don't keep well, so don't plan on them for long-term storage.

Green (English) Peas

In times past, this was the most common type of pea eaten as a green vegetable. Times change, and nowadays we're far more likely to have sugar-snap peas or snow peas rather than genuine shelled green peas. That's too bad, because fresh green peas — also called English peas, garden peas, and shelling peas — are deliciously sweet. If you don't grow them, look for them at farmers' markets or roadside stands in summer — just be sure that you're buying English peas, not sugar-snap peas which have edible pods (and generally cost a lot more). Look for plump pods that are swollen with fat peas; the pods should not be shriveled or brown, an indication that they've been off the plants too long. Like corn, fresh peas have natural sugars that begin turning to starch shortly after picking, so they are best when shelled and processed within a few hours of picking. (For more information about pea varieties, please read Beans and Peas: A General Discussion on page 153.)

To shell the peas, grasp the stem remnant and pull it down sharply along the length of the pod; this should "unzip" the pod so you can gently scrape the peas out and into a bowl. The pods are inedible; add them to the compost pile. Steam-blanch the shelled peas for 3 minutes or blanch

DEHYDRATOR/CONVECTION OVEN

Use screens on trays or racks; for small peas, use solid liner sheets. Stir peas after about 2 hours. Green peas generally take 5 to 9 hours at 125°F.

OVEN (NON-CONVECTION)

Use screens on racks; for small peas, use baking sheets. Stir peas several times during drying. At 125°F, green peas may take as little as 5 hours to dry, or as long as 13 hours.

Vegetables are not recommended for sun-drying (see page 42)

in boiling water for 2 minutes. Drain and chill in ice water, then drain thoroughly before spreading on trays. Frozen peas work well for dehydrating and need no pretreatment; simply dump them onto the trays and start dehydrating (they will thaw quickly).

DONENESS TEST: Shrunken, brittle, hard, and wrinkled; they should shatter if squeezed firmly.

YIELD: 1 pound of fresh green peas (in the shell) yields about ½ cup dried. When rehydrated, 1 cup of dried green peas yields about 2 cups.

TO USE: To rehydrate, hot-soak for 30 minutes to 1 hour, or cold-soak overnight. Add rehydrated peas to soups or stews for additional cooking, or simmer in the soaking water until tender for use as a plain vegetable or for use in recipes. Dried peas may also be powdered for use in soups or casseroles.

Recipes in this book featuring dried green peas:

- Homesteader's Meat and Vegetable Stew
- Purée of Green Pea Soup
- Shepherd's Pie

Snow Peas and Sugar-Snap Peas

Both of these pea varieties have edible pods. Snow peas are very flat and have tiny peas inside. Sugar-snap pea pods are swollen with peas that are often nearly full-size; they resemble fresh green (English) peas (see listing above), but the pods of English peas are tough and inedible, so be sure of what you're getting at the market! Please read Beans and Peas: A General Discussion on page 153 for information about shell peas. Snow peas and sugar-snap peas — together referred to here as peapods — lose their crisp crunch when they've been rehydrated; they have a cooked texture.

DEHYDRATOR/CONVECTION OVEN	OVEN (NON-CONVECTION)
Snow peas generally take 5 to 8 hours at 125°F; sugar-snap peas may take up to 15 hours.	At 125°F, snow peas may take as little as 4½ hours to dry, or as long as 12 hours; sugar-snap peas may take up to 20 hours.

Vegetables are not recommended for sun-drying (see page 42)

Peapods are best when blanched before dehydrating; they should be bright green but still crisp. Snow peas take about 2 minutes in steam or 1 minute in boiling water; sugar-snap peas should be blanched for 3 minutes in steam or 1½ minutes in boiling water. Chill in ice water and blot dry before spreading on trays in a single layer.

DONENESS TEST: Crispy or brittle, darkened, with a papery feel. Sugar-snap peas will look lumpy; the peas inside the pods should be completely dry when cut open.

YIELD: 1 pound of fresh peapods yields 1½ to 2 cups dried. When rehydrated, 1 cup of dried peapods yields about ¾ cup.

TO USE: Dried snow peas rehydrate quickly and may be added without rehydrating to soups and stews that will cook for at least 30 minutes longer; sugar-snap peas need to cook for at least 45 minutes. To rehydrate for use as a cooked vegetable or for use in recipes, cover peapods with boiling or hot water and soak until no longer hard, 15 to 45 minutes, then simmer in soaking water until tender. Dried peapods are very easy to powder; the powder adds delicious flavor and valuable nutrients to broth and other soups.

Bell Peppers and Pimientos

Available in a rainbow of colors, bell peppers are found in supermarkets year-round, and the quality is usually good even in winter (although they are shipped in from Mexico and other countries, so tend to be expensive). Pimientos are heart-shaped peppers that are red when ripe; most are sweeter and more flavorful than standard red bell peppers, but some varieties of pimiento peppers are hot. Although pimientos are seen most often as the stuffing for green olives or as a bottled garnish, they can be purchased fresh and also work well for dehydrating. Bell peppers and pimientos can be grown in a garden that has abundant sun and rich soil. Whether you buy them or grow them, choose peppers that are firm and glossy, with tight skins; wrinkles or soft spots indicate that the pepper has been stored too long and is not suitable for dehydrating.

To prepare peppers for dehydrating, it's easiest to cut the sides off the bell peppers in four slabs, as though cutting the sides off a cube; this is more efficient than trying to cut away the stem as though it were the core of a strawberry. The sides are easier to cut into strips or pieces than a curved half-pepper, and almost all of the seeds remain with the central portion of the pepper. Cut the white riblike membranes off the bottom of the central piece, then remove any white membranes or seeds from the side pieces. Cut the sides into ¼-inch strips or dice into ½-inch squares; cut the strips into shorter pieces if you like, or leave them long. The bottom piece is usually lumpy, and works best when diced; you can also trim the flesh around the stem and dice it. Pimientos can be cut in the same way, although they are not very cubelike (but the basic principle of cutting the sides away from the center remains the same). Bell peppers and pimientos require no pretreatment.

Recipes in this book featuring dried bell peppers or pimientos:

- Camper's Corn Chowder
- Minestrone Soup Mix in a Jar
- Scalloped Asparagus
- Scalloped Corn
- Southwestern Jerky Stew
- Vegetable and Herb Dip Mix in a Jar
- Vegetable Broth Powder
- Vegetable Flakes

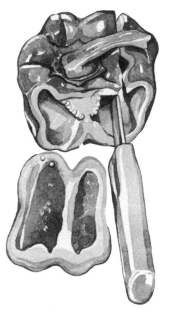

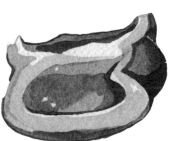

preparing a bell pepper

DEHYDRATOR/CONVECTION OVEN	OVEN (NON-CONVECTION)
Use screens on trays or racks. Strips and diced peppers generally take 6 to 10 hours at 125°F.	Use screens on racks. Stir and rearrange pieces several times during drying. At 125°F, strips and diced peppers may take as little as 5 hours to dry, or as long as 15 hours.

Vegetables are not recommended for sun-drying (see page 42)

DONENESS TEST: Leathery and shriveled; thicker areas will have no moisture inside.

YIELD: 1 quart of diced fresh peppers yields about 1 cup dried. When rehydrated, 1 cup of dried diced pepper yields about 1⅓ cups.

TO USE: Dried bell and pimiento peppers may be added without rehydrating to soups and stews that will cook for at least 45 minutes longer; for each ¼ cup fresh bell pepper or pimiento called for in a recipe, substitute 2 heaping tablespoons dried diced pepper or pimiento. To rehydrate for use in meatloaf, eggs, or other recipes, hot-soak for 30 minutes to 1 hour, or cold-soak overnight. Rehydrated bell peppers are soft like cooked peppers, rather than crunchy like raw bell peppers.

Chile Peppers

Dozens of varieties of chile peppers are now available in the seed catalogs and in the supermarkets; heat levels vary quite a bit. Poblano, Anaheim, Ancho, Pasilla, Rocotillo, and Santa Fe peppers are fairly mild; most other chile peppers are hotter; and some, such as habañero and Scotch bonnet peppers, are unbelievably hot. Some have fairly thin flesh and are usually dried whole; these include cayenne peppers, habañeros, Mirasol peppers, Tabasco peppers, and Thai peppers. Other chile peppers, including jalapeños and poblanos, have thicker flesh and are cut up before dehydrating.

Thin-fleshed chile peppers can be strung up whole and allowed to dry against a sunny wall, or even in the kitchen or attic. In the Southwest, strings or wreaths of dried chile peppers are called *ristras* and are considered edible art. To make your own, thread a stout needle with heavy thread and pierce the stems of fresh thin-fleshed chile peppers, pushing them together. The threaded peppers can be hung in any warm, dry location and look particularly stunning against an adobe wall in the sun. Once dry, the peppers are hung in the kitchen, to be pulled off and crumbled as needed. You may also dry whole thin-fleshed chile peppers in your dehydrator, on a sun-drying rack, or in your oven, as directed below.

To dehydrate jalapeños and other relatively small, thicker-fleshed chile peppers, slice them crosswise into rings that are about ⅛ inch thick. You may also cut off the stem and halve the pepper vertically, then use a small spoon to scrape out the seeds and ribs (wear rubber gloves when cutting chile peppers to prevent burning your hands). The pepper halves can be dried as is, although poblanos and larger chile peppers are best when cut into strips or 1-inch chunks. Thin-fleshed chile peppers can simply be arranged whole, in a single layer, on screens. No matter the shape or cutting method, chile peppers need no pretreatment; simply spread the peppers out on the screens in a single layer. If you're drying sliced peppers, place an empty tray with a solid liner sheet (or a baking sheet, if drying in the oven or a homemade dehydrator) underneath the trays with the chile peppers; otherwise you may end up with pepper seeds on the foods below. Note: Pickled jalapeño slices, sold as a garnish for tacos and other foods, dehydrate quite nicely; simply spread them on trays and dehydrate like fresh chile pepper slices.

Recipes in this book featuring dried chile peppers:

- Chili Powder Blend
- Sausage Sauce for Spaghetti
- Southwestern Jerky Stew

DRYING METHODS: CHILE PEPPERS

DEHYDRATOR/CONVECTION OVEN

Use screens on trays or racks. Depending on the size, cutting method, and thickness, chile peppers will take anywhere from 4 to 15 hours at 125°F.

SUN-DRYING

Spread whole, thin-fleshed chile peppers on screens in a single layer. Gently stir and turn peppers after 5 or 6 hours. Chile peppers will probably take 1 to 2 days to dry completely. Thin-fleshed chile peppers may also be strung and dried as described above.

OVEN (NON-CONVECTION)

Use screens on racks. Stir and rearrange pieces several times during drying. Depending on the size, cutting method, and thickness, chile peppers will take anywhere from 4 to 24 hours at 125°F.

DONENESS TEST: Shrunken, leathery, dark, and wrinkled; slices may be curled and will have pale centers.

YIELD: Yield varies when working with chile peppers, depending on the type of pepper and preparation before dehydrating. Generally, thin-fleshed whole peppers will take up about half the amount of storage space as they occupied when fresh. A cup of chile pepper slices will generally shrink down to ½ to ⅔ cup when dried, depending on variety. Dried chile peppers are generally used in the dried form, so rehydrating yields are not given.

TO USE: Use as you would purchased dried chile peppers. Add one or two small dried chile peppers to pickles when canning. Crumble dried chile peppers for use in sauces or stews. Grind to use in chili powder (be careful of the dust, which will irritate eyes and nose). Dried chile pepper slices rehydrate quickly and may be added without rehydrating to soups and stews that will cook for at least 30 minutes longer.

Potatoes

Although they don't rehydrate as well as commercially freeze-dried potatoes, home-dehydrated potatoes are convenient for camping and hiking trips or wherever weight is a consideration. They must be watched carefully during storage, for any hint of moisture will cause the entire batch to mold.

Any variety can be dehydrated. Scrub potatoes well, especially if you plan to dehydrate them with the peels on; the peels are tough when the potatoes are rehydrated but add fiber. Cut into ½-inch-square sticks (like French fries), ¼- to ⅛-inch slices, or ½-inch cubes. As you cut the potatoes, add them to a bowl of acidulated water to inhibit browning. Steam-blanch for 6 to 8 minutes or blanch in boiling water for 5 to 6 minutes. Chill in ice water, then drain and pat dry. For additional protection against browning, dip in light honey dip; this does not make the potatoes taste sweet and is especially recommended if you choose not to blanch the potatoes prior to dehydrating. Frozen diced potatoes also work well for dehydrating and do not need to be blanched or dipped; simply spread them on trays while still frozen and begin dehydrating.

DEHYDRATOR/CONVECTION OVEN

For cubed potatoes, use screens on trays or racks. Potatoes generally take 7 to 12 hours at 125°F; thinner slices dry more quickly.

OVEN (NON-CONVECTION)

For cubed potatoes, use screens on racks. Stir pieces and rearrange slices several times during drying. At 125°F, potatoes will take 6 to 18 hours to dry.

Vegetables are not recommended for sun-drying (see page 42)

DONENESS TEST: Slices will be crisp, brittle, and somewhat translucent, with a dry, leathery surface. Cubes and French-fry cuts will be hard or brittle and must have no moisture in the center.

YIELD: 1 pound of fresh potatoes yields about 1 cup dried. When rehydrated, 1 cup of dried potatoes yields 1 to 1⅓ cups.

TO USE: To rehydrate, hot-soak for 45 minutes to 1¼ hours; the soaking water will be starchy and works well as the liquid for making bread. Add rehydrated potatoes to soups or stews for additional cooking, or simmer in the soaking water until tender for mashing, frying, or use in recipes.

Radishes

Red radishes look the best when dehydrated, but white radishes may also be used. Choose firm radishes, preferably with the greens still attached, and make sure that the greens look fresh rather than wilted. Trim off the roots and top ends, and then wash well. Slice ⅛ inch thick. No pretreatment is needed.

DEHYDRATOR/CONVECTION OVEN

Use screens on trays or racks. Radish slices generally take 7 to 10 hours at 125°F.

OVEN (NON-CONVECTION)

Use screens on racks. Stir pieces several times during drying. At 125°F, radish slices will take 6 to 14 hours to dry.

Vegetables are not recommended for sun-drying (see page 42)

Recipes in this
book featuring
dried radishes:

- Southwestern
  Jerky Stew

DONENESS TEST: Shrunken, curled, and leathery to brittle, with a papery surface; the edges of red radishes will be a rich maroon color.

YIELD: 1 pound of fresh radishes yields ⅓ to ½ cup dried. When rehydrated, 1 cup of dried radish slices yields about 1⅓ cups.

TO USE: Eat crisp slices as a snack, alone or with cheese dip. Crumble crisp slices and scatter over salad, or add to potato salad or coleslaw. To rehydrate for use as a cooked vegetable, simmer for about 20 minutes in an equal amount of boiling water. Season to taste with salt, pepper, and butter. Rehydrated radishes may be added to recipes, but they will no longer be crunchy like a fresh radish. Dried radishes may also be powdered and used to add a tangy flavor to dips, soups, or casseroles.

Salsify

Looking like a cross between a carrot and a parsnip, salsify is also called the vegetable oyster because it has the taste of the sea. Look for it during the winter months; like parsnips, it needs to be sweetened by frost before picking. Salsify has very coarse skin, so it is always peeled before use. Slice crosswise about ⅛ inch thick; if the salsify is very narrow, cut it at an angle so the slices are wider. Salsify discolors quickly after cutting, so you should drop pieces into a bowl of acidulated water as you go. When all pieces have been cut, you may drain and spread them directly on the trays; for best results, however, steam-blanch for 4 minutes or blanch in boiling water for 3 minutes before dehydrating.

Gardening alert: Salsify has a tendency to spread rapidly and may even be considered invasive in some locations.

DRYING METHODS: SALSIFY

DEHYDRATOR/CONVECTION OVEN
Use screens on trays or racks. Salsify generally takes 9 to 15 hours at 125°F.

OVEN (NON-CONVECTION)
Use screens on racks. Stir pieces several times during drying. At 125°F, salsify will take 8 to 20 hours to dry.

Vegetables are not recommended for sun-drying (see page 42)

DONENESS TEST: Crisp and leathery, with no moisture inside. Salsify that has been blanched will have a deep cream color; unblanched pieces may be brownish.

YIELD: 1 pound of fresh salsify yields about 1 cup dried. When rehydrated, 1 cup of dried salsify yields about 1¼ cups.

TO USE: Slices may be eaten in the dried form as a snack or mixed with other dried vegetables. Small slices may be added in dried form to tossed salads. Dried salsify may be chopped and used as a casserole topping. To rehydrate, hot-soak for 30 minutes to 1 hour, or cold-soak overnight. Add rehydrated salsify to soups or stews for additional cooking, or simmer in the soaking water until tender for use as a plain vegetable or for use in recipes. Dried salsify may also be powdered for use in soups or casseroles.

Recipes in this book featuring dried salsify:

- Mock Fried Oysters

- Salsify and Celery Chowder

Scallions (Green Onions)

Also called green onions, scallions are common in both the spring garden and year-round in the supermarket. If you're growing your own scallions, pull them before the bulbs have swollen and become rounded. Dried scallion slices make a nice accent and are used as a seasoning. To prepare for dehydrating, wash the scallions thoroughly and trim off the root ends. Cut the entire onion, including the green tops, into ¼- to ½-inch pieces. No pretreatment is necessary. If possible, use a temperature of 115°F or lower for dehydrating; the green tops may scorch at higher heat. If you dry them at 125°F in the same load as other vegetables, keep the greens separate from the white pieces and remove them as soon as they become dry.

Recipes in this book featuring dried scallions:

- Potato Pancakes with Parsnips or Turnips

- Purée of Green Pea Soup

- Tabouli Salad

DRYING METHODS: SCALLIONS

DEHYDRATOR/CONVECTION OVEN
Use screens on trays or racks. Stir pieces after an hour of drying. Scallions generally take 5 to 8 hours at 115°F; the tops dry more quickly.

OVEN (NON-CONVECTION)
Use screens on racks. Stir pieces several times during drying. At 115°F, scallions may take as little as 4 hours to dry, or as long as 10 hours; the tops dry more quickly.

Vegetables are not recommended for sun-drying (see page 42)

Vegetables are not recommended for sun-drying (see page 42)

DONENESS TEST: Crisp, lightweight, and somewhat shriveled; the tops will be dark green and very crisp.

YIELD: 1 cup of sliced scallions yields about ⅓ cup dried.

TO USE: Dried scallions rehydrate quickly and may be added to soups and stews directly, without rehydrating. Thinner dried slices are also good sprinkled as a garnish on salads, soups, egg dishes, or casseroles.

Squash (Winter) and Pumpkins

As used here, the term "winter squash" refers to squash with hard, inedible rinds; firm, dense flesh; and a hollowed core with large, woody seeds. Common varieties include acorn, buttercup, butternut, kabocha, and Hubbard. Pumpkins are also a type of winter squash; large jack-o'-lantern types don't work well for dehydrating, but small "pie pumpkins" can be dehydrated like other winter squash. Spaghetti squash, although technically a winter squash, has flesh that pulls apart into strands; it doesn't dehydrate well. (Summer squash have thin, edible skins and tender, somewhat watery flesh embedded with small, soft seeds; see Zucchini and Other Summer Squash on page 196 for more information.)

Cut or break off the stem, then cut the squash or pumpkin in half. Use a spoon to scoop out the seeds, also scraping out the surrounding stringy material. Carefully cut off the rind; it's tricky to cut around curvy areas and can take a fair amount of pressure to get the job done, so always cut away from yourself and beware of slippery hands. (Some cooks prefer to slice the unpeeled squash and cut the rind off individual pieces, but it can be very difficult to slice through the rind on some squash.) Cut the squash in halves or quarters, depending on size, then slice ¼ inch thick; for diced squash, cut into ⅜- to ½-inch cubes. Blanch in steam or boiling water until cooked about halfway through; this usually takes 3 to 5 minutes in steam or 2 to 3 minutes in boiling water, but timing varies depending on the type and age of the squash. Chill in ice water, then drain and pat dry.

Winter squash or pumpkin can also be cooked until completely tender, then mashed before dehydrating; spread the mash about ½ inch thick on solid liner sheets or baking sheets lined with kitchen parchment and dehydrate until dry. Cooked squash can also be puréed to make leather, which can be powdered and used like pumpkin or squash purée; the cooked

DEHYDRATOR/CONVECTION OVEN

For cubes, use screens on trays or racks. For mashed squash or pumpkin, use solid liner sheets or line baking sheets with kitchen parchment; as the mash begins to dry, stir it occasionally and break or tear it into smaller pieces until it is crumbly. Winter squash slices or cubes generally take 7 to 12 hours at 125°F; mashed squash may take up to 18 hours.

OVEN (NON-CONVECTION)

Mashed squash or pumpkin may take longer than 18 hours and is not recommended. For cubes, use screens on racks. Stir and rearrange pieces several times during drying. At 125°F, winter squash may take as little as 6 hours to dry, or as long as 18 hours.

Vegetables are not recommended for sun-drying (see page 42)

purée is also used to add body to watery fruits when making fruit leathers (see chapter 8 for leather instructions). When rehydrated, mashed squash has more texture than powdered puréed squash.

DONENESS TEST: Shrunken and deeply colored. Cubes will be hard, with no moisture in the center. Slices will be leathery to hard. Mashed squash will be dry and crumbly to leathery, with a rough surface; larger crumbles must have no moisture in the center.

YIELD: 1 pound of fresh winter squash or pumpkin yields ¾ to 1 cup dried slices or cubes; mashed squash yields about 1¼ cups of crumbles. When rehydrated, 1 cup of dried winter squash slices, cubes, or mash crumbles yields about 1½ cups.

TO USE: To rehydrate slices or cubes, hot-soak for 45 minutes to 1¼ hours, or cold-soak overnight. Add rehydrated winter squash slices or cubes to soups or stews for additional cooking, or simmer in the soaking water until tender for use as a plain vegetable or for use in recipes. To rehydrate mashed squash or pumpkin, stir measured crumbles into an equal amount of boiling water, then remove from the heat and let stand until cool, stirring occasionally; if the mixture is too thick, add a little additional water. Dried winter squash slices or cubes may also be powdered for use in soups or casseroles.

Recipes in this book featuring dried winter squash:

- Curried Winter Squash Soup Mix in a Jar
- Pumpkin and Peach Cookies
- Squash or Pumpkin Bread

Sweet Potatoes

Recipes in this
book featuring
dried sweet
potatoes:

- Orange-
  Glazed Sweet
  Potatoes

Often referred to (incorrectly) as yams, sweet potatoes are better for dehydrating than white potatoes because their additional sugar keeps them more tender when rehydrated. Choose sweet potatoes with deeply colored flesh; these are better than the pale-fleshed varieties, which are often mealy. Dried sweet potatoes must be watched carefully during storage, for any hint of moisture will cause the entire batch to mold.

Scrub sweet potatoes well, especially if you plan to dehydrate them with the peels on; the peels are tough when the sweet potatoes are rehydrated but add fiber. Cut into ½-inch-square sticks (like French fries), ¼- to ⅛-inch slices, or ½-inch cubes. As you cut the sweet potatoes, add them to a bowl of acidulated water to inhibit browning. Steam-blanch for 5 to 7 minutes or blanch in boiling water for 4 to 5 minutes. Chill in ice water, then drain and pat dry. For additional protection against browning, dip in light honey dip; this is especially recommended if you choose not to blanch the sweet potatoes prior to dehydrating.

Another option is to bake whole, unpeeled sweet potatoes at 350°F until just tender, about 45 minutes. Let them cool completely, then cut off the skins and cut up the sweet potato as desired. Sweet potatoes that have been prebaked dehydrate more quickly.

DRYING METHODS: SWEET POTATOES

DEHYDRATOR/CONVECTION OVEN

For cubed sweet potatoes, use screens on trays or racks. Sweet potatoes generally take 9 to 15 hours at 125°F; thinner slices and prebaked sweet potato pieces dry more quickly.

OVEN (NON-CONVECTION)

Cubes or French-fry cuts may take longer than 18 hours to dry and are not recommended. For slices, stir and rearrange pieces several times during drying. At 125°F, sliced sweet potatoes may take as little as 9 hours to dry, or as long as 18 hours; prebaked sweet potato slices dry more quickly.

Vegetables are not recommended for sun-drying (see page 42)

DONENESS TEST: Slices will be hard but still a bit flexible, with a dry, leathery surface. Cubes and French-fry cuts will be hard or brittle and must have no moisture in the center.

YIELD: 1 pound of fresh sweet potatoes yields about 1 cup dried. When rehydrated, 1 cup of dried sweet potatoes yields 1 to 1⅓ cups.

TO USE: To rehydrate, hot-soak for 45 minutes to 1¼ hours. Add rehydrated sweet potatoes to soups or stews for additional cooking, or simmer in the soaking water until tender for mashing, frying, or use in recipes.

Tomatillos

Although husked tomatillos look like small green tomatoes, they are actually a relative of the ornamental Chinese lantern. Tomatillos are used in southwestern and Mexican cooking, and provide a tangy, "green" flavor to stews, soups, and salsas. Like tomatoes, tomatillos are actually fruits, so sun-drying works well for them; follow the instructions for sun-drying tomatoes on page 195. When drying tomatillos in a dehydrator or oven, a temperature of 135 to 145°F is recommended to speed drying.

Tomatillos grow inside a papery husk which dries and splits when the fruits are ripe. When buying tomatillos at the store, choose individual tomatillos with a dry husk and bright green fruit; if you see black spots or if the husk is wet, pass that one by. To prepare them for dehydrating, pull off and discard the papery husk. The fruits have a sticky surface, so you need to wash them in cold water, rubbing the surface with your fingers until no longer sticky. Cut out the small core at the top, then slice the tomatillos ¼ inch thick. Tomatillos require no pretreatment.

Recipes in this book featuring dried tomatillos:

- Green Salsa with Dried Tomatillos

DRYING METHODS: TOMATILLOS

DEHYDRATOR/CONVECTION OVEN
Use screens on racks or trays. Tomatillo slices generally take 7 to 12 hours at 145°F.

OVEN (NON-CONVECTION)
Use screens on racks. Turn and rearrange slices several times during drying. At 145°F, tomatillo slices may take as little as 7 hours to dry, or as long as 18 hours.

For sun-drying, follow the instructions for tomatoes on page 195

DONENESS TEST: Shrunken, leathery or brittle, and wrinkled; the insides will be pale and the skins will be darkened somewhat.

YIELD: 1 pound of fresh tomatillos yields about 1⅓ cups of loosely packed dried slices. When rehydrated, 1 cup of dried slices yields about 1¼ cups.

TO USE: To rehydrate tomatillos, hot-soak for about 30 minutes. Add rehydrated tomatillos to soups or stews for additional cooking, or simmer in the soaking water until tender for use in recipes.

Tomatoes

Tomatoes come in many varieties and sizes, from small cherry and grape tomatoes, to huge beefsteak varieties. Both green and ripe tomatoes may be dehydrated, although only round slicing tomatoes are recommended for dried green tomatoes. Low-acid varieties, however, turn black and should not be dehydrated unless puréed, mixed with a little vinegar or lemon juice, and dried as a leather; see chapter 8 for information.

Although tomatoes are used as vegetables, they are actually fruits, so sun-drying works well. When drying tomatoes in a dehydrator or oven, a temperature of 135 to 145°F is recommended to speed drying.

Ripe tomatoes are prepared differently than green tomatoes. Most ripe tomatoes should be peeled (skinned) before dehydrating, although this isn't necessary with small tomatoes such as cherry, grape, and plum (Roma); however, plum tomatoes will dry more quickly and have a more vibrant color when dried if peeled before dehydrating.

To peel ripe tomatoes, drop them, a few at a time, into a large pot of furiously boiling water. When the skins begin to split (usually 30 to 60 seconds), transfer them to a sinkful of cold water and slip off the skins. When all the tomatoes have been peeled, cut out the cores. Slice round tomatoes crosswise ¼ to ½ inch thick, and cut the slices into halves or quarters if you like; whole tomatoes can also be cut into ½-inch chunks. Whether peeled or not, plum tomatoes should be cut in half if small or into quarters if large. Cherry tomatoes and grape tomatoes should not be peeled, but need to be cut in half before dehydrating; place on trays with the cut side up to start. To speed drying of plum, saladette, grape, and cherry tomato halves, "pop" each tomato half midway through drying by pressing on the skin side with your thumbs to turn the flesh inside out; return to trays and continue drying.

Recipes in this book featuring dried tomatoes:

- Green Tomatoes and Okra
- Italian Green Tomatoes
- Minestrone Soup Mix in a Jar
- Southwestern Jerky Stew
- Stewed Okra and Rice
- "Sun-Dried" Tomato Pesto
- Tabouli Salad
- Vegetable Broth Powder

For dried green tomatoes, you'll get the best results with slicing varieties rather than cherry tomatoes or the other small varieties. Pick tomatoes while still green and firm, before they begin to ripen inside. Green tomatoes should not be peeled; simply cut out the core, then slice the tomatoes crosswise ¼ to ½ inch thick, or cut into ½-inch chunks.

DRYING METHODS: TOMATOES

DEHYDRATOR/ CONVECTION OVEN

For chunks or small tomatoes, use screens on trays or racks. Turn slices, halves, or quarters after 2 to 4 hours, or when the top sides are dry, and stir chunks several times during drying. Slices or chunks generally take 8 to 12 hours at 145°F. Plum tomatoes and halved small tomatoes take much longer. Some pieces will be dry after about 12 hours, while others may take as long as 24 hours; skinned plum tomatoes dry more quickly than unskinned.

SUN-DRYING

Turn slices, halves, or quarters after about a half-day of drying, or when the tops are dry; stir chunks when they can be separated. Slices or chunks will probably take 1 to 3 days to dry completely. Plum tomatoes and halved small tomatoes may take up to 5 days.

OVEN (NON-CONVECTION)

Plum tomatoes and halved small tomatoes will take longer than 18 hours and are not recommended. For chunks, use screens on racks; slices should be fine when placed directly on the racks unless the racks have really large gaps and the slices are small. Turn slices when the top sides are dry, and stir chunks several times during drying. At 145°F, sliced and chunked tomatoes may take as little as 7 hours to dry, or as long as 18 hours.

DONENESS TEST: Dried tomatoes should be deep red, not black; black tomatoes are probably a low-acid variety and should not be consumed. Sliced tomatoes will be leathery to crisp and much thinner than when fresh. Chunks will be leathery and will feel springy when squeezed; there must be no moisture in the center, and if the chunks feel squishy rather than springy, they aren't dry enough. Plum tomatoes and halved small tomatoes will be twisted, shrunken, leathery, and flexible or springy when squeezed; there must be no moisture in the thickest parts.

YIELD: 1 pound of fresh tomatoes generally yields about 1 cup dried. When rehydrated, 1 cup of dried tomatoes yields about 1½ cups.

TO USE: Dried sliced tomatoes or chunks rehydrate quickly and may be added without rehydrating to soups, casseroles, and stews that will cook for at least 30 minutes longer. To rehydrate slices for use in recipes, place on a plate or platter and spray with warm water, then let soak for 1 hour, turning and spraying occasionally with more water. Rehydrate chunks or smaller pieces by soaking in warm water to cover for 1 hour or more. For fried green tomato slices, dip rehydrated slices in flour and sauté in butter. Dried tomatoes are very easy to powder; the powder adds delicious flavor and valuable nutrients to broth and other soups.

Zucchini and Other Summer Squash

As used here, the term "summer squash" refers to squash with thin, edible skins and tender, somewhat watery flesh embedded with small, soft seeds. Zucchini are the most common summer squash; yellow squash (straight or crookneck) and pattypan squash are two other common varieties. (Winter squash have hard rinds, firm flesh, and a core with large, woody seeds; see Squash (Winter) and Pumpkins on page 190 for more information.)

Choose small to medium-size squash, which will have very small seeds. If you have monster zucchini in the vegetable patch, it's better to use it fresh for zucchini bread, although you could quarter it and cut away the seedy center, then use the rest of it for dehydrating.

To prepare summer squash for dehydrating, cut off the stem remnant and small, hard knob at the bottom of the squash. Slice unpeeled squash crosswise ⅛ to ¼ inch thick; if the slices are large, you might want to halve or quarter them. You may also cut summer squash into ⅜-inch cubes or shred very coasely; the fine julienne blade of a food processor or mandoline work best for shreds. Summer squash requires no pretreatment.

DEHYDRATOR/CONVECTION OVEN

For cubes, use screens on trays or racks. For shreds, use solid liner sheets or baking sheets lined with kitchen parchment; fluff the shreds every hour until they no longer stick together. Slices and cubes generally take 7 to 10 hours at 125°F; shreds dry more quickly.

OVEN (NON-CONVECTION)

For cubes, use screens on racks. For shreds, use baking sheets lined with kitchen parchment; fluff the shreds every hour until they no longer stick together. Stir and rearrange slices or cubes several times during drying. At 125°F, sliced or cubed summer squash may take as little as 5½ hours to dry, or as long as 15 hours; shreds dry more quickly.

Vegetables are not recommended for sun-drying (see page 42)

DONENESS TEST: Crisp or brittle, lightweight and shrunken with dark, puckered edges; cubes should have no moisture inside.

YIELD: 1 pound of fresh summer squash yields about ¾ cup dried. When rehydrated, 1 cup of dried summer squash yields about 1½ cups.

TO USE: Slices may be eaten in the dry form as snacks; they also work well when crumbled and sprinkled on soups or salads as a garnish. Dried summer squash rehydrates quickly. Shreds may be added without rehydrating to soups and stews that will cook for at least 10 minutes longer; slices and cubes should cook for at least 20 minutes. Rehydrated summer squash is very soft and is not very good as a solo cooked vegetable. Dried summer squash is very easy to powder; the powder adds delicious flavor and valuable nutrients to broth and other soups.

Recipes in this book featuring dried summer squash:

- Vegetable and Herb Dip Mix in a Jar
- Vegetable Broth Powder

Recipes Using Dried Vegetables

THE RECIPES ARE listed alphabetically by the type of vegetable used (asparagus, beets, broccoli, and so on). Dried ingredients from this book are highlighted in **bold type**.

Scalloped Asparagus

Makes 4–6 servings

- 1 cup water
- 1 cup **dried asparagus pieces**
- 1 tablespoon **diced dried pimiento**
- 1 cup milk, approximate
- 3 tablespoons butter
- 3 tablespoons all-purpose flour
- ½ teaspoon salt
- 2 hard-cooked eggs, shelled and sliced
- ¼ cup grated cheese

1. Heat the water to boiling in a saucepan. Stir in the asparagus and pimiento; remove from the heat and let stand for 30 minutes. Near the end of the rehydrating time, preheat the oven to 350°F. Lightly grease a shallow casserole; set aside.

2. Return the saucepan with the asparagus to the heat and simmer until tender, 15 to 20 minutes. Drain, reserving the cooking liquid. Add enough milk to the cooking liquid to equal 1½ cups.

3. In another saucepan, melt the butter and blend in the flour and salt. Gradually stir in the milk mixture. Cook over low heat, stirring constantly, until smooth and thickened. Carefully stir in the drained vegetables and hard-cooked egg slices. Transfer to the prepared casserole; sprinkle the top with the cheese. Bake for 30 to 45 minutes, or until lightly browned.

String Beans with Tarragon

Makes 4 servings

2	cups water
¾	cup **dried green or wax beans**
2	tablespoons **dried chopped onion**
4	bacon strips, diced
1	tablespoon **Tarragon Vinegar** (see page 240)
¼–½	teaspoon salt

1. Heat the water to boiling in a saucepan. Add the beans and onion; cover, remove from the heat and let stand for 30 minutes.

2. Cook the bean mixture over low heat, covered, until the beans are plump and tender, 15 to 20 minutes. Meanwhile, sauté the diced bacon in a small skillet until crisp and brown. Drain the bacon.

3. Add the drained bacon, vinegar, and salt to the cooked green beans. Mix lightly and serve hot.

Harvard Beets

Makes 6 servings

1	cup water
1	cup **dried diced or julienned beets**
⅓	cup sugar
1	tablespoon cornstarch
½	teaspoon salt
½	cup white vinegar
2	tablespoons butter
1	teaspoon **dried chopped onion**

1. Heat the water to boiling in a saucepan. Stir in the dried beets. Cover and cook over low heat for 30 to 40 minutes, or until tender.

2. Near the end of the cooking time, stir together the sugar, cornstarch, and salt in a separate nonreactive saucepan. Add the vinegar and stir well. Cook over very low heat until smooth and thickened, stirring constantly. Add the butter, onion, and tender beets. Cook over very low heat for 15 to 20 minutes to blend flavors, stirring frequently. Serve warm or chilled.

Dried Vegetable Trio

Makes 4–6 servings

2	cups water
¾	cup **dried cauliflower pieces**
½	cup **dried broccoli pieces**
½	cup **dried carrot slices**
2	tablespoons butter
½	teaspoon salt

1. Heat the water to boiling in a saucepan; remove from the heat. Stir in the cauliflower, broccoli, and carrots. Cover and set aside for 30 minutes.

2. Cook the vegetables in the soaking water over medium heat, covered, until tender, 15 to 20 minutes. Lift the vegetables out of the liquid onto a serving dish. Add the butter and salt to the cooking liquid and cook until the butter is melted and the liquid has cooked down to ½ cup. Pour over the vegetables and serve immediately.

Baked Brussels Sprouts with Crumb Topping

Makes 4–6 servings

1 cup water

1 cup **dried Brussels sprouts**

4 tablespoons butter

3 tablespoons all-purpose flour

½ teaspoon mustard powder

¼ teaspoon salt

1 cup milk

½ cup dried breadcrumbs

1. Heat the water to boiling in a saucepan; remove from the heat. Stir in the Brussels sprouts, then cover and set aside for 30 minutes. Near the end of the rehydrating time, preheat the oven to 350°F; grease a medium casserole and set aside.

2. Cook the Brussels sprouts in the soaking water over medium heat, covered, until tender, 15 to 20 minutes. Drain, reserving the liquid. Transfer the Brussels sprouts to the prepared casserole and set aside.

3. In the same saucepan, melt 2 tablespoons of the butter. Blend in the flour, mustard powder, and salt. Gradually stir in the milk and reserved cooking liquid. Cook, stirring constantly, until smooth and thickened. Pour the sauce over the Brussels sprouts in the casserole.

4. Melt the remaining 2 tablespoons butter in a microwave-safe bowl or small saucepan. Mix the breadcrumbs with the melted butter; scatter over the Brussels sprouts. Bake for about 25 minutes, until lightly browned.

Sweet and Tangy Cabbage with Apples

Makes 6 servings

2	tablespoons butter
2	cups **dried cabbage shreds**
1	cup **dried apple slices**
2	cups boiling water
2	tablespoons all-purpose flour
¼	cup brown sugar, packed
1½	teaspoons finely chopped **dried lemon zest**
	Salt and freshly ground black pepper

1. Melt the butter in a large skillet over medium heat. Add the cabbage, apple slices, and boiling water. Cover and simmer until the cabbage and apples are tender, 30 to 40 minutes.

2. Sprinkle the cooked cabbage mixture with the flour, stirring constantly to prevent lumps. Stir in the brown sugar, lemon zest, and salt and pepper to taste. Cover and simmer for 5 minutes longer to blend flavors.

Carrot-Oat Cookies

Makes about 4 dozen cookies

1	cup brown sugar, packed
⅔	cup milk
½	cup vegetable shortening
3	eggs
1	cup **dried shredded carrots**
2	cups all-purpose flour
1	teaspoon baking powder
½	teaspoon baking soda
½	teaspoon ground cinnamon
½	teaspoon salt
1½	cups old-fashioned rolled oats
1½	cups **dried seedless grapes** or chopped **dried plums**
½	cup chopped nuts
1	tablespoon finely chopped **dried orange zest**

1. Preheat the oven to 350°F. Lightly grease two baking sheets; set aside.

2. Combine the brown sugar, milk, shortening, and eggs in a large mixing bowl; beat with a fork until well blended. Stir in the carrots; set aside for 10 minutes.

3. Sift together the flour, baking powder, baking soda, cinnamon, and salt into a medium bowl. Stir in the oats, grapes, nuts, and orange zest. Add to the carrot mixture, stirring with a wooden spoon until just combined.

4. Drop rounded teaspoons of the dough onto the baking sheets, keeping about 2 inches apart; refrigerate the unused dough. Bake for 10 to 12 minutes or until lightly browned. Transfer the cookies to a cooling rack. Cool the baking sheets and repeat until all dough has been baked.

Scalloped Corn

Makes 4–6 servings

3	cups water
1½	cups **dried corn kernels**
2	teaspoons **dried diced pimiento**
4	tablespoons butter
2	tablespoons all-purpose flour
½	teaspoon salt
	Freshly ground black pepper
2	eggs, beaten
½	cup dried breadcrumbs
	Dash of ground paprika

1. Heat the water to boiling in a medium saucepan; remove from the heat. Stir in the corn and pimiento. Let stand for 30 minutes.

2. Cover the corn mixture and cook over low heat, stirring occasionally, until tender, about 30 minutes. Meanwhile, preheat the oven to 350°F. Lightly grease a medium casserole; set aside.

3. When the corn is tender, drain, reserving the soaking liquid in a measuring cup. Add water to the soaking liquid to equal 1 cup. In another saucepan over medium-low heat, melt 2 tablespoons of the butter and whisk in the flour. Gradually add the 1 cup cooking liquid, whisking constantly. Cook over low heat, whisking frequently, until thickened. Add the salt, and pepper to taste. Remove from the heat and add the eggs, stirring constantly. Mix in the drained corn and pimiento. Pour into the prepared casserole.

4. Melt the remaining 2 tablespoons butter in a small skillet over medium heat, and then stir in the breadcrumbs. Sprinkle over the top of the casserole; dust with paprika. Set in a shallow pan of very hot water and bake for 45 to 50 minutes.

Eggplant and Tomato Casserole

Makes 6 servings

12 **dried eggplant slices**

2 cups boiling water

1 egg

⅓ cup milk

¼ teaspoon salt

3 tablespoons vegetable oil

½ pound mozzarella cheese, sliced

3 medium tomatoes, sliced

1 tablespoon olive oil

½ teaspoon dried oregano

1. Place the eggplant slices in a heatproof bowl. Pour the boiling water over and soak at room temperature for 1 to 2 hours, or let cool and soak overnight in the refrigerator.

2. When you're ready to cook, preheat the oven to 350°F. Lightly grease a large casserole; set aside.

3. Drain the eggplant slices and pat dry; set aside. With a fork, beat together the egg, milk, and salt in a flat dish. Heat the vegetable oil in a large skillet over medium heat. Dip the eggplant slices in the egg mixture. Add a single layer to the skillet and brown lightly on both sides. Transfer the browned slices to the prepared casserole; top with some of the cheese and tomatoes. Continue cooking the eggplant and layering with cheese and tomatoes, ending with cheese. Brush the top layer of cheese with olive oil; sprinkle with oregano. Bake for 30 minutes. Serve hot.

Creamed Greens Soup

Makes 4 servings

This is a very basic cream soup; feel free to jazz it up with herbs or spices.

- 3 tablespoons butter
- 3 tablespoons all-purpose flour
- ½ teaspoon salt

  Pinch of ground nutmeg
- 3 cups whole or 2 percent milk
- 1 cup lightly packed **dried spinach, kale, beet greens, or dandelion greens**

1. In a large nonreactive saucepan, melt the butter over medium-low heat. Sprinkle in the flour, salt, and nutmeg, whisking constantly, and cook for about 3 minutes. Slowly add the milk in a thin stream, whisking constantly, and cook until the mixture is smooth and lightly thickened, about 5 minutes. Remove from the heat and stir in the dried greens; cover and let stand for 30 minutes.

2. Return the saucepan to medium-low heat and cook until the mixture is hot. Serve immediately.

Stewed Okra and Rice

Makes 4–6 servings

- 3 cups boiling water
- 1 cup **dried okra slices**
- 1 cup **dried tomato chunks or broken-up slices**
- ¼ cup **dried chopped onion**
- ¼ cup uncooked white rice
- 2 tablespoons vegetable oil
- ½ teaspoon salt

1. Combine water, okra, tomatoes, onion, rice, oil, and salt in a medium nonreactive saucepan. Cover and cook over low heat, stirring occasionally, for 30 to 45 minutes, or until the rice is cooked and the vegetables are tender.

Onion and Bacon Pie

Makes 6–8 servings

3	cups boiling water
1½	cups **dried onion slices**
	Pastry for one 9-inch piecrust
6	bacon strips
2	eggs plus 1 egg yolk
¾	cup sour cream or yogurt
½	teaspoon snipped **dried chives**
⅛	teaspoon **dried caraway seeds**
	Salt and freshly ground black pepper
	Ground paprika

1. Combine the boiling water and onion slices in a heatproof bowl. Set aside to soak for 45 minutes.

2. Near the end of the soaking time, preheat the oven to 425°F. Fit the pastry into a 9-inch pie plate, decoratively fluting the edges. Refrigerate until needed.

3. Fry the bacon until crisp in a medium skillet over medium heat. Remove and drain on paper towels. Pour off all but 3 tablespoons of the bacon drippings. Drain the onion slices, reserving the soaking liquid for soups or other uses. Fry the onion slices in the bacon drippings until golden but not browned, stirring often. Set aside to cool slightly.

4. Combine the eggs, egg yolk, sour cream, chives, caraway seeds, and salt and pepper to taste in a mixing bowl. Beat with a fork until smooth. Crumble the bacon into large pieces and add to the egg mixture; stir in the onion slices. Pour into the prepared pie shell. Sprinkle with paprika.

5. Bake for 10 minutes, then reduce the heat to 350°F and bake for 25 to 30 minutes longer, until set in the center. Serve hot or warm.

Slow-Cooker Pork Chops with Root Vegetables

Makes 4 servings

1⅓ cups **dried parsnip, rutabaga, or turnip slices** (all one type, or a mix)

½ cup **dried carrot slices**

2 cups boiling water

¼ cup **dried apple slices**

4 boneless pork chops, 4–5 ounces each

Salt and freshly ground black pepper

¼ cup all-purpose flour

1 tablespoon vegetable oil

4 teaspoons ketchup

4 teaspoons brown sugar, packed

1 teaspoon crumbled **dried basil leaves**

3 tablespoons minced fresh onion

2 teaspoons butter, cut up

1. Place the parsnips and carrots in a slow cooker. Stir in the boiling water. Let stand for 45 minutes, stirring several times (do not turn on the slow cooker).

2. Cut the dried apple slices in half, then scatter them over the vegetables.

3. Season the pork chops with salt and pepper to taste, then dip them into the flour, shaking off excess. Heat the oil in a medium skillet over medium-high heat, then brown the pork chops on both sides. Arrange the browned pork chops in a single layer on top of the apples and vegetables.

4. Top each chop with 1 teaspoon ketchup and 1 teaspoon brown sugar; sprinkle the basil over all. Scatter the onion evenly on top of the chops, and dot with the butter. Set the slow cooker to low and cook for 7 to 8 hours, or until the pork chops are tender. Serve pork chops, apples, and vegetables with the juices from the slow cooker.

Potato Pancakes with Parsnips or Turnips

Makes 6 servings

1	cup **dried parsnip or turnip pieces**
1	cup boiling water
1	large baking potato, peeled and cut into 1-inch cubes
1	tablespoon **dried scallion pieces**, chopped
1	egg, beaten
¼	cup all-purpose flour
½	teaspoon salt
¼	teaspoon freshly ground black pepper
	Canola oil for frying
1½	cups prepared applesauce

1. Combine the parsnips and boiling water in a heatproof bowl. Set aside to soak for 30 minutes; then drain the turnips, reserving the soaking liquid for soups or other uses.

2. Heat a large pot of water to boiling over high heat. Add the potato cubes and drained turnips. Cook until the potatoes are tender, about 12 minutes, then drain, discarding the water. Transfer the potato mixture to a mixing bowl; stir in the scallion pieces. Set aside for 10 minutes. Meanwhile, line a plate with paper towels; set aside.

3. Mash the cooled potato mixture with a potato masher until fairly smooth. Stir in the egg, flour, salt, and pepper, mixing very well.

4. Pour about ¼ inch of oil into a large heavy skillet. Heat over medium heat until the surface is shimmering but not smoking. Use a quarter-cup dry measure to scoop up about ¼ cup of the potato mixture; carefully place it in the skillet. Repeat with the remaining potato mixture, dividing evenly to make 6 patties. Flatten the tops slightly with a spatula. Fry until nicely browned, then carefully turn and brown the second side. Transfer to the paper towel–lined plate and allow to stand for about a minute to blot off excess oil. Serve with applesauce.

Purée of Green Pea Soup

Makes 4–6 servings

- 2 cups water
- 1 cup **dried green peas**
- 2 tablespoons **dried scallion pieces**
- ½ teaspoon salt
- Pinch of ground nutmeg
- ½ cup cream
- 2 tablespoons butter

1. Heat the water to boiling in a saucepan. Remove from the heat and stir in the peas and scallion pieces. Cover and set aside to soak for 30 minutes.

2. After soaking, place the saucepan over medium heat and cook, covered, until the peas are tender, about 20 minutes. Stir in the salt and nutmeg. Process the peas and cooking water through a food strainer, food mill, or blender. Return to the saucepan. Add the cream and butter. Heat over medium-low heat until just simmering; do not boil. Serve hot.

Chili Powder Blend

Makes about ¼ cup

- 2 tablespoons chopped or crumbled **dried Ancho chile peppers** or other mild variety
- 2 teaspoons **dried cumin seeds**
- 2 teaspoons crumbled **dried oregano leaves**
- 2 teaspoons ground paprika
- 1 teaspoon **dried garlic slices**
- ½–1 teaspoon chopped or crumbled **dried cayenne chile peppers** or other hot variety

Chile and *chili* are not interchangeable words. *Chile* refers to the hot peppers themselves — some hotter than others — while *chili* powder is a blend of dried chile peppers and other spices. *Chili* is also the name of the familiar stewlike dish that includes chili powder. Got it?

Combine all ingredients in a small electric coffee mill/spice grinder, and process until fine. Use for chili, barbecue sauce, bean dishes, meatloaf, and wherever you want a taste of the Southwest.

Mock Fried Oysters

Makes 4–6 servings

- 1¾ cups water
- 1¾ cups **dried salsify slices**
- 2 eggs
- 1 tablespoon butter, melted
- ½ teaspoon salt
- ⅛ teaspoon freshly ground black pepper
  Fine dried breadcrumbs for coating
  Canola oil for frying

1. Heat the water to boiling in a saucepan. Remove from the heat and stir in the salsify; cover and set aside to soak for 30 minutes.

2. After soaking, place the saucepan over medium heat and cook, covered, until the salsify is tender, about 20 minutes. Drain, discarding the liquid (unless you want to save it for making fish soup). Mash the salsify with a potato masher or electric mixer until fluffy. Add 1 egg, the melted butter, salt, and pepper; blend well with a fork. Shape into 12 oyster-sized patties.

3. Beat the remaining egg in a flat dish. Dip the patties into the beaten egg, then into the breadcrumbs. Set aside on a plate while you heat the oil; this resting time helps the coating to adhere.

4. Line a plate with paper towels. Pour about ¼ inch of oil into a large heavy skillet. Heat over medium heat until the surface is shimmering but not smoking. Carefully add the salsify patties. Fry until nicely browned, then carefully turn and brown the second side. Transfer to the paper towel–lined plate and allow to stand for about a minute to blot off excess oil. Serve hot.

Salsify and Celery Chowder

Makes 4–6 servings

 2 cups water

1½ cups **dried salsify slices**

 ½ cup **dried celery slices**

 6 tablespoons butter

 6 tablespoons all-purpose flour

 1 quart whole or 2 percent milk

   Salt and freshly ground black pepper

   Oyster crackers

1. Heat the water to boiling in a saucepan. Remove from the heat and stir in the salsify and celery; cover and set aside to soak for 30 minutes.

2. After soaking, place the saucepan over medium heat and cook, covered, until the salsify and celery are tender, about 20 minutes. Drain, discarding the liquid (unless you want to save it for making fish soup).

3. Melt the butter in another saucepan over medium-low heat. Sprinkle in the flour, whisking constantly, and cook for about 3 minutes. Slowly add the milk in a thin stream, whisking constantly, and cook until the mixture is smooth and lightly thickened, about 5 minutes. Add the cooked salsify and celery. Season with salt and pepper to taste. Serve with oyster crackers.

Squash or Pumpkin Bread

Makes 1 loaf

¾ cup **dried mashed-squash or mashed-pumpkin crumbles***

1 cup boiling water

1 cup sugar

½ cup vegetable oil

2 eggs

1¾ cups all-purpose flour

1 teaspoon baking soda

½ teaspoon cinnamon

½ teaspoon salt

¼ teaspoon ground cloves

¼ teaspoon baking powder

½ cup **dried plum chunks** or ⅓ cup **dried cranberries**, optional

⅓ cup coarsely chopped nuts

1. Stir together the mashed-squash crumbles and boiling water in a heat-proof bowl. Let stand until fully rehydrated, 30 to 45 minutes, stirring several times; stir in an additional tablespoon or two of cold water if it seems to need it, and use a fork to mash any large chunks you notice.

2. When the squash is rehydrated, preheat the oven to 350°F. Grease and flour a 9- by 5-inch loaf pan; set aside.

3. Combine the sugar, oil, eggs, and rehydrated squash in a large mixing bowl; beat with a fork until smooth. Sift together the flour, baking soda, cinnamon, salt, cloves, and baking powder, and add to the squash mixture, stirring with a wooden spoon until just moistened. Stir in the plums and nuts. Scrape the mixture into the prepared loaf pan.

4. Bake for 1 hour 10 minutes, or until a tester inserted in the center comes out clean. Cool on a wire rack for 15 minutes, and then turn the loaf out onto the rack to cool completely before slicing.

---

* This recipe is for winter squash or pumpkin (not summer squash). You may substitute ¾ cup dried pumpkin powder, made from pumpkin leather, for the mashed-pumpkin crumbles.

Pumpkin and Peach Cookies

Makes about 2 dozen cookies

½	cup **dried mashed-pumpkin crumbles***
½	cup boiling water
4	tablespoons butter
½	cup sugar
1	egg
½	teaspoon vanilla extract
1	cup all-purpose flour
½	teaspoon baking powder
½	teaspoon baking soda
½	teaspoon ground cinnamon
¼	teaspoon salt
1	cup chopped **dried peaches or apricots**

1. Stir together the mashed-pumpkin crumbles and the boiling water in a heatproof bowl. Let stand until fully rehydrated, 30 to 45 minutes, stirring several times; stir in an additional tablespoon or two of cold water if it seems to need it, and use a fork to mash any large chunks you notice.

2. When the pumpkin is rehydrated, preheat the oven to 350°F. Grease several large baking sheets; set aside.

3. Place the butter in a large mixing bowl; beat with an electric mixer until fluffy. Add the sugar and beat until creamy. Add the egg, rehydrated pumpkin, and vanilla, and beat well. Sift together the flour, baking powder, baking soda, cinnamon, and salt into another mixing bowl. Stir in the peaches. Add the flour mixture to the pumpkin mixture about a cup at a time, beating well after each addition.

4. Drop heaping teaspoons of the dough onto the baking sheets, about 2 inches apart; refrigerate any unused dough. Bake for 12 to 15 minutes or until lightly browned. Transfer the cookies to a cooling rack. Cool the baking sheets and repeat until all dough has been baked.

* This recipe is for winter squash or pumpkin (not summer squash). You may substitute ½ cup dried squash or pumpkin powder, made from squash or pumpkin leather, for the mashed-squash crumbles.

Orange-Glazed Sweet Potatoes

Makes 4–6 servings

This is a nice side dish at holiday time; it goes very well with roasted poultry or ham.

- 3 cups water
- 3 cups **dried sweet potato slices**
- ⅔ cup sugar
- 1 tablespoon cornstarch
- ½ teaspoon salt
- ½ teaspoon finely chopped **dried orange zest**
- 1 cup orange juice
- 2 tablespoons butter

1. Heat the water to boiling in a nonreactive saucepan. Remove from the heat and stir in the sweet potatoes; cover and set aside to soak for 30 minutes.

2. After soaking, place the saucepan over low heat and cook, covered, until the sweet potatoes are tender, about 15 minutes. Meanwhile, preheat the oven to 350°F. Lightly grease a medium casserole; set aside.

3. Drain the sweet potatoes and place in the prepared casserole, reserving the soaking liquid for soups or other uses. Combine the sugar, cornstarch, salt, and orange zest in another nonreactive saucepan. Gradually add the orange juice, stirring constantly. Cook over low heat until thickened, stirring frequently. Add the butter and boil for 1 minute, stirring constantly. Pour over the sweet potatoes. Cover and bake for 1 hour, basting occasionally with the sauce.

Green Salsa with Dried Tomatillos

Makes about 1 cup

½   fresh jalapeño pepper, cut vertically

½   small white onion, cut into 2 pieces and separated

2   garlic cloves

1   tablespoon olive oil

1¼   cups **dried tomatillo slices**

¾   cup boiling water

3   tablespoons finely chopped cilantro leaves

1   tablespoon lime juice, more as needed

½   teaspoon salt, more as needed

1. Preheat the oven to 375°F. Line a small rimmed baking sheet with heavy-duty foil. Place the jalapeño pepper half, onion pieces, and whole garlic cloves on the foil. Drizzle the oil over the vegetables, turning to coat. Roast until the vegetables are soft and beginning to brown, about 30 minutes; turn the vegetables several times during roasting. Remove from the oven and set aside to cool.

2. Meanwhile, while the vegetables are roasting, prepare the tomatillos. Heat a dry cast-iron skillet over medium to medium-low heat. Add a few of the dried tomatillo slices and cook, pressing down on the slices with a spatula, until just lightly browned, about 5 seconds; don't over-brown them. Turn and brown the second side. Transfer the browned tomatillos to a heatproof bowl and repeat with the remaining slices, a few at a time. Stir in the boiling water; set aside for 30 minutes, stirring occasionally.

3. When the tomatillos have soaked for 30 minutes and the vegetables have cooled enough to handle, scrape the seeds out of the jalapeño pepper and cut off the stem; pull off and discard the blistered skin. Add the cleaned jalapeño and the roasted onions and garlic to a food processor, then add the tomatillos and their soaking liquid. Pulse a few times to chop everything to a medium-fine texture; don't over-process and turn it into a purée.

4. Transfer the chopped vegetable mixture to a glass or ceramic bowl. Stir in the cilantro, lime juice, and salt. Taste and add additional lime juice or salt as you prefer. Serve with tortilla chips, tamales, burritos, or any other dish that is served with salsa. Refrigerate leftover salsa.

"Sun-Dried" Tomato Pesto

Makes about 1½ cups

This make-ahead mixture is great on pasta, grilled chicken, and vegetables and also makes a nice topping for bruschetta.

1	cup **dried tomato chunks, diced halves, or broken-up slices**
½	cup boiling water
1	cup fresh basil leaves
2–3	tablespoons pine nuts, optional
1½	teaspoons crumbled **dried oregano leaves**
1	small garlic clove
¼	cup olive oil, plus additional to top off jar

1. Combine the tomatoes and water in a small heatproof bowl. Stir well and set aside to soften for about 10 minutes. Drain off and discard the water (or save it to add flavor to soups or stews). Pat the tomatoes lightly dry with paper towels.

2. Combine the drained tomatoes, basil, pine nuts, oregano, and garlic in a food processor or blender. Pulse a few times until chopped to medium consistency. Add the oil and process until smooth. Pack the pesto tightly into a clean glass jar and cover with a thin layer of olive oil. Keep refrigerated, and use as needed.

Italian Green Tomatoes

Makes 4–6 servings

12	**dried green tomato slices**
	Warm water as needed
1	egg
3	tablespoons all-purpose flour
½	teaspoon salt
½	cup vegetable oil
¼	pound mozzarella cheese, grated
¼	cup minced onion
1	cup tomato sauce
½	teaspoon sugar
¼	teaspoon crumbled **dried oregano leaves**
¼	teaspoon salt

1. Place the tomato slices on a large platter and spray generously with warm water. Let them soak for 30 minutes, turning and spraying occasionally with more warm water.

2. Near the end of the soaking time, preheat the oven to 350°F. Lightly grease a 1½-quart casserole; set aside.

3. Drain the tomato slices. Beat the egg in a flat bowl. Stir together the flour and salt in another flat bowl. Heat 6 tablespoons of the oil in a large skillet over medium heat. Dip the tomato slices one at a time in the egg and then into the flour mixture; shake off excess flour and transfer them to the skillet. Working quickly, repeat with additional slices until the skillet is filled but not crowded with a single layer of tomatoes. Sauté the tomato slices until golden brown on both sides. As they are browned, arrange them in layers in the prepared casserole alternately with grated cheese.

4. When all slices are browned, cool the skillet slightly and wipe out with a paper towel. Add the remaining 2 tablespoons oil to the skillet and place over low heat. When the oil is warm, add the onion and sauté until transparent but not browned. Add the tomato sauce, sugar, oregano, and salt. Simmer for 5 minutes, then pour over the tomatoes and cheese in the casserole. Bake for 20 to 25 minutes, or until the cheese has melted.

Green Tomatoes and Okra

Makes 4–6 servings

- 2 cups water
- 12 **dried green tomato slices**
- ½ cup **dried onion slices or chopped pieces**
- 1 cup **dried ripe tomato chunks**
- ½ cup **dried okra slices**
- 2 tablespoons butter
- Salt and freshly ground black pepper
- 1 teaspoon crumbled **dried parsley leaves**

Heat the water to boiling in a large nonreactive saucepan. Add the green tomato slices, onion, ripe tomato chunks, and okra. Simmer for 30 minutes, stirring occasionally. Stir in the butter, and add salt and pepper to taste. Sprinkle with parsley.

Vegetable Flakes

Makes about ¾ cup

Keep a jar of these flakes in the pantry, and then sprinkle them into casseroles, salad dressings, potato salad, egg dishes, or soups.

- ½ cup **dried carrot slices**
- 2 tablespoons **dried celery slices**
- ½ cup **dried onion slices**, firmly packed
- ½ cup **dried diced bell peppers**
- 2 tablespoons crumbled **dried parsley leaves**

1. Combine the carrots and celery in a blender. Pulse a few times until coarsely chopped. Add the onion and peppers. Pulse until the vegetables have been chopped into fine flakes; don't over-process or you'll end up with powder. Transfer the flaked vegetables to a small bowl and stir in the parsley. Store in a tightly sealed glass jar; shake or stir before using to distribute ingredients evenly.

Vegetable Broth Powder

Makes ½–⅔ cup

Use this in place of purchased granulated bouillon, or mix with water as directed and use the broth in place of vegetable broth or chicken broth in recipes. Feel free to tinker with the ingredients, depending on what you have on hand.

- ½ cup **dried diced bell peppers**
- ½ cup **dried zucchini slices**
- ¼ cup **dried tomato slices**,* cut into chunks before measuring
- ¼ cup **dried mushrooms**
- ¼ cup **dried onion slices** or **dried chopped onion**
- 2 tablespoons **dried celery slices**, or ¼ cup **dried celery leaves**
- 2 tablespoons crumbled **dried parsley leaves**
- 1 tablespoon crumbled **dried basil leaves**
- 1 tablespoon salt or salt substitute, optional
- 1 teaspoon crumbled **dried oregano or marjoram leaves**
- ½ teaspoon **dried garlic powder**
- 1 teaspoon ground paprika
- ½ teaspoon ground white pepper

1. Combine the bell peppers, zucchini, tomatoes, mushrooms, onion, and celery in a blender. Cover tightly, then pulse a few times to chop the vegetables. Add the parsley, basil, salt, oregano, and garlic. Cover tightly, then process on high until finely ground. Let the dust settle for about a minute. Pour into a fine wire-mesh strainer set over a mixing bowl and stir with a spoon to sift the powder into the bowl. Return any vegetable pieces remaining in the strainer to the blender and process until fine; repeat as necessary. Add the paprika and white pepper to the sifted mixture in the bowl; stir until thoroughly mixed. Store in a tightly sealed glass jar.

2. To make vegetable broth, combine 1 heaping teaspoon of the powder with 1 cup boiling water. It may not dissolve completely, but will work fine in recipes. If you want to sip it as a hot beverage, stir occasionally.

* Dried tomato slices tend to be easier to powder than dried plum tomatoes. You may have a few tomato flakes that refuse to be powdered; save them to add to soup or stew.

Mock Chicken Broth Powder

Makes about 1 cup

This vegetarian mixture can be substituted for chicken bouillon granules in recipes. Nutritional yeast — also called brewer's yeast — provides great flavor and nutrition; look for it at health-food stores. It provides a surprisingly "chicken-y" flavor to the broth powder.

- ⅓ cup **dried chopped onion**
- ¼ cup **dried mushrooms**
- ¼ cup **dried shredded carrots**
- 2 tablespoons **dried celery slices**, or ¼ cup **dried celery leaves**
- 1 cup nutritional yeast powder (see headnote)
- 1 tablespoon salt
- 1 tablespoon crumbled **dried parsley leaves**
- 1 teaspoon **dried thyme leaves**
- 1 teaspoon crumbled **dried dill leaves**
- 1 teaspoon crumbled **dried marjoram leaves**
- 1 teaspoon ground turmeric
- ½ teaspoon ground white pepper

1. Combine the onion, mushrooms, carrots, and celery in a blender. Cover tightly, then pulse a few times to chop the vegetables. Add the yeast powder, salt, parsley, thyme, dill, and marjoram. Cover tightly, then process on high until finely ground. Let the dust settle for about a minute. Pour into a fine wire-mesh strainer set over a mixing bowl and stir with a spoon to sift the powder into the bowl. Return any vegetable pieces remaining in the strainer to the blender and process until fine; repeat as necessary. (If there are a few flakes left that won't turn to powder, don't worry about it; simply save them to add to soup or another dish.) Add the turmeric and white pepper to the sifted mixture in the bowl; stir until thoroughly mixed. Store in a tightly sealed glass jar.

2. To make mock chicken broth, combine 1 heaping teaspoon of the powder with 1 cup boiling water. It may not dissolve completely but will work fine in recipes. If you want to sip it as a hot beverage, stir occasionally.

dried basil leaves

CHAPTER 6

Herbs and Spices

FROM A CULINARY STANDPOINT, *herbs* are tender (non-woody) plants whose leaves and/or flowers are used in the immature stage of the plant's growth as seasoning; basil leaves, oregano leaves, and chamomile flowers are common herbs. In addition, some tender plants have other parts — seeds, roots, and bulbs — that are used at the mature stage of the plant's growth as seasoning; examples include anise seeds, gingerroot, and garlic. These parts of the plants are referred to as *spices*. Fruits and leaves of some shrubs and trees are also used as spices; examples include juniper berries and sassafras leaves.

Drying Herbs

THE LEAVES AND FLOWERS OF HERB PLANTS have been used for centuries to add flavor and color to foods; indeed, herbs are among the ingredients that define many dishes. Herbs get much of their flavor and fragrance from volatile oils that are sensitive to both heat and light. These oils begin to diminish as soon as the plants are harvested and continue to fade as the herbs dry. Although dried herbs are never as flavorful as fresh herbs, they are still valuable and worth keeping in the kitchen.

To preserve as much of their flavor as possible, herbs should be dried at very low temperatures and with adequate air circulation, out of direct sunlight. Commercial processors use equipment that combines gentle heat, high airflow, specialized ventilation, and often dehumidification to dry herbs before they deteriorate. Even with this type of setup, it takes days to dry a batch of herbs for commercial production.

There are several methods for drying herbs at home; see Listing of Herbs below for suggestions for each type of herb. Dehydrators and home ovens that run at very low temperatures can be used to dry some herbs, but this approach is not practical for plants like basil, which have large, tender leaves on tender stems. If the entire sprig is placed in the dehydrator, the stem will wilt and everything will clump together, hindering drying. For efficient drying in a dehydrator or oven, the basil leaves must be pulled off the stems and laid *individually without overlapping* on trays, then dried at low temperatures for perhaps 12 hours. If you have more than one or two basil plants to dry, your dehydrator will be running for days to process this single herb. However, with very little work you can prepare dozens of plants or stems and set them aside for air-drying, then let time do the work — and you can dry as many different types of herbs as you like at the same time.

Some herbs with small or stout leaves on tough stems work fairly well in a manufactured dehydrator or home oven. Thyme is one example; the leaves are much smaller and firmer than basil, and the wiry stems don't collapse during drying so the leaves don't clump together. Many of these plants tend to be sprawling and tangled, however, so you have to cut them into small sprigs to fit between the dehydrator trays, or dry just one or two trays' worth at a time, leaving space between the trays for the tangle of herbs.

Again, air-drying is a great solution because you can tie up these tough-stemmed herbs if practical, and if not, you can simply pile the uncut stems loosely into a paper bag and set it aside until the leaves dry — a boon at the end of the season, when you have a tangled mass of thyme, oregano, or other loose-growing herbs to dry.

Harvesting and Preparing Herbs for Drying

Pick leafy herbs when they are tender and flavorful, generally just before the plant flowers. Flower heads of herb plants such as dill and chamomile must be gathered before the seeds develop.

Don't try to "pick" herbs as you might daisies. Cut them with scissors or pruning shears. Leave 4 inches of stem on leafy annuals; for leafy perennials, cut only one-third the growth. This permits further growth and future harvesting. If frost threatens at the end of the season, however, cut the whole plant off at the base.

Hose herbs off the day before you plan to dry them, and then cut the stems the next day as soon as the sun has dried off the dew. If your herbs seem dirty, rinse them very quickly under running water or spray. Line the basket of a salad spinner with paper towels, add the herbs, and spin until the leaves are completely dry.

As you prepare the herbs for drying, keep an eye out for insects, stray blades of grass, or other unwanted materials, picking them out as you go. Also pick off and discard any withered, blackened, or damaged leaves.

Listing of Herbs

Here is a list of the most common herbs, grouped according to the growth pattern and recommended drying methods.

- **BUNCHING HERBS WITH LARGE LEAVES:** These herbs can be tied into a bunch and are best when air-dried. If dried in a dehydrator or oven, leaves should be pulled off the stems and spread on trays in a single layer without overlapping. This group includes basil, bay leaves, catnip, chervil, cilantro, lemon balm, lemon verbena, mint, parsley, and sage. Some people prefer to use a needle and thread to string individual sprigs of basil, rather than drying it in a bunch; this method hastens drying and prevents the leaves from sticking together as they dry.

- **HERBS ON THICK, MOIST STEMS:** These herbs can't be air-dried because the tender stems are too thick and moist and would spoil before the leaves were dry; dry these leaves in a dehydrator or oven. This group includes celery leaves, dill leaves, fennel leaves, and lovage.

- **SMALLER-LEAVED HERBS ON TOUGH OR WIRY STEMS:** These herbs can be air-dried, dried in a dehydrator, or oven-dried. Dry whole sprigs, with the leaves still attached to the stems. This group includes marjoram, oregano, rosemary, savory, tarragon, and thyme.

- **FLOWER HEADS OF HERBS:** Flower heads can be air-dried, dried in a dehydrator, or oven-dried. This group includes chamomile flowers and dill flowers.

- **CHIVES** are in a class by themselves. These long, hollow leaves have no stems, so are handled differently. For air-drying, tie a handful of full-length chives into a bundle and dry like bunching herbs, then snip into short lengths once dry. For drying in a dehydrator or oven, snip the chives into ¼-inch pieces, and then spread on trays covered with solid liner sheets or on a baking sheet covered with kitchen parchment.

Air-Drying Herbs

Step 1.

Gather a selection of clean, square-bottomed paper bags, including small lunch bags, large grocery bags, and anything in between. You'll also need kitchen twine, a place to hang bunches or bags of herbs, and push-pins, tacks, nails, or another system to hang the bunches.

Step 2.

Get the herbs ready; see Harvesting and Preparing Herbs for Drying, on page 225.

Step 3.

Working with one type of herb at a time, gather a small handful of stems. If the stems are fairly straight and the leaves are growing in an orderly fashion, bunch the stems and tie the ends together tightly with kitchen twine, and then tie a loop on one end of the twine; the bunch is ready for hanging. If the stems are tough or wiry and grow in a large, open tangle that is hard to gather into a bunch, place them loosely into a paper bag without tying; you may dry small batches of each herb in a lunch bag, or a large number of stems in a grocery bag, as long as the stems are loosely packed. If you're drying chamomile or dill flower heads, place the long stems heads down into paper bags.

Step 4.

Hang the tied bunches on a rafter (or other location) in a warm, airy room; the heads should point downward and should not be exposed to direct sunlight. Small paper bags can be tacked to a rafter or set on a table; large paper bags can be set on a table (or on the floor, if they won't be disturbed). The tops of all bags should be partially or fully open.

Step 5.

Check the herbs periodically until they are completely dry; this generally takes one to four weeks. Process and store the dried herbs as described in Storing and Using Herbs, on page 231.

TIPS FOR AIR-DRYING HERBS

- As an option when tying a bunch of stems together, place the bunch inside a paper lunch bag with the stems sticking out of the top, then wrap kitchen twine tightly around the bag and stems together and tie securely. Cut several open slits in the sides of the bag, and hang the bag as directed. The bag protects the herbs from dust and light and also catches any leaves that may fall off the bunch during drying.

- You could hang a rod from the ceiling, and then loop the kitchen twine around the rod for hanging.

- Another option is to stretch a piece of sturdy cord between two walls, then slip paper clips onto the cord and hang the bunches from the paper clips.

Drying Herbs in a Dehydrator

Step 1.

Place a solid liner sheet on a dehydrator tray and position it on the bottom level; the solid sheet will catch small leaves that fall through the screens. Place screens on the other dehydrator trays.

Step 2.

Get the herbs ready; see Harvesting and Preparing Herbs for Drying, on page 225.

Step 3.

For herbs with large, tender leaves, pull individual leaves off the stems and arrange on the screens in a single layer without overlapping. For smaller-leaved herbs on tough or wiry stems, place entire sprigs on the screens; if you have a stacking-tray dehydrator, cut the sprigs into pieces that will fit between the trays, and if you have a box-style dehydrator, remove empty trays as necessary so the herbs fit into the dehydrator without cutting into small pieces. For flower heads, spread individual flowers or small flower clusters on screens. Place the trays of herbs in the dehydrator.

Step 4.

Run the dehydrator at 100 to 105°F until the herbs are dry. Small leaves and flowers may take anywhere from 2 to 8 hours; large leaves may take up to 18 hours.

Step 5.

When the herbs are dry, process and store them as described in Storing and Using Herbs, on page 231.

TIPS FOR DRYING HERBS IN A DEHYDRATOR

- Don't dry herbs in a batch with vegetables or fruits, because those foods add so much moisture to the air that the herbs will take too long to dry

- Dry each type of herb separately if possible to keep the flavors from blending.

- Check herbs frequently near the end of drying time, and remove them as soon as they are dry; over-drying causes flavor loss.

- A home-built dehydrator can be used for drying herbs but isn't ideal because the herbs will be exposed to strong light during drying.

Drying Herbs in an Oven

Step 1.

Prepare racks for oven drying and line them with screens; see page 50 for more information. Position an empty baking sheet on the bottom of the oven; the baking sheet will catch small leaves that fall through the screens.

Step 2.

Get the herbs ready; see Harvesting and Preparing Herbs for Drying, on page 225.

Step 3.

For herbs with large, tender leaves, pull individual leaves off the stems and arrange on the screens in a single layer without overlapping. For smaller-leaved herbs on tough or wiry stems, place entire sprigs on the screens; if the sprigs are in a bulky tangle, pull them apart or cut up as necessary so they fit between the oven racks. For flower heads, spread individual flowers or small flower clusters on screens.

Step 4a.

If you have a **convection oven**, place the racks of herbs in the oven and adjust the oven to run on the convection setting at 100°F; see more information on using convection ovens on page 46. Monitor the temperature and adjust the setting as needed, continuing until the herbs are dry. Small leaves and flowers may take anywhere from 2 to 8 hours; large leaves may take up to 18 hours.

Step 4b.

If you have a **non-convection oven that has no pilot light**, preheat it to 200°F, turn it off, and place the racks of herbs in the oven. Prop the door open with a ball of foil, positioning it to turn off the oven light switch. Let the herbs dry in the oven for 6 to 8 hours (or overnight). If the herbs are not fully dry, leave the racks on the counter until drying is complete.

Step 4c.

If you have a **non-convection oven with a pilot light**, place the racks of herbs in the oven without preheating it; the heat from the pilot light will dry the herbs slowly. Prop the door open with a ball of foil, positioning it to turn off the oven light switch. Small leaves and flowers may take anywhere from 2 to 10 hours; large leaves may take up to 20 hours.

Step 5.

When the herbs are dry, process and store them as described in Storing and Using Herbs, on page 231.

TIPS FOR DRYING HERBS IN AN OVEN

- Don't dry herbs in a batch with vegetables or fruits, because those foods add so much moisture to the air that the herbs will take too long to dry.

- Dry each type of herb separately if possible to keep the flavors from blending.

Storing and Using Herbs

When properly dried, herb leaves and flowers will be crumbly and brittle. If you've dried small herb leaves on the stems, strip them off before storing. Work over a large baking sheet to catch leaves as they fall, or hold the bunch inside a large, clean paper bag as you strip the leaves. Discard the stems. Herbs retain better flavor if the leaves are stored whole and then crumbled just prior to use. If you wish to prepare herb blends, however, you'll have to crumble most herbs before combining them with others. Some, such as sage, oregano, and marjoram, may be coarsely crumbled in the hands. Stiffer leaves, such as rosemary, savory, and tarragon, may be finely crushed with a rolling pin. Bay leaves are used whole; thyme leaves are so small that they may be used whole or crumbled lightly just before use.

Flowers that have been dried in a dehydrator or oven are ready to store as soon as they are dry. If you've air-dried the flower heads, use a small pair of scissors to snip the individual flowers off the stems; pick through the flowers to remove any stray bits of stem that may have broken off. Discard all stems.

Store dried herbs in tightly sealed glass jars. Small jars retain the delicate flavors better than large ones, which lose aroma each time the jar is opened; if you have a large batch of herbs, divide them among several jars. To keep dried herbs at their best, always keep the herbs in a dry, cool, dark place. Don't store them in a cabinet near a stove, radiator, or refrigerator, because the heat can cause flavor loss.

Dried herbs are used in the dry state, without refreshing in water. The flavor of dried herbs is much more pronounced than that of fresh herbs, so use smaller amounts. As a general rule, when substituting dried herbs in a recipe that calls for fresh, use one-third as much dried herbs as indicated for fresh herbs in the recipe (so if the recipe calls for 1 tablespoon of a chopped fresh herb, use 1 teaspoon of the dried herb). It is easy to add more, but the overpowering flavor of too much can spoil a carefully planned dish.

Drying Spices

SPICES ARE PLANT PARTS that are traditionally dried and used for seasoning. Seeds are perhaps the most common spices that come from herbaceous plants, and many of the seed-bearing spice plants can be grown easily in the home garden. Various roots, bulbs, and fruits may also be harvested and dried to use as spices; garlic is the most familiar, but others such as juniper berries and gingerroot can also be grown at home.

Seeds from Herbs

Herb plants with seeds that are used as spices include anise, caraway, celery, coriander (cilantro), cumin, dill, fennel, and mustard. Harvest the plants when the seeds are turning brown — too early means the seeds have not ripened, too late means the seed crop may fall to the ground and be lost. Insects sometimes hide in seed heads; if this is a problem, dip the seed heads briefly in boiling water before drying, although doing so may cause some seeds to fall out of the head and also lengthens drying time.

Although herbaceous seed heads are lightweight and open, they are large and delicate, so most are best dried in paper bags rather than in a dehydrator. Cut off the stems fairly low down on the plant to avoid jostling the heads too much and knocking out the seeds. Slip the stems, seed heads–first, into a paper bag; if the heads are large and bulky or if you have a lot of them, use a large paper grocery bag. Leave the bag open at the top, and set it in an out-of-the-way spot. Dry the seed heads until the stalks are brittle and the seeds are completely dry; this may happen in a few days or may take a week or more. Many seeds will fall out on their own as the seed heads dry; if the heads seem dry but there are still seeds attached, jostle the bag to shake them out, or place them on a waxed paper–lined baking sheet and shake them to loosen the seeds.

If you have a box-style or home-built dehydrator, you can dry the seed heads by using only one or two trays to allow more room for the heads. Snip off all but a very short piece of stem; some seeds may fall out as you do this, so hold the head over a bowl. Place the heads stem-side-up on the trays, and dehydrate at 100°F until the heads are dry and the seeds are falling out; this may happen as quickly as an hour, so keep an eye on it. You could also place the heads on a baking sheet lined with kitchen parchment, then put them into a barely warm oven that has been pre-heated and turned off.

When the seeds have fallen out of the heads, pick through them to remove bits of stem and the flower remnants. If the seeds have dropped out but don't appear to be fully dry, scatter them on solid liner sheets and place them in a 100°F dehydrator or just-warm oven for a brief period.

Many seeds are ground finely before use; cumin, for example, is much more common in the ground form than as whole seeds. An electric coffee grinder/spice mill is the best tool for this, although a mortar and pestle may also be used; blenders and food processors don't work well for grinding seeds.

Leaves, Roots, Bulbs, and Fruits

Because this category includes several types of plant parts, each listing below includes specific instructions for dehydrating as well as use.

- **FILÉ POWDER** is both a spice and a thickener. Made from the leaves of the sassafras tree, filé is used to season and thicken Cajun or Creole stews, particularly gumbo. Harvest sassafras in early fall, before the leaves develop their fall color. For a dehydrator, spread individual leaves thinly on trays or racks lined with screens; dehydrate at 100°F until very crisp, generally 6 to 8 hours. For air-drying, snip off small, leafy branches, then tie the branches together and hang until dry. Process the dried leaves to a fine powder in a blender, then shake through a fine wire-mesh strainer to remove any bits of hard stem. Store in a tightly sealed glass jar. Add filé powder to the stew off the stove, just before serving, or let individuals stir it into their bowls as needed; it becomes stringy or slimy if boiled.

- **GARLIC** is familiar to most cooks in both the fresh and dried form, so its uses don't need explanation here. To prepare garlic cloves for dehydrating, peel off the papery husks. For **garlic flakes**, slice the fresh cloves crosswise ⅛ inch thick; you may also cut the fresh cloves into ¼-inch slices, dehydrate those, then pulse the dried slices in the blender to make flakes (this method involves less cutting time but more dehydrating time). For **chopped garlic**, chop the cloves into rough chunks. Spread over solid liner sheets or baking sheets lined with kitchen parchment. Dehydrate at 100 to 110°F, stirring occasionally, until crisp and very dry, generally 4 to 6 hours. Store as is, or make **garlic powder** by chopping in an electric coffee grinder/spice mill.

- **GINGERROOT** is dried and ground for use in many baked goods. To prepare for dehydrating, scrape the thin skin off the root, then slice the root very thinly or chop coarsely. Spread on solid liner sheets or baking sheets lined with kitchen parchment. Dehydrate at 110 to 125°F until brittle and completely dry, generally 2 to 3 hours. Grind to a powder in an electric coffee grinder/spice mill, then sift through a fine wire-mesh strainer, discarding any fibrous material that remains in the strainer. Use as you would purchased ground ginger.

- **JUNIPER BERRIES** are the fruit of the common juniper shrub; although they look like a berry (and are called berries), they are actually cones. Their smell is familiar to anyone who's ever had a martini, since it is the juniper berry that gives gin its distinctive taste. In the kitchen, they are used in the marinade for sauerbraten and other hearty meat dishes. Pick juniper berries from the shrubs in late summer or fall; they should be pale blue with a dusty finish. Make certain you're harvesting from a true juniper; Eastern red cedar has similar-looking fruits, but the needles are flat rather than pointed. Dry juniper berries on a baking sheet at room temperature for a week or two or in a dehydrator at 100°F for 2 or 3 hours. Store whole dried juniper berries in glass bottles. To use, add a few to meat marinades, or use as directed in recipes calling for purchased juniper berries.

- **LEMONGRASS BULBS** come from a plant with long, bladelike leaves. The bulbs are used in Asian cooking, particularly Thai and Vietnamese dishes. Lemongrass bulbs are best used fresh, as they lose flavor when dried; however, lemongrass can be hard to find in markets, so you may want to dehydrate some to have it available whenever you want it. To dry the bulbs, the use of a dehydrator is recommended. Cut off the bulb where it just begins to change color from white to pale green, then cut off the fibrous roots at the base. Cut the bulb in half vertically, then rinse in plenty of cold water to clean out any dirt that's hidden between the layers. Slice the bulb halves crosswise, about 1/8 inch thick. Spread on dehydrator screens and dry at 125°F until brittle, 3 to 4 hours. To use, pound to a powder with a mortar and pestle or grind in an electric coffee grinder/spice mill. Stir the powder into soy sauce or other liquids being used in recipes that call for lemongrass paste, using twice the amount of powder as you would of fresh lemongrass paste.

- **ROSE HIPS** are the fruits of the rose bush. They are rich in vitamin C and are often used for tea; they also can be steeped to make jelly or stewed and strained to make jam and spreads. Harvest ripe rose hips starting in late fall, when they are beginning to dry; the hips persist through winter and are sweetened and softened by frost. The hips have coarse hairs inside that irritate the throat; to remove these, use a small pair of scissors to cut the hips lengthwise, and then scrape out the seeds and hairs with the tip of a table knife. Spread the split hips out on dehydrator screens and dry at 90 to 100°F until they are leathery, generally 4 to 6 hours. Rose hip tea benefits from the addition of other herbs such as lemon balm or mint.

- **SHALLOTS** are like small onions, with an onion-garlic flavor. To prepare shallots for dehydrating, peel off the papery skin, then trim off the tip and roots. Slice crosswise ⅛ inch thick, or chop coarsely. Spread over solid liner sheets or baking sheets lined with kitchen parchment. Dehydrate at 100 to 110 F, stirring occasionally, until crisp and very dry, generally 4 to 6 hours.

Recipes Featuring Herbs and Spices

HERBS AND SPICES ARE USED in recipes throughout this book as a supporting actor; there are too many to list with each type of herb or spice above. Below are some recipes that highlight herbs and spices specifically. As in previous chapters, dried ingredients from this book are highlighted in **bold type**.

Poultry Seasoning

Makes about ¼ cup herb blend

This mixture of herbs is used in stuffing for poultry, veal, and pork. It can also be sprinkled on poultry prior to cooking.

    1   tablespoon crumbled **dried sage leaves**
    1   tablespoon **dried thyme leaves**
    1   tablespoon crumbled **dried marjoram leaves**
    1   tablespoon crumbled **dried savory leaves**
    1   tablespoon broken **dried rosemary leaves**

1. Combine all ingredients, crumbling together to blend.

2. Store in a tightly sealed glass jar. To use, add 1 or 2 teaspoons of mixture to any stuffing recipe.

Dried Italian Herb Mix

Makes about ½ cup herb blend

- 2 tablespoons crumbled **dried basil leaves**
- 1½ tablespoons crumbled **dried parsley leaves** (preferably flat-leaf)
- 2 teaspoons crumbled **dried oregano leaves**
- 1 teaspoon crumbled **dried marjoram leaves**
- ½ teaspoon broken **dried rosemary leaves**
- ½ teaspoon **dried thyme leaves**

1. Combine all ingredients, crumbling together to blend.

2. Store in a tightly sealed glass jar. Use to season meat, fish, pasta, and vegetable dishes.

Fines Herbes

Makes about ½ cup herb blend

This classic French herb mixture offers a delicate combination of flavors that works particularly well with chicken or fish; it's also excellent added to egg dishes and sprinkled over hot, cooked vegetables.

- 2 tablespoons crumbled **dried chervil leaves**
- 2 tablespoons crumbled **dried parsley leaves**
- 2 tablespoons crumbled **dried tarragon leaves**
- 1 tablespoon **dried snipped chives**
- 1 tablespoon crumbled **dried marjoram leaves**

1. Combine all ingredients, crumbling together to blend.

2. Store in a tightly sealed glass jar. Use as directed in recipes that call for *fines herbes*, or try adding about ½ teaspoon to chicken, fish, or egg dishes.

Herbes de Provence Mix

Makes about 1 cup herb blend

3 tablespoons **dried fennel seeds**

3 tablespoons crumbled **dried marjoram leaves**

3 tablespoons **dried thyme leaves**

3 tablespoons crumbled **dried savory leaves**

2 tablespoons crumbled **dried basil leaves**

2 tablespoons broken **dried rosemary leaves**

2 tablespoons crumbled **dried oregano leaves**

1. Crush the fennel seeds lightly with a mortar and pestle. Combine in a mixing bowl with the marjoram, thyme, savory, basil, rosemary, and oregano, crumbling together to blend.

2. Store in a tightly sealed glass jar. Use to season meat, poultry, fish, pasta and vegetable dishes.

Simple Herb Tea

Makes 2 servings

Here are instructions for making a simple tea from dried herbs. Use all one kind of herb or a mix.

2½ tablespoons crumbled **dried catnip leaves, chamomile flowers, lemon balm leaves, lemon verbena leaves, or mint leaves**

2 fresh lemon slices, optional

1. Place the herbs in a heated teapot. Pour 2 cups of boiling water over the herbs. Cover and let steep for 5 minutes.

2. Strain the tea, and serve hot or cold, with lemon and/or sweeteners, if you like.

Peppermint-Rosemary Tea Blend

Makes ½ cup dry tea blend

  ¼ cup crumbled **dried peppermint leaves**

  ¼ cup coarsely broken **dried rosemary leaves**

1. Combine peppermint and rosemary, crumbling together to blend. Store in a tightly sealed glass jar.

2. To make tea for two, place 2 tablespoons of the tea blend in a heated teapot. Add 2 cups of boiling water; cover and let steep for 5 minutes.

3. Strain the tea; serve hot or cold, plain or sweetened with sugar or honey.

Rose Hip Tea

Makes 2 servings

  2 tablespoons **dried rose hip halves**

1. Combine the rose hips with 2 cups of cold water in a small saucepan. Cover and slowly bring to a boil. Simmer over low heat for 15 minutes.

2. Mash the hips with a fork, and then strain the liquid. Drink hot or cold with a spoonful of lemon juice and honey or sugar, if you like.

Rose Hip Sparkle Tea

Makes 6 servings

  2 tablespoons **dried rose hip halves**

  3 tablespoons crumbled **dried peppermint leaves**

  1 tablespoon crumbled **dried orange zest**

1. Simmer rose hips in 1½ quarts water in a nonreactive saucepan for 15 minutes. Remove from the heat.

2. Add the peppermint leaves and orange zest, and let steep for 5 minutes. Strain the tea; serve hot or cold, plain or sweetened with sugar or honey.

Tarragon Vinegar

Makes 1½ quarts

- 1 quart red wine
- 1 pint cider vinegar
- 2 tablespoons crumbled **dried tarragon leaves**
- ¼ teaspoon **dried chopped garlic**
- 2 whole cloves

1. Stir together the wine, vinegar, tarragon, garlic, and cloves in a nonreactive saucepan. Let stand for 2 hours.

2. Simmer for 15 minutes over low heat; remove from the heat and set aside until cool. Strain through a paper coffee filter and pour into a sterilized bottle; seal tightly for storage.

White Wine Vinegar with Herbs

Makes 1 quart

- 2 cups white wine vinegar
- 2 cups dry white wine
- 1 teaspoon crumbled **dried lemon balm leaves**
- ½ teaspoon crumbled **dried tarragon leaves**
- ⅛ teaspoon **dried chopped garlic**
- 3 **dried bay leaves**
- 2 whole cloves

1. Stir together the vinegar, wine, lemon balm, tarragon, garlic, bay leaves, and cloves in a nonreactive saucepan. Place over medium-low heat. Bring slowly to a boil, cover, and simmer for 10 minutes.

2. Remove from the heat and set aside until cool. Strain through a paper coffee filter and pour into a sterilized bottle; seal tightly for storage.

Sage Vinegar

This simple technique works well with other herbs.

Makes 1 quart

- 1   quart white wine vinegar
- 1   tablespoon coarsely crumbled **dried sage leaves**

1. Heat the vinegar to boiling in a nonreactive saucepan over medium heat. Remove from the heat and stir in the sage leaves. Cover and let stand at room temperature for 24 hours.

2. Strain through a paper coffee filter and pour into a sterilized bottle; seal tightly for storage.

Tangy Seasoned Rice Vinegar

Makes 1 quart

- 1   quart unseasoned rice vinegar
- 1   tablespoon **dried lemongrass bulb**
- 1   tablespoon **dried snipped chives**
- 3–4 **dried gingerroot slices**
- 3–4 **dried garlic flakes**

1. Combine the vinegar, lemongrass, chives, gingerroot, and garlic in a nonreactive saucepan. Heat just to boiling, then cover and reduce the heat and simmer for 15 minutes. Remove from the heat and let stand for 3 hours.

2. Strain through a paper coffee filter and pour into a sterilized bottle; seal tightly for storage.

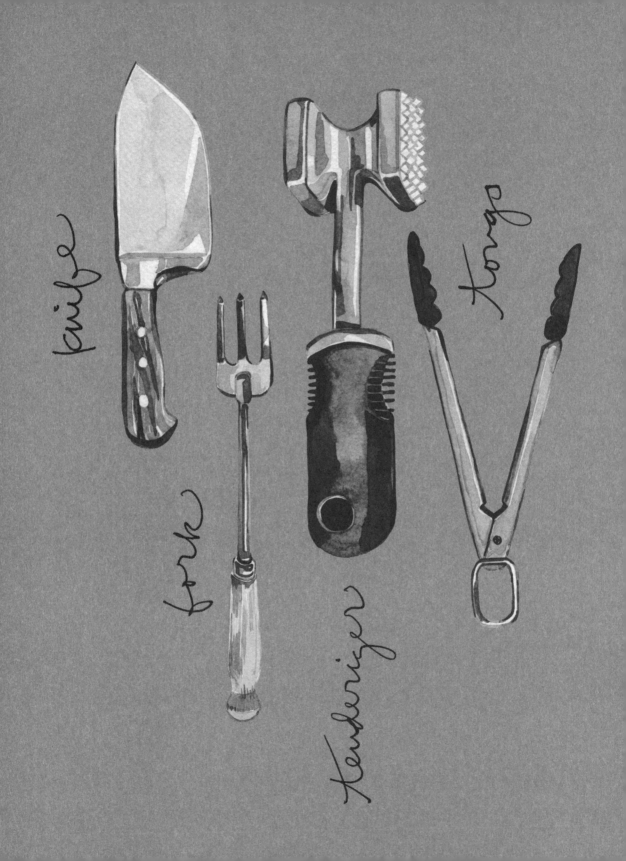

knife

fork

tenderizer

tongs

CHAPTER 7

Meat and Poultry
(Including Jerky)

THE DRIED MEATS and poultry in this chapter are primarily for use in mixes packed for camping or other similar situations in which the food will be used fairly quickly. While they can be stored at cool room temperature for a few weeks, home-dried meat and poultry will turn rancid or develop off tastes during long-term storage unless they are kept refrigerated or, preferably, frozen. For long-term storage, you're better off simply freezing raw meat and poultry. The frozen raw meats and poultry will be far more versatile and will have a better texture when cooked than your dried versions. Dried meat cubes, for example, are fairly firm when rehydrated (like boiled beef) and will never return to a juicy, tender state, although ground meat and thinner pieces such as jerky rehydrate more successfully. However, it is worth pointing out that if the power is lost for days or weeks, your home-dried meats and poultry will still be edible, while those that were frozen while raw will need to be cooked and consumed, pronto.

Red meat and poultry may be dried in a dehydrator or oven. A dehydrator with rectangular trays accommodates jerky strips more efficiently than one with round trays. As mentioned in the section on sun-drying in chapter 3, modern food science tells us that meats should no longer be dried in the sun due to risk of bacterial growth. Instructions are not given in this book for sun-drying meats; should you choose to do so, the basic techniques are the same as those used for fruits.

In the past, plain meats and fish were sun-dried or air-dried from the raw state; indeed, this practice is still common in some countries. For food safety reasons, however, meat and poultry to be dried should be fully cooked before dehydrating to kill pathogens that might remain in meats that were dried without cooking.

Jerky is thin strips of meat that have been treated with salt and, often, other seasoning, then dehydrated (or smoked) until completely dry and chewy. Traditionally, jerky is dried with no precooking, and most cooks today still follow that practice with no problems. However, contemporary studies published by the USDA have concluded that for *complete* safety, even jerky should be cooked before dehydrating. This book includes instructions for both traditional jerky prepared from raw meat and for jerky prepared with precooked meat; the choice is up to you.

Meat and poultry should be dehydrated at temperatures higher than those used for vegetables or fruits. A target temperature of 140°F is recommended for most meat and poultry; 145°F is recommended for ground meat or poultry. For safety reasons, meat and poultry should not be dehydrated at temperatures lower than 130°F.

Below you'll find specific instructions for dehydrating beef, lamb, venison, bison, chicken, and turkey, as well as full instructions, marinades, and seasoning blends to prepare jerky from red meat and poultry. (For instructions on drying soups, baked beans, and other prepared foods that

A NOTE ABOUT DAIRY PRODUCTS

Most dairy products should not be dried at home. Eggs have a risk of bacterial contamination; if you need dried eggs for camping mixes or other uses, buy commercially dried and pasteurized egg powder from the camping store. Milk is simply too "wet" to make it worth drying at home because it takes too long to be practical. Shredded cheese can be dried, but it still needs to be stored in the refrigerator or freezer and it has an odd texture; it's not worth the bother.

contain meats or poultry, see "Dehydrating Prepared Foods" starting on page 282.) Approximate drying times are given for a dehydrator or oven at 140 or 145°F, depending on the cut being dehydrated. If you dehydrate at a higher or lower temperature, your times will change accordingly; variables such as humidity and the total amount of food in your dehydrator will also affect drying time, sometimes dramatically, so use the times given as a general guideline.

Each listing also includes suggestions for using the dried meat or poultry, including a list of recipes in this book that use each type of dried product. The recipes are at the end of this chapter.

Dehydrating Meat and Poultry

RED MEAT SUCH AS beef, lamb, venison, and bison is composed of both lean and fat portions, and while the lean portion keeps fairly well when dried, the fat portion will soon turn rancid. To minimize this, only lean cuts should be dried, and all possible fat should be removed before drying. When working with venison, you must be certain that the carcass was properly dressed so there was no contamination by fecal matter; if you don't know for sure, don't dehydrate the venison.

When choosing chicken or turkey, select only perfectly fresh cuts; poultry that has been languishing in the butcher's meat case should not be used for dehydrating. Duck and goose meat is generally not dehydrated because it is too fatty, although skinless breast meat can be used for jerky following the instructions for beef.

Ground red meat and poultry has more fat than lean whole-muscle meat, but it can be dehydrated with special procedures. The dried ground meat can be kept at room temperature for a week or two, making it safe to carry on a camping trip, but it should be refrigerated or frozen for long-term storage. Most cuts of pork don't work well for dehydrating because of their high fat content, but lean portions of ham and Canadian-style bacon may be dried.

Leftover cooked roasts can also be dehydrated, as long as they have been properly handled. Roasts that are allowed to sit on the sideboard for hours before being refrigerated are not suitable for dehydrating; neither are fatty roasts or those that have been simmered with gravy or rich sauce. To prepare leftover cooked roasts, slice ¼ to ½ inch thick and cut into cubes, then proceed as directed below, bypassing the cooking step.

Red Meat and Poultry Cuts

For beef, lamb, venison, and bison, choose a lean roasting cut and trim off any exterior fat; for venison, also trim away any areas that were damaged by shot. For chicken and turkey, boneless, skinless breasts are preferable; thighs may be used but have intramuscular fat and veins that need to be removed, making them more difficult to work with. Timing on all cooking methods below will depend on the size of the cut, so times are not given.

- For **whole red-meat cuts**, trim off all external fat. Place the meat on a roasting rack and bake at 350°F until the internal temperature at the thickest part reaches 160°F. For thinner cuts, steam the meat or simmer it in a small amount of water until it reaches 160°F. Red-meat cuts may also be cooked it in a pressure cooker according to the manufacturer's instructions, using no added fat.

- For **whole or halved turkey breasts or whole turkey thighs**, remove the skin and trim off any external fat; poultry may be roasted with the bone in or boneless. Place the poultry on a roasting rack and bake at 350°F until the internal temperature at the thickest part reaches 165°F. You may also cook it in a pressure cooker according to the manufacturer's instructions, using no added fat.

- For **chicken breasts or thighs** or **smaller portions of turkey breasts or thighs**, remove the skin and bones and trim off any external fat. Steam the poultry or simmer it in a small amount of water until the internal temperature at the thickest part reads 165°F.

Preheat the dehydrator or oven to 140°F near the end of the cooking time. Allow the cooked meat or poultry to cool enough to handle, and then remove any bones. Cut the meat or poultry into ½-inch cubes, discarding any fat, gristle, or tendons you encounter. Spread the cubes evenly on the dehydrator trays, keeping a bit of space between them. Place immediately into the preheated dehydrator or oven.

When the meat or poultry is completely dry, pat with paper towels while still warm to remove any oil on the surface. Cool the cubes completely before packing. Keep in the refrigerator or freezer for long-term storage.

Recipes in this book featuring dried meat or poultry cubes:

- Homesteader's Meat and Vegetable Stew

- Stovetop Chicken and Noodle Casserole

DEHYDRATOR/CONVECTION OVEN

Use screens on trays or racks. Precooked meat or poultry cubes generally take 4 to 8 hours at 140°F.

OVEN (NON-CONVECTION)

Use screens on racks. Stir pieces several times during drying. At 140°F, precooked meat or poultry cubes may take as little as 4 hours to dry, or as long as 12 hours.

DONENESS TEST: Very hard and dry; difficult to cut with a knife. If the cubes feel springy, they aren't dry enough.

YIELD: 2 pounds of uncooked, boneless red meat or poultry yield 2½ to 3 cups of dried cubes. When rehydrated, 1 cup of dried red meat or poultry cubes yields 1½ to 1¾ cups.

TO USE: To rehydrate, combine in a saucepan with water to cover very generously. Heat to boiling and remove from the heat, then soak at room temperature for 1 hour. Simmer the soaked meat in its soaking liquid over medium-low heat until no longer hard, about 1 hour. Use in any recipe calling for cooked meat or poultry; the rehydrated meat will have a firm, boiled texture. Include the simmering liquid in the recipe if possible, as it contains much of the flavor from the meat or poultry.

Ground Red Meat and Poultry

Recipes in this book featuring dried ground meat:

- Borscht (Beet Soup)
- Shepherd's Pie

Buy the leanest ground beef, lamb, bison, or poultry you can find; if possible, have the butcher custom-grind a lean roast or skinned poultry. For venison, have the processor grind a very lean mixture. Fry in a large skillet over medium heat, stirring frequently to break up chunks, until the meat loses its raw color completely and is evenly crumbled; if the meat is sticking to the skillet, add a little water but do not add any oil or other fat. Transfer the cooked meat or poultry to a wire-mesh strainer and rinse with hot water, shaking the strainer to rinse the mixture evenly. Let drain thoroughly; meanwhile, place screens on your dehydrator racks or trays, then cover the screens with paper towels. Spread the drained meat or poultry in a thin layer on the paper towel–lined trays. The suggested temperature for drying is 145°F.

DEHYDRATOR/CONVECTION OVEN

Stir the ground meat or poultry every 2 hours. Ground meat or poultry generally takes 4 to 7 hours at 145°F.

OVEN (NON-CONVECTION)

Stir the ground meat or poultry every hour, moving crumbles from the edges of the racks to the center and vice versa. At 145°F, ground meat or poultry may take as little as 3½ hours to dry, or as long as 11 hours.

DONENESS TEST: Hard, dark, and crumbly; if the crumbles feel springy or soft when squeezed, they are not dry enough.

YIELD: 1 pound of extra-lean raw ground meat or poultry yields 1 to 1⅓ cups of dried ground crumbles. When rehydrated, 1 cup of dried ground crumbles yields about 1½ cups.

TO USE: The dried ground crumbles may be added without rehydrating to soups and stews that will cook for at least 45 minutes longer. To rehydrate for use in recipes calling for cooked ground meat or poultry, hot-soak at room temperature until no longer hard, 1 to 2 hours.

Ham and Canadian-Style Bacon

Select lean, ready-to-eat ham or Canadian-style bacon. Trim off all fat. Because they are ready-to-eat products, ham and Canadian-style bacon may be dried without further cooking. Ham, however, will be more tender when rehydrated if it is heated through before drying; bake it as you would a ham to be served hot. Slice ham and Canadian-style bacon ³⁄₁₆ inch thick or slightly thinner, then cut into ¼- to ½-inch strips that are no longer than 2 inches.

The dried meat will be oily on the surface. Pat with paper towels while still warm to remove any beads of oil on the surface, and place a fresh paper towel in the storage container with the blotted meat.

Recipes in this book featuring dried ham or Canadian-style bacon:

- Camper's Corn Chowder

- Ham and Apple Dumplings

DEHYDRATOR/CONVECTION OVEN
Use screens on trays or racks. Ham and Canadian-style bacon pieces generally take 5 to 10 hours at 145°F.

OVEN (NON-CONVECTION)
Use screens on racks. Stir and rearrange pieces several times during drying. At 145°F, ham or Canadian-style bacon pieces may take as little as 5 hours to dry, or as long as 15 hours.

DONENESS TEST: Stiff, with a deep rose color; the center should look completely dry when a piece is cut.

YIELD: 1 pound of ham or Canadian-style bacon yields about ¾ cup of dried pieces. When rehydrated, 1 cup of dried ham or Canadian-style bacon pieces yields about 1¼ cups.

TO USE: To rehydrate, combine in a skillet with water to cover generously. Cover and cook over low heat for about 1 hour, or until the meat is tender. Drain and use in any cooked dish calling for cooked ham or Canadian-style bacon. The rehydrated meat will have a firm texture.

Jerky

Recipes in this book featuring dried ground meat:

- Southwestern Jerky Stew

Jerky is an ideal trail food since it's high in protein and can be eaten plain with no additional preparation. It can also be used to make a tasty stew; see Southwestern Jerky Stew on page 264 for one version. Whole-muscle jerky is made of strips of lean meat that have been marinated in a flavorful liquid or sprinkled with a salt mixture; in some marinades, the salt comes from a condiment such as soy sauce or teriyaki sauce. Most commercial processors prepare jerky using curing compounds that include sodium nitrate and sodium nitrite, which act as preservatives. Home cooks can buy a curing salt blend that contains these chemicals, and many recipes use curing salt to prepare the jerky before dehydrating or smoking. These chemicals are controversial, however, due to studies over the last few decades that point to them as possible carcinogens. Recipes in this book do not include curing salts.

By its very nature jerky is chewy, but you can decide how much chewing you want to do. Meat that is cut with the grain before drying will be very chewy when dried because you have to bite and chew through the long muscle fibers, which have been toughened by drying. Meat that is prepared by slicing across the grain will be easier to chew when dried but it will also be more brittle. Jerky prepared from ground meats will be much more tender because the muscle fibers have been broken up by grinding. No matter which direction you cut it, whole-muscle meat is easiest to cut if it is partially frozen first, just enough so it feels "crunchy" when pierced with the tip of a thin knife. A countertop electric meat slicer makes quick work of the job, but a very sharp chef's knife will also work.

Most recipes for homemade jerky don't include any preliminary cooking; raw meat is marinated or seasoned and put directly into the dehydrator or low-temperature oven (or, more traditionally, smoked, a technique that is not covered in this book). Jerky has been made for years without precooking, and you may choose to prepare your jerky from raw meat. Recent studies, however, suggest that pathogens including *E. coli* may survive the traditional jerky-making process *even if the jerky is prepared in a dehydrator set to 160°F*, the temperature used to assure safety of red meats. According to a USDA paper* updated in November 2011, the problem is that although the dehydrator may be running at 160°F, the moisture-laden air inside the dehydrator is absorbing most of the heat; the meat itself doesn't reach that temperature for some time, and by then the bacteria have become heat-resistant and more likely to survive. This is a special concern when making jerky from ground meat, which is far more likely than whole-muscle meat to harbor *E. coli, Salmonella,* and other dangerous pathogens. For *complete* safety, jerky — especially that made from ground meat — should be precooked until the meat reaches 160°F (165°F for poultry). Instructions for precooking meat and drying it to prepare jerky are on pages 256–257.

Whether you precook the meat or not, jerky should be dehydrated at temperatures above 130°F; a range of 135 to 145°F is ideal. Because temperatures can fluctuate inside a dehydrator, a temperature of 140°F is recommended here. Use a manufactured dehydrator or an oven (convection or standard) to dehydrate jerky; the home-built dehydrator is not recommended because it may end up operating at temperatures too high for the tolerance of the fan.

---

* The USDA paper is available by searching for "Jerky and food safety" at www.fsis.usda.gov.

No matter how you make jerky, consider its shelf life short. Keep it in plastic bags or glass jars so it will not absorb moisture, and store the containers in the refrigerator or freezer for maximum safe storage. Eat the jerky within 6 months.

FOUR STEPS

Preparing Traditional Jerky from Whole Cuts

This version does not include precooking; see page 256 if you wish to precook the jerky before drying it.

Step 1.

Choose lean cuts of beef, venison, bison, turkey, or chicken. Trim off any external fat, then freeze the meat until it's firm enough to slice easily. Meanwhile, prepare a marinade following one of the recipes on pages 258–259 (or any other that you prefer); each recipe is enough for 1 pound of meat, but you can increase the quantities proportionally if you're preparing more than a pound.

Step 2.

Slice the partially frozen meat or poultry $1/8$ to $3/16$ inch thick, cutting with or across the grain as you prefer (see text on page 251). Cut the slices into strips 1 inch wide and any length you prefer. Pour a little of the marinade into a glass baking dish. Arrange a single layer of strips on top of the marinade; pour a thin layer of marinade over the meat strips. Repeat with remaining meat strips and marinade, pouring any remaining marinade over the top layer. Cover the dish and refrigerate overnight.

Step 3.

Drain the jerky after marinating, discarding the marinade; pat the jerky lightly with paper towels. Arrange the strips on trays or racks in a single layer with a little space between the strips. Place in the dehydrator; if using an oven, place an empty baking sheet on the bottom rack to catch drips.

Step 4.

Dehydrate at 140°F until the jerky is leathery but still flexible; blot the meat with paper towels while still warm if the surface is oily. Jerky will generally take 3 to 6 hours in a dehydrator or convection oven; jerky dried in a non-convection oven may be done in the same range or may take close to twice as long. One pound of raw meat will generally yield about ½ pound of jerky.

About Ground-Meat Jerky (Including Poultry)

Jerky made with ground meat is still pleasantly chewy, but it is much more tender than jerky made from whole-muscle cuts. Purchased ground beef, bison, turkey, chicken, and even ground venison typically have a fair amount of fat, however, and this means that your jerky will turn rancid more quickly than jerky made from very lean, whole-muscle cuts. When you buy ground beef, look for the leanest grind you can find; most super-lean ground beef has 5 to 8 percent fat, while standard ground beef often has 15 percent fat — sometimes even more. Ground poultry breast meat is generally leaner than ground dark poultry. For even leaner ground meat or poultry, buy lean roast or skinless poultry and have the butcher grind it for you. If you have a good meat grinder, you can do this at home; a food processor can be used but tends to produce uneven results.

As discussed above in the section on whole-muscle jerky, the USDA recommends that all meat used for jerky should be precooked to an internal temperature of 160°F for red meat (165°F for poultry). This is probably more important for ground meat, which is more likely to be contaminated with pathogens than whole-muscle meat. Precooking instructions for ground-meat jerky are on page 257. After precooking, the jerky is dehydrated at a lower temperature to avoid toughening it by too-rapid dehydrating.

Ground meat — and throughout the rest of this section, this term refers to ground beef, bison, venison, and poultry — needs to be shaped into strips that are similar in shape to pieces of whole-muscle jerky. During dehydrating, the ground meat will shrink more than whole-muscle cuts, so the ideal size for ground-meat strips is 3/16 inch thick, 1¼ inches wide, and about 4 inches in length. The biggest challenge is making strips that are even in thickness. Here are some techniques to shape ground meat into strips for jerky.

- **Jerky guns** look like cookie presses used to make spritz cookies, but they have a flat nozzle at the end so the meat comes out in a flat strip. Some jerky guns work quite well, but others tend to jam up or squirt the meat out in uneven lumps.

- **Pastry bags** that are used to pipe cream-puff pastry and frosting can be used. Fit the bag with a large round tip, fill it with the meat mixture, and pipe "ropes" of the desired length onto a baking sheet (if you plan to precook the meat) or directly onto the dehydrator tray, keeping them

pastry bag

jerky gun

about an inch apart; draw a wet spatula across each rope to flatten individually. Another option is to pipe numerous ropes at 1-inch intervals onto a sheet of kitchen parchment, then lay another sheet of parchment on top and use a rolling pin to flatten them all at once; use a spatula to carefully transfer the strips to the dehydrator trays. (Once you've used a pastry bag for ground meat, it should be reserved only for that; don't use it to pipe frosting or dough.)

- **Hand-rolling** also works if you don't have a pastry bag. Simply roll about 2 tablespoons of the seasoned meat mixture between your palms to form a rope, then proceed as directed above for ropes made with a pastry bag.

Preparing Traditional Jerky from Ground Meat

This version does not include precooking; see page 257 if you wish to precook the jerky before drying it.

Step 1.

Combine lean ground meat with one of the ground-meat jerky seasoning blends on pages 259–260, mixing very well. For best results, cover the meat and refrigerate it overnight to allow the flavors to blend; you may also proceed directly to shaping the strips.

Step 2.

Line dehydrator trays or racks with screens. Shape the ground meat into strips, using one of the techniques described on pages 253–254.

Step 3.

Arrange the strips on the screens in a single layer with a little space between the strips. Place in the dehydrator or oven; if using an oven, place an empty baking sheet on the bottom oven rack to catch drips.

Step 4.

Dehydrate at 145°F for 2 hours, then blot with paper towels, turn the strips over, and blot the second side. Continue dehydrating until the jerky is leathery but still flexible; blot the meat with paper towels while still warm if the surface is oily. Jerky will generally take 4 to 7 hours in a dehydrator or convection oven; jerky dried in a non-convection oven may be done in the same range or may take close to twice as long. One pound of raw ground meat will generally yield about ⅓ pound of jerky.

Preparing Precooked Jerky

Follow these instructions if you want to precook the meat strips before dehydrating. Jerky prepared with whole cuts is less chewy and somewhat thicker when the meat is precooked than when it is dehydrated from the raw state. Whether made from whole cuts or ground meat, jerky that is precooked dehydrates more quickly than jerky prepared from raw meat.

FOUR STEPS

Preparing Precooked Jerky from Whole Cuts

Step 1.

Prepare a marinade and slice the meat as directed in steps 1 and 2 in Preparing Traditional Jerky from Whole Cuts, on page 252. Combine the sliced meat and the marinade in a glass bowl, separating the slices and ensuring that all sides are exposed to the marinade. Set aside to marinate at room temperature for 45 minutes to 1 hour, stirring occasionally.

Step 2.

Lay the marinated slices flat in a large skillet, preferably nonstick. Ideally, the skillet should be large enough to hold all the slices in a single layer, but some overlapping is acceptable because the meat shrinks quickly during cooking. Pour the marinade into the skillet. Place the skillet over medium heat. When the mixture is simmering, adjust the heat to maintain the simmer and begin turning over individual meat strips, also moving them around in the skillet from the center to the edges of the pan. Turn the strips continuously, ensuring that each strip is turned and

repositioned several times. Simmer until the meat is cooked through, 3 to 5 minutes; don't cook any longer than necessary. Remove the skillet from the heat.

Step 3.

Use tongs to transfer the meat to trays or racks; set them over a baking sheet or a large piece of foil to catch drips. Place in the dehydrator; if using an oven, place an empty baking sheet on the bottom rack to catch drips.

Step 4.

Dehydrate at 140°F until the jerky is leathery but still flexible; blot the meat with paper towels while still warm if the surface is oily. Jerky made from whole cuts that has been precooked will generally take 2 to 3 hours in a dehydrator or convection oven; jerky dried in a non-convection oven may be done in the same range or may take close to twice as long. One pound of raw meat will generally yield about ½ pound of jerky.

Preparing Precooked Jerky from Ground Meat

Step 1.

Season the ground meat as directed in step 1 in Preparing Traditional Jerky from Ground Meat, on page 255. Cover the meat and refrigerate it overnight to allow the flavors to blend.

Step 2.

When you are ready to shape the jerky the next day, position an oven rack so it is 5 to 6 inches below the broiler. Preheat the broiler. Make a few tiny meatballs, about $3/8$ inch thick, from the ground meat; these will be used to confirm doneness. Shape the rest of the ground meat into strips, using one of the techniques described on pages 253–254. Transfer the strips to a rimmed baking sheet in a single layer. Put one or two of the tiny meatballs on the baking sheet near the jerky, close to the edge of the sheet rather than in the center.

Step 3.

Place one baking sheet of strips in the oven, 5 to 6 inches below the broiler. Cook until the top side has lost its raw color but is not browned, generally 2 to 3 minutes. Remove the sheet from the oven and carefully turn the strips; it's easiest if you slip a fork underneath a strip, then use a second fork to flip the strip over. Return the sheet to the oven and cook until the meat is cooked completely through, 2 to 3 minutes longer. Test the temperature of one of the tiny meatballs, or cut it in half to check for doneness. The center of the tiny meatballs should read 160°F for red meat, 165°F for poultry; the balls are thicker than the jerky strips, and also away from the hottest area of the broiler, so if the balls are cooked through you know that the jerky strips are too. Remove the baking sheet from the oven and blot the top sides of the strips with paper towels.

Step 4.

Line dehydrator trays or racks with screens. Arrange the precooked strips on the screens in a single layer with a little space between the strips; flip each strip over as you arrange them so the blotted side is down. Now blot the top sides of the strips with paper towels. Place trays in the dehydrator; if using an oven, place an empty baking sheet on the bottom oven rack to catch drips.

Step 5.

Dehydrate at 145°F until the jerky is leathery but still flexible; blot the meat with paper towels while still warm if the surface is oily. Jerky made from ground meat that has been precooked will generally take 3 to 5 hours in a dehydrator or convection oven; jerky dried in a non-convection oven may be done in the same range or may take close to twice as long. One pound of raw ground meat will generally yield $1/3$ to $1/2$ pound of jerky, depending on the leanness of the ground meat.

Recipes for Jerky Marinades and Seasoning Blends

ON THE FOLLOWING PAGES are some mixtures that are used to flavor red meat or poultry before it's dried to make jerky; salt (or salty ingredients) in the mixtures also helps preserve the meat after it's dried. Each recipe makes enough for 1 pound of meat or poultry; increase measurements proportionally as needed if you're making a larger batch. To use any of the recipes, simply stir together the ingredients and proceed as directed in the step-by-step instructions referenced below.

The four marinades on these two pages are for use with cut slices of red meat or poultry. If you're drying the slices without precooking, follow the marinating instructions in step 2 of Preparing Traditional Jerky from Whole Cuts on page 252. If you're precooking the slices before drying them, follow the marinating instructions in step 1 of Preparing Precooked Jerky from Whole Cuts on page 256.

The three seasoning blends on page 260 are for use with ground meat or poultry. The seasoning blend is combined with the raw ground meat or poultry, which is then shaped into flat strips. If you're drying the strips without precooking, follow the seasoning instructions in step 1 of Preparing Traditional Jerky from Ground Meat on page 255. If you're precooking the strips before drying them, follow the seasoning instructions in step 1 of Preparing Precooked Jerky from Ground Meat on page 257.

Sportsman's Marinade for Red Meat

- ⅓ cup Worcestershire sauce
- ⅓ cup soy sauce
- 2 tablespoons honey or maple syrup
- 2 tablespoons ketchup
- 1 teaspoon liquid smoke, optional
- ½–1 teaspoon coarsely ground black pepper
- 1 garlic clove, finely minced

Barbecue Marinade for Red Meat or Poultry

1 cup barbecue sauce

1 tablespoon liquid smoke, optional

1 tablespoon Worcestershire sauce

1 teaspoon **Chili Powder Blend** (see page 210) or purchased chili powder blend

Dash cayenne pepper

Red-Hot Marinade for Red Meat

¾ cup beer

¼ cup teriyaki sauce

1 tablespoon pickle juice

2 teaspoons cracked black peppercorns

2 teaspoons **dried onion flakes**

1 teaspoon liquid hot red pepper sauce

½ teaspoon Cajun seasoning blend

Pineapple Marinade for Poultry

¾ cup pineapple juice

½ cup white wine

¼ cup honey

¼ cup minced raw onion

2 tablespoons kosher salt

2 teaspoons freshly ground black pepper

2 garlic cloves, finely minced

Simple Ground-Meat Jerky Seasoning

1 tablespoon Worcestershire sauce

1 teaspoon seasoned salt

¼ teaspoon **dried onion flakes**

Garlicky Ground-Meat Jerky Seasoning

2 tablespoons crumbled **dried parsley leaves**

1 tablespoon finely minced fresh garlic

1½ teaspoons salt

½ teaspoon crumbled **dried marjoram leaves**

½ teaspoon freshly ground black pepper

Chili-Spiced Ground-Meat Jerky Seasoning

1 tablespoon lime juice

2 teaspoons **Chili Powder Blend** (see page 210) or purchased chili powder blend

½ teaspoon **dried onion flakes**

¼ teaspoon **ground cumin seeds**

Recipes Using Dried Meat and Poultry

AS IN PREVIOUS CHAPTERS, dried ingredients from this book are highlighted in **bold type**.

Homesteader's Meat and Vegetable Stew

Makes 6 servings

- 3¼ cups water
- 1½ cups **dried beef or venison cubes**
- ½ cup **dried carrot slices**
- ½ cup **dried green peas**
- ½ cup **dried green beans**
- ½ cup **drled parsnip slices**
- ¼ cup **dried celery slices**
- 1 tablespoon **dried chopped onion**
- ¼ cup all-purpose flour

  Salt and freshly ground black pepper

1. Heat 1½ cups of water to boiling in a Dutch oven over high heat. Stir in the beef cubes, then reduce the heat to medium-low and simmer for 1 hour, or until the meat is no longer hard.

2. While the meat is simmering, place the carrots, peas, green beans, parsnip, celery, and onion in a heatproof bowl. Add 1½ cups boiling water and set aside to soak.

3. When the meat is no longer hard, add the carrot mixture and any remaining soaking liquid to the beef. Simmer for 30 minutes longer. Blend the flour and ¼ cup cold water in a cup. Gradually stir the flour mixture into the stew mixture and cook, stirring constantly, until the gravy is thickened. Season with salt and pepper to taste.

Stovetop Chicken and Noodle Casserole

Makes 6 servings

1	quart chicken broth
2	cups **dried chicken cubes**
3	tablespoons **dried celery slices**
¼	cup **dried mushroom slices**, optional
1	tablespoon **dried onion flakes**
2	cups curly egg noodles
	Salt and freshly ground black pepper
1½	tablespoons crumbled **dried parsley leaves**

1. Heat the chicken broth to boiling in a Dutch oven over high heat. Stir in the chicken cubes and celery, then reduce the heat to medium-low and simmer for 1 hour, or until the chicken is no longer hard.

2. Add the mushrooms and onion, and simmer for 15 minutes longer. Add the noodles and increase heat so the mixture is boiling gently. Cook for 10 to 15 minutes, until the noodles are tender. Add salt and pepper to taste. Sprinkle with parsley.

Shepherd's Pie

Makes 4 or 5 servings

2½	cups water	
1¼	cups **dried ground lamb or beef**	
⅓	cup **dried diced carrots or carrot slices**	
¼	cup **dried green peas**	
3	tablespoons **dried chopped onion**	
2½	tablespoons **dried celery slices**	
1	**dried bay leaf**	
½	teaspoon crumbled **dried basil leaves**	
½	teaspoon salt	
¼	teaspoon ground white pepper or black pepper	
¼	teaspoon crumbled **dried marjoram leaves**	
2	tablespoons butter	
1½	tablespoons all-purpose flour	
¾	cup whole milk	
2–2½	cups prepared mashed potatoes	

1. Heat the water to boiling in a large saucepan over high heat. Remove from the heat; stir in the lamb, carrots, peas, onion, celery, and bay leaf. Cover and set aside to soak for 30 minutes, stirring once or twice.

2. After the soaking time, preheat the oven to 350°F. Lightly grease a 1½-quart casserole; set aside. Heat the lamb mixture in the saucepan over medium-low heat until simmering, then cook, covered, for 10 minutes. Remove from the heat. Remove and discard the bay leaf. Stir the basil, salt, pepper, and marjoram into the lamb mixture.

3. Melt the butter in a small saucepan over medium-low heat. Sprinkle in the flour, stirring constantly with a whisk or fork, and cook for about 3 minutes. Add the milk in a thin stream, whisking constantly, and cook until thickened and bubbly, about 2 minutes. Stir the thickened milk mixture into the lamb mixture and transfer the filling to the prepared casserole.

4. Spread the mashed potatoes evenly over the top. Bake until the filling is bubbly and the top is lightly browned, 40 to 45 minutes.

Ham and Apple Dumplings

Makes 4 servings

- 2 quarts water
- ½ cup **dried ham pieces**
- 1 cup **dried apple slices**
- 2 tablespoons brown sugar, packed
- 1 cup all-purpose flour
- 1 teaspoon baking powder
- ¼ teaspoon salt
- 2 tablespoons butter, melted
- 1 egg
- ½ cup milk, approximate

1. Combine the water and ham in a Dutch oven. Heat to boiling over high heat, then reduce the heat and simmer for 1 hour, or until the ham is no longer hard. Add the apples and simmer for 30 minutes longer. Stir in the brown sugar and let the mixture simmer while you prepare the dumplings.

2. To prepare the dumplings, sift together the flour, baking powder, and salt into a mixing bowl. Stir in the butter, egg, and enough milk to make a stiff batter. Drop batter in golf-ball-size clumps into the simmering liquid in the Dutch oven. Simmer for 10 minutes, then cover and cook for 10 minutes longer.

Southwestern Jerky Stew

Makes 4 servings

The seasoning used to make the jerky will flavor the stew. This stew is based on posole, a traditional stew or soup from Mexico that is now common in the Southwest.

- 3½ cups water
- 3 ounces **whole-muscle jerky**, cut into ¾- to 1-inch chunks (about 1 cup chunks)
- ⅔ cup **dried Poblano or other mild chile pepper chunks**

²⁄₃ cup cut-up **dried plum tomato halves**, cut into 1-inch chunks before measuring

½ cup **dried onion slices**, firmly packed

⅓ cup **dried diced bell peppers**

½ teaspoon **dried garlic flakes**, or 2 fresh garlic cloves, sliced

1 cup chicken broth, or 1 teaspoon **Mock Chicken Broth Powder** (see page 221) mixed with 1 cup boiling water

½ teaspoon **Chili Powder Blend** (see page 210) or purchased chili powder blend

1 (15.5 ounce) can white or yellow hominy, drained and rinsed*

1 teaspoon crumbled **dried oregano leaves**

Garnishes for serving (any or all, as you wish): Crumbled **dried radish slices** or fresh sliced radishes, diced avocado, chopped fresh cilantro, lime wedges, chopped fresh white onion, hot pepper sauce

1. Combine the water and jerky in a nonreactive soup pot or large saucepan. Heat to boiling over high heat. Remove from the heat and let soak for 1 hour.

2. After the soaking time, add the chile peppers, plum tomatoes, onion slices, bell peppers, and garlic to the soup pot. Heat to boiling over medium-high heat, then lower the heat so that the mixture bubbles gently; cook, stirring occasionally, for 20 minutes. Stir in the chicken broth and chili powder; cook for 25 minutes longer or until the jerky and vegetables are tender.

3. Stir in the drained hominy and oregano. Reduce the heat and simmer for 10 minutes longer. Serve the hominy in soup plates, with garnishes as desired.

* Hominy is made by soaking fresh corn in lye or a lime solution, which removes the skins and swells the kernels, making them chewy. If you can find dried hominy, soak it overnight and cook until tender, then use 1½ cups of that in the stew.

plum roll-up

apricot roll-up

grape roll-up

CHAPTER 8

Leathers, Baby Food, and Prepared Foods

LEATHERS have almost as many names as they have uses. In pioneer days, settlers made thin, dried sheets of cooked fruits and vegetables to preserve fresh foods that would otherwise have gone to waste. They called them "papers" because of their paperlike thinness or "leathers" because of their pliable, leathery texture. Today fruit leathers are sometimes called fruit taffy because of their delicious candylike taste. Leathers usually are rolled in plastic wrap, giving them their other common name, roll-ups.

Baby foods are also easy to make in your dehydrator using fresh fruits and vegetables; the principles are the same as making fruit and vegetable leathers. See page 281 for more information. Prepared foods such as sauerkraut, excess tomato paste, and thick soups may also be dehydrated in the same way as leathers; see page 282 for some ideas.

Fruit and Vegetable Leathers

THE BASIC CONCEPT OF LEATHERS is simple. Fruits and vegetables are puréed, spread on a solid sheet, and dehydrated until most of the moisture has been removed and the purée turns into a flexible, leathery sheet. Cooked or raw produce can be used. Leathers made from cooked foods will appear bright and shiny. Those made from uncooked foods appear dull but have a fresher flavor.

Fruit leathers also may be softened in water and used as a pie filling, as a dessert topping for ice cream or pudding, or as a flavoring for yogurt. Children love fruit leathers, which are a wonderful, more healthful alternative to candy. Winter squash and other vegetables also work well for leathers; squash leathers may be reconstituted and used as cooked squash or in recipes that call for pumpkin purée. Finally, some fruit and vegetable combinations make leathers that are delicious out of hand snacks.

Leathers can be prepared in a manufactured or home-built dehydrator, in a convection oven, or in a non-convection oven that can be set low enough for dehydrating; a target temperature of 135°F is recommended. If you're thinking of purchasing a manufactured dehydrator and you plan to prepare a lot of leathers, there are some things to consider. Ventilation is essential for preparing leathers, so don't bother with cheap manufactured dehydrators that lack a fan. Box-style dehydrators are more efficient for making leathers than stackable-tray models. In a stackable-tray model the air blows vertically through a central hole. Although well-designed stackable models provide ventilation around the sides of the trays as well as through the middle, a good bit of the vertical airflow is interrupted by the solid sheets. In contrast, the air in a box-style dehydrator blows sideways across the trays, providing even ventilation to all trays. Leathers that are prepared in a stackable-tray model will have a hole in the middle, while those prepared in box-style dehydrators, in a home-built dehydrator, or in an oven will be solid in the middle. If using a non-convection oven, be sure to use a fan as described on page 53 to provide ventilation.

If you live in an area where sun-drying is an option, you can easily sun-dry fruit leathers. Set up baking sheets as described in Solid Sheets to Hold Purées on page 272, then sun-dry according to the instructions on pages 41–46. Make sure your leathers are well protected from insects during sun-drying; the protective netting or cheesecloth needs to wrap entirely around the bottoms of the baking sheets to prevent insects from crawling into openings.

Making Purées for Leather

Fruit and vegetable purées may be prepared with different types of kitchen equipment, using either raw or cooked foods. Here is a list of equipment, along with pros and cons of each.

- A **blender** works great; you may need to add a little liquid to loosen the mixture, particularly if blending raw fruits or vegetables. The purée may not be completely smooth and even. Seeds and skins need to be removed before blending.

- A **food mill** produces smooth purée and also holds back skins and seeds, a real benefit when working with seedy fruits such as raspberries and blackberries. Food mills are bulky to store and a nuisance to clean.

food mill

- A **wire-mesh strainer** can be used for soft-cooked fruits and vegetables; this method also works for very soft, overripe raw fruits. Place the strainer over a bowl, add the cut-up fruits or vegetables, and stir vigorously with a wooden spoon or rubber spatula to force the flesh through. Be sure to scrape the outside (bottom) of the strainer to collect the purée that may be adhered there. Skins and seeds will remain in the strainer and can be discarded easily. The purée will be very smooth.

hand-cranked strainer

- A **hand-cranked strainer** is a great choice if you plan to make a lot of leathers or if you have other uses for puréed fruits and vegetables. These countertop appliances have a large hopper to hold the food, with a crank-operated auger-style grinder below. When the handle is cranked, the prepared food is crushed and forced through a fine filter. Victorio and Squeezo are two common brands.

- A **food processor** has the power to prepare smooth purées, but for small batches they are less efficient than a blender because the food tends to spatter around the sides, away from the blade. As with a blender, seeds and skins need to be removed before processing.

- A **potato masher** can be used for soft-cooked fruits and vegetables, but the leather will have a lumpy texture and may not dry evenly. This is the least satisfactory method of making a purée.

Most fruits can be puréed and dehydrated to make leather. Some can be puréed raw; others are best when cooked. Choose fruits that are fully ripe or even slightly overripe (but not spoiled). Frozen fruits work great and require no cooking; simply thaw and purée. Fruits that are high in water content and low in pectin, including blackberries, blueberries, and raspberries, make thin or weak purées that become brittle rather than leathery when dried. These are best when combined with apples, bananas, peaches, or other fruits with more body.

The blender is the best tool for raw fruits such as apples that are somewhat firm when ripe; it also works for very soft raw fruits. Prepare the raw fruit carefully, removing stems, seeds, pits, and any tough or inedible portions. Apples and pears should be peeled and cored. Even fruits with soft skins such as apricots and peaches should be skinned (pages 73 and 98) because the leather will be grainy if the skins are included in the purée. Cut away any damaged or bruised areas, then cut the fruit into smaller pieces if necessary. Process in the blender until smooth, adding a little water or fruit juice if necessary to loosen the mixture. You may also blend in flavorings such as vanilla extract or cinnamon, or liquid sugar such as honey or maple syrup. The purée is now ready for dehydrating.

Raw fruits that are very soft, including bananas, ripe apricots and peaches, plums, ripe mangoes, and berries, can be processed in a food mill. Wash the fruit, remove any large pits or stones, and cut away any damaged or bruised areas; bananas and mangoes should be peeled, but skinning isn't necessary for apricots, peaches, and plums. Cut the fruit into smaller pieces if necessary, then process in the food mill; discard the seeds and skins that are left behind in the food mill. Stir any flavorings such as vanilla extract or ground cinnamon, and any liquid sugar such as honey or maple syrup, into the purée, then spread it on the trays.

Some fruits are better when cooked before puréeing. Rhubarb, for example, has a high water content and is somewhat fibrous when raw; cooking makes it more suitable for leather. Cooking also dissolves any granulated or brown sugar that needs to be added to tart fruits. Below you'll find a few recipes to get you started, but feel free to try your own fruit combinations.

Fruits may also be combined with cooked sweet potatoes, winter squash, or carrots to make leathers for snacking. These root vegetables provide structure and bulk to the low-pectin or watery fruits mentioned above. Sweet potatoes, winter squash, and carrots are also naturally sweet, and the combination leathers will taste like fruit, not vegetables. The recipe for Mixed Berry and Sweet Potato Leather on page 279 gives you an idea of the possibilities.

Tomato leather is a convenient product to keep in the pantry, particularly when it's dried in small circles as described in Tips for Making Leathers on page 274. It can be rehydrated and used in recipes calling for tomato paste; with a little more water, it becomes a stand-in for tomato sauce. Tomatoes are very watery and should be cooked down before puréeing. A food mill is better for tomatoes than the blender because the food mill strains out the seeds and skins. Follow the instructions in the Tomato Leather recipe on page 279.

Pie pumpkins and other winter squash may be cooked until soft, scooped out of the shell (if not peeled before cooking), then puréed and dried as a leather; when rehydrated, pumpkin leather can be used in recipes for pie and other baked goods that call for pumpkin purée, and rehydrated squash can be used as a cooked vegetable. The pumpkin or squash leather may be stored in a roll, then broken up and mixed with enough boiling water to reconstitute. As an option, you may dehydrate the pumpkin or squash leather until very crisp and dry, then process it in a blender; the resulting powder reconstitutes easily when mixed with a little boiling water. Rehydrated pumpkin or squash purées have a much smoother texture than mashed pumpkin or mashed squash that has been dried; see pages 190–191 for information if you prefer cooked pumpkin or squash with a little more texture.

Solid Sheets to Hold Purées

No matter what type of equipment you use, you need solid sheets of some sort to hold the purée. Manufactured dehydrators have special solid liner sheets made specifically for each model; some dehydrators come with a few solid liner sheets, while with other models, you must purchase them. Some sheets work fine as is and will release the finished leather with no problems, but others should be coated lightly with cooking spray to make removal of the leather easier; try a small batch of leather to see how yours perform.

If you're using a home-built dehydrator or your oven, or drying in the sun, nonstick baking sheets with a smooth, undamaged surface work well; for best results, mist them lightly with cooking spray. Another option is to line baking sheets with kitchen parchment; the leather will not have a totally flat surface because the parchment wrinkles during drying. Heavyweight plastic wrap can be used instead to line baking sheets. The gentle heat won't melt the wrap, although some may choose to avoid plastic wrap due to concerns about chemicals they release. When using plastic wrap, tape the edges to the baking sheet with freezer tape; this holds the wrap in place during filling and dehydrating. Another option is to buy flexible cutting mats, which are thin sheets of polypropylene sold at discount stores and cookware shops; ensure that the mats are dishwasher safe, which means they will stand up to the gentle heat of dehydrating. Use metal binder clips from the office-supply store to clip the flexible mat to a cake-cooling rack, or use them to line baking sheets.

Drying temperatures for leathers and purées should be about the same as those used for fruits; a target temperature of 135°F is recommended. Below are step-by-step instructions for making leathers from fruits, vegetables, or combinations, as well as eleven recipes for various leathers.

Making Fruit and Vegetable Leathers

Step 1.

Prepare the purée as directed in Making Purées for Leather on page 269, using one of the recipes on pages 275–279 or your own combination.

Step 2.

Prepare trays or racks as described in Solid Sheets to Hold Purées on page 272. Pour the purée onto a sheet, spreading it out into a circle or rectangle that is about ¼ inch thick; most dehydrator trays and full-size baking sheets will hold 1½ to 2 cups purée. (See tip on page 274 for a suggestion to make smaller, fun-size leathers.) Use the back of a large spoon to spread out the purée so the center is about ⅛ inch thick; the edges should be ¼ inch thick because the edges dry more quickly than the center.

Step 3a.

For dehydrators and oven-drying: Dry at 135°F until the leather can be peeled off the sheet without sticking. Turn the leather over and continue drying; for speedier results, place the turned leather onto another tray or rack lined with a screen rather than a solid sheet. When properly dried, leather should be flexible and dry to the touch, with no sticky spots; it should remain flexible. Total drying time generally ranges from 6 to 15 hours, depending on the moisture content of the purée and the efficiency of your dehydrator or oven.

Step 3b.

For sun-drying: Place the baking sheets with the purée in a well-ventilated spot in full sun, raising them off the ground as directed on page 44. Drape fine-mesh nylon netting or cheesecloth over the baking sheet, propping it up in the corners with cans or inverted glasses so the fabric doesn't touch the purée. Tuck the fabric underneath the trays to create a barrier all around the baking sheet; if there is even the slightest gap, insects will crawl through and contaminate your leather. Dry until the leather can be peeled off the sheet without sticking, generally 6 to 8 hours. Turn the leather over and continue sun-drying until the leather is dry to the touch, with no sticky spots; it should remain flexible. Leathers generally take 1 to 2 days; bring the baking sheets inside at night.

Step 4.

Transfer the leather while still slightly warm to a sheet of plastic wrap large enough to hold the entire leather. Roll up the leather and wrap together, twisting the ends. Label them clearly; many leathers look similar and it's hard to tell what you've got. Store wrapped leathers in tall glass jars or other canisters. Leathers can be kept at room temperature for many months but may also be stored in the refrigerator to maintain a fresher flavor; bring to room temperature before eating.

TIPS FOR MAKING LEATHERS

- For additional flavor and texture, sprinkle the fruit purée with chopped nuts, finely chopped dried fruits, sunflower seeds, granola, or shredded coconut before dehydrating. Leathers with nut or coconut toppings should be refrigerated for long-term storage.

- Make fun-size leather drops by pouring the purée onto the sheets in small portions. A tablespoon or two produces bite-size droplets; one-quarter cup of purée will produce a circle about 3 inches across.

- Dry small amounts of salsa, barbecue sauce, and other sauces, and then carry the dried "sauce leathers" with you on camping trips. This saves weight and space and also allows you to carry sauces that would otherwise need refrigeration.

- Use two different purées of contrasting colors in a single leather. Spoon them in concentric circles or spread them next to each other in lines, and then draw a knife across them to make swirls. You could also spoon small amounts of one color on top of the other to make big polka dots.

- When making tomato leather to use later as paste or sauce, add herbs and some diced onion to the tomato mixture when cooking.

- For a quick and easy leather purée, mix 1½ cups of smooth applesauce with a jar of strained baby apricots or other baby fruit.

NONREACTIVE COOKWARE

Many recipes in this book call for nonreactive saucepans or mixing bowls. These recipes have high-acid foods such as fruits or tomatoes. The acid reacts with aluminum, imparting an off flavor to the food (and the aluminum cookware may turn black if the acid is high enough). Stainless steel saucepans are the best choice; for mixing bowls, use Pyrex, glass, or ceramic bowls.

Recipes for Fruit and Vegetable Leathers

EACH RECIPE makes 1½ to 2 cups of purée. Spread the purée on a solid liner sheet and dry as directed in Making Fruit and Vegetable Leathers on page 273.

Raw Apple Leather

2 cups peeled, cored, and chopped apples

½ cup apple cider

¼ teaspoon ground cinnamon

Combine the apples, cider, and cinnamon in a blender. Process until smooth.

Cooked Apple Leather

4 medium apples, peeled, cored, and cut into 1-inch chunks

½ cup water

¼ cup honey or maple syrup

1. Combine the apples and water in a medium nonreactive saucepan. Cook over medium heat until tender, stirring occasionally.

2. Process through a food mill or wire-mesh strainer. Stir in the honey.

Maple-Kissed Apple Leather

3   large Granny Smith or other tart apples

5   tablespoons pure maple syrup

1   tablespoon apple juice or orange juice

½   teaspoon vanilla extract

1. Peel and core the apples, and then cut into ½-inch chunks.

2. Combine the cut-up apples with the maple syrup, apple juice, and vanilla in a nonreactive saucepan. Cover and cook over medium-low heat, stirring frequently, until the apples are very soft, about 10 minutes.

3. Process in a food processor until smooth, or through a food mill or wire-mesh strainer.

Cooked Apricot or Peach Leather

2   cups sliced apricots or peaches

½   cup sugar

½   cup water

¼   teaspoon ground cinnamon or nutmeg

1. Combine the apricots, sugar, water, and cinnamon in a medium nonreactive saucepan. Cover and cook over low heat until the fruit is very soft, about 10 minutes.

2. Remove from the heat and uncover; set aside to cool for 15 minutes.

3. Process in a blender until smooth, or through a food mill or wire-mesh strainer.

Banana Leather

4   medium bananas, heavily flecked with brown

½   cup finely chopped pecans or walnuts, optional

1. Peel the bananas and break into pieces. Process through a food mill or wire-mesh strainer. Spread the purée on a solid sheet and sprinkle the chopped nuts over the top.

2. Refrigerate the finished leather for long-term storage.

Pumpkin Leather

1½   cups canned pumpkin or cooked puréed fresh pumpkin

⅓   cup honey

¼   teaspoon ground cinnamon

⅛   teaspoon ground nutmeg

⅛   teaspoon ground cloves

Stir the pumpkin, honey, cinnamon, nutmeg, and cloves together in a mixing bowl.

Raspberry-Banana Leather

2   cups fresh raspberries

¼   cup sugar

1   teaspoon lemon juice

1   large banana, fully ripe or heavily flecked with brown

1. Combine the raspberries, sugar, and lemon juice in a medium nonreactive saucepan. Mash with a potato masher to start the juices flowing. Cook over medium heat, stirring frequently, until very soft, about 5 minutes.

2. Process through a wire-mesh strainer to remove the seeds. Add the raspberry purée and the banana to a blender; process until smooth.

Strawberry-Rhubarb Leather

1½ cups sliced strawberries

1¼ cups cut-up red rhubarb stalks

¾ cup sugar

½ teaspoon vanilla extract

1. Combine the strawberries, rhubarb, sugar, and vanilla in a medium nonreactive saucepan. Heat to simmering over medium-low heat, stirring to dissolve sugar. Cook, uncovered, for 10 minutes; the rhubarb and strawberries should be very soft.

2. Remove from the heat and set aside for 15 minutes to cool somewhat, then process in a blender until smooth.

Tropical Leather

1½ cups cut-up peaches, skinned before cutting up

2 tablespoons sugar

1 tablespoon lemon juice

1 tablespoon water

1 cup cut-up mango pieces, skinned before cutting up

½ medium banana

1. Combine the peaches, sugar, lemon juice, and water in a microwave-safe mixing bowl. Microwave on high until the mixture is bubbling around the edges, about 2 minutes. Stir well; microwave for 1 minute longer. Remove from the microwave and set aside for 15 minutes to cool somewhat.

2. Add the peach mixture, mango, and banana to a blender; process until smooth.

Mixed Berry and Sweet Potato Leather

1 medium orange-fleshed sweet potato such as a garnet yam

2 cups frozen mixed berries (measured while still frozen)

⅓ cup sugar

¼ cup orange juice

1. Use a fork to poke holes at 1-inch intervals all over the sweet potato; this prevents it from exploding in the microwave. Wrap the sweet potato in a damp paper towel. Microwave on high until just tender when pressed, 3 to 5 minutes. (As an option, you can bake the sweet potato in a 400°F oven until tender, 40 to 60 minutes. Set aside to cool while you prepare the berries.)

2. Combine the berries (thawed or still frozen), sugar, and orange juice in a medium nonreactive saucepan. Heat to a very gentle boil over medium heat. Boil gently for 10 minutes or until the berries are very soft, stirring occasionally. Remove from the heat and set aside to cool for 15 minutes.

3. While the berries are cooling, peel the sweet potato and cut into 1-inch cubes. Measure 1 cup of the cubes; refrigerate any remaining sweet potato for other uses.

4. Combine the 1 cup of sweet potato cubes with the cooled berry mixture in a blender. Process until smooth.

Tomato Leather

Any quantity tomatoes

1. Core ripe tomatoes and cut into quarters. Cook over low heat in a covered nonreactive saucepan for 15 to 20 minutes.

2. Process through a food mill, hand-cranked strainer, or wire-mesh strainer to remove seeds. Pour the purée into a skillet or wide, shallow pan. Add salt to taste; if using low-acid tomatoes, also add 2 teaspoons lemon juice or white vinegar to each quart of purée.

3. Cook over low heat until thickened, stirring frequently.

Homemade Baby Food

NUTRITIOUS, ADDITIVE-FREE BABY FOOD is a pleasure to make at home in your dehydrator or oven. The process is basically the same as making leathers, except the finished leather should be more brittle so it can easily be powdered. A thin purée, higher heat, and sufficient drying time produce a leather that is brittle enough to powder easily. Sugars, spices, and other flavorings usually are not added to baby food.

Toddlers who are ready for a bit more texture can also be accommodated with dehydrated foods. To prepare food for a toddler, add crisply dehydrated vegetables or fruits to a blender and pulse briefly to make flakes; the finer the flake, the smoother the baby food. Combine ¼ cup flakes with ½ cup boiling water, stir, and let cool to serving temperature; add a little more water if needed. This makes about ¾ cup of slightly chunky toddler food.

Preparing Puréed Baby Food

Step 1.

Cook fruits or vegetables until very soft by steaming, boiling, or microwaving. Process through a food mill, wire-mesh strainer, or hand-cranked strainer, or purée in a blender until very smooth. The purée may be slightly looser and more watery than those used for regular leathers.

Step 2.

Prepare trays or racks as described in Solid Sheets to Hold Purées, on page 272. Pour the purée onto a sheet, spreading it out into a circle or rectangle that is about ⅛ inch thick overall; most dehydrator trays and full-size baking sheets will hold 1½ cups of the thinner baby-food purée.

Step 3.

Dry at 135 to 150°F until the leather can be peeled off the sheet without sticking; don't worry if it cracks in spots. As the leather begins to dry, break or tear it up into smaller pieces, turning and rearranging them periodically. Your goal is to have flat crumbles or thin pieces that are totally dry and very brittle. Total drying time generally ranges from 12 to 20 hours, depending on the moisture content of the purée and the efficiency of your dehydrator or oven.

Step 4.

Cool the dried crumbles and pieces. Store in a glass jar; alternately, you may powder the crumbles and pieces right away and store small jars of powder.

Step 5.

To rehydrate the baby food, grind to a fine powder in a blender or electric coffee grinder/spice mill. Mix a small amount of powder with a small amount of warm water, stirring until moist, smooth, and of the desired consistency.

Dehydrating Prepared Foods

PREPARED FOODS such as sauerkraut, baked beans, and thick soups can be dehydrated, then used to make quick and easy meals at home. Not only will you save money by making these ready-to-go meals yourself, but you'll be able to make them to suit your family's tastes.

Home-dried prepared foods are also great for camping and backpacking. At camp, they can easily be rehydrated to produce a quick meal that costs far less than purchased freeze-dried food mixes. For more ideas, see Mixes for Camping and Backpacking on page 315.

While they can be stored at cool room temperature for a few weeks, home-dried prepared foods that are high in fat or that contain meat will turn rancid or develop off tastes during long-term storage unless they are kept refrigerated or, preferably, frozen. To rehydrate, simply add some boiling water and stir well, then let stand for a short time until the food is rehydrated. Heat before serving, adding a little more water if needed.

Use the same solid sheets used when making leathers; see Solid Sheets to Hold Purées, on page 272. Spread the food out evenly, about ¼ inch thick, and stir or turn frequently during drying. Use a target temperature of 150°F in a manufactured dehydrator or in the oven. If using a home-built dehydrator, don't exceed 140°F; this works fine but will take longer. Sun-drying is not recommended for prepared foods.

Almost any prepared food that's thick enough to hold its shape on a baking sheet can be dehydrated.

- **SAUERKRAUT** should be drained well and rinsed briefly. Spread thinly on sheets and dry until crisp and completely dry, stirring and breaking up the sauerkraut as it begins to dry.

- **BAKED BEANS** are best when cooked until somewhat dry before dehydrating. If there is meat in the beans, break or cut it up into very small pieces. Spread the mixture thinly on sheets, and crumble as it begins to dry. Continue drying and crumbling until the beans are in clusters of two or three; the sauce will be caked around the beans. The beans should be completely hard and dry inside, and some may "pop" like popcorn. Keep refrigerated or frozen for long-term storage.

- **THICK SOUPS** such as split pea or potato chowder should be cooked longer or prepared with less liquid so the mixture is thick enough to just hold its shape in a spoon; if you're dehydrating leftover soup, cook it a bit to thicken it before dehydrating. If the soup contains meat, break or cut it up into very small pieces. Spread the soup ¼ inch thick on sheets, and crumble as the mixture begins to dry. Continue drying and crumbling until the soup is in small crumbles, with no moisture in the center of any. If the soup contains meat, keep refrigerated or frozen for long-term storage.

- **TOMATO PASTE** is often used in small quantities, leaving you with a partial can of unused paste. The leftover paste can be spread out in a thin layer and dried in a solid sheet like a leather, but it's often more useful to dry it in 1-tablespoon droplets; when you have a recipe that calls for 1 tablespoon of tomato paste, simply add one dried droplet.

- **COOKED RICE** and rice pilaf can be dried, and then used like "instant rice" for future meals. This is particularly useful for brown rice and wild rice, which take a long time to cook. Spread the rice ¼ inch thick on sheets and stir frequently during drying. Dehydrate until the rice is hard.

- **SALSA** dehydrates wonderfully and is easy to rehydrate. Spoon off any thin liquid, then spread the salsa on sheets about ¼ inch thick. Dry until the salsa can be peeled off the sheet, then turn and continue drying until crisp and brittle, crumbling the mixture as it starts to become brittle.

- **BARBECUE SAUCE** can be spread on solid sheets and dehydrated to make leather that's great for camping or just to have in the pantry. To use, tear into small pieces and rehydrate with a little boiling water.

- **LEFTOVER VEGETABLES** can be chopped up, then spread on dehydrator sheets and dried until crisp and moisture-free. Use the dried vegetables to add flavor and body next time you're making a soup or stew.

crackers | crisps

CHAPTER 9

Snacks, Cereal, and Specialties

IN THE PREVIOUS CHAPTERS, you learned how the dehydrator can be used to dry prepared foods that will be later rehydrated and used as though they were freshly cooked. Here, you'll learn how the dehydrator can also be used to prepare tasty snacks, cereal, jam, pasta, and even a homemade veggie burger blend that's gluten-free, vegan, and totally delicious.

Snacks

A SURPRISING VARIETY of tasty snacks can be made entirely in your dehydrator. Some, such as crisp caulifloweretes and thinly sliced cucumbers, parsnips, turnips, and zucchini, have already been discussed in chapter 5, Vegetables. In this section, however, the flavor gets taken up a notch with seasonings or marinades applied before drying. The dehydrator can also be used to make tasty crackers and vegetable-based chips.

Most recipes in this section use a target temperature of 145°F to dry the foods quickly and produce pleasant crispness. A manufactured dehydrator or convection oven works best, but the home-built dehydrator can be used if you dehydrate at 140°F or below. A non-convection oven is too difficult to control for thin-sliced crisps.

Some of the foods in this chapter are commonly used in raw-food and living-food diets, though the temperatures used here exceed 118°F, the top temperature for preparing foods that may still be considered acceptable in the context of the raw-food diet. If you are following a raw- or living-food diet, adjust the temperatures as described on page 18. Use only scrupulously fresh vegetables — preferably organic — and adhere to rigorous standards of cleanliness to reduce your risk of food-borne illnesses. If you have a manufactured dehydrator, you can load the dehydrator in the evening and run it overnight at 110 to 115°F; the snacks should be done in the morning.

Many of these snacks fit with other special diets as well. Vegans can enjoy a variety of vegetable-based snacks; some of the recipes are vegan with no adaptation, while others would require the use of vegan Parmesan cheese. Those who are gluten-intolerant will find a variety of healthful, gluten-free snacks here. For reduced-sodium diets, regular salt can be replaced with reduced-sodium or sodium-free versions, or eliminated entirely, in any of the snack recipes below that call for salt.

As in previous chapters, dried ingredients from this book are highlighted in **bold type**.

Vegetable Crisps, Chips, and Treats

Here are some healthful and delicious alternatives to potato chips, commercial crackers, and other purchased snack foods that are laden with fat, sodium, and empty calories. *Crisps* are made from dehydrated, thinly sliced raw vegetables; they are crisp but not crunchy like potato chips or commercial crackers. Other raw vegetables can be seasoned and dehydrated to make tasty, crispy treats too; below you'll find some ideas that may inspire you to try a few combinations of your own. There's also a recipe to make vegetable tortilla chips that are as tasty and crunchy as commercial chips, with loads less sodium and fat.

Slice raw vegetables as thinly as possible when making vegetable crisps. A mandoline works best; see page 19 for information on this specialty kitchen tool. A food processor with a very thin slicing blade is the next best alternative. The vegetables must be cut to fit the processor's feed tube, but slicing is quick and easy. Use light rather than heavy pressure when pushing the vegetables through the food tube. Of course, a good sharp chef's knife works well, too. Vegetable crisps don't keep for long periods; store them in tightly sealed containers, and enjoy within a few weeks for the best flavor and crispness.

Asian-Seasoned Beet Crisps

Makes 4 servings

Add a little sesame oil to the leftover marinade, and then use it as a salad dressing for mixed greens.

- ¼ cup rice vinegar
- 2 tablespoons finely chopped cilantro leaves
- 1 teaspoon sugar
- 1 teaspoon soy sauce, regular or reduced sodium
- ½ teaspoon finely minced fresh gingerroot
- 2 medium beets, 4–5 ounces each

1. Stir together the vinegar, cilantro, sugar, soy sauce, and gingerroot in a medium mixing bowl.

2. Peel the beets with a swivel-bladed vegetable peeler. Cut crosswise into slices 1⁄16 inch thick, adding to the vinegar mixture as you slice. When all the beet slices have been added, gently stir the mixture, separating the slices to ensure that all are coated with the marinade. Set aside to marinate for 1 hour, stirring and separating slices once or twice.

3. Drain the slices and arrange on trays or racks in a single layer. Dehydrate at 145°F until crisp and dry, 7 to 8 hours.

Cauliflower Popcorn

Makes 2–3 servings

In this healthful snack, cauliflower florets are cut to look like large popcorn kernels. Nutritional yeast — also called brewer's yeast — provides great flavor and nutrition; look for it at health-food stores.

- 4 cups orange or white cauliflower (from about ½ head), broken into small florets before measuring*
- 1 teaspoon olive oil
- 2 tablespoons finely grated Parmesan cheese
- 1 teaspoon nutritional yeast powder, optional
- ¼ teaspoon salt

1. Steam-blanch the florets for 3 minutes. Chill in ice water, then drain and pat dry with paper towels.

2. Place the blanched, dried florets in a large mixing bowl. Add the oil; toss well with your fingertips to lightly coat each piece of cauliflower with the oil. Sprinkle about half of the Parmesan, nutritional yeast, and salt over the cauliflower and toss well, then sprinkle the remaining Parmesan, yeast, and salt into the bowl and toss thoroughly.

3. Line dehydrator trays or racks with solid sheets. Spread the florets over the sheets, piling loosely; it will shrink as it dries. Dehydrate at 145°F for 2 to 3 hours or until the florets are beginning to dry. Stir gently and continue dehydrating until crisp and dry; total drying time will be 5 to 7 hours.

---

* See the instructions on page 166 for a suggested method of cutting up the cauliflower. Use florets that are about ½ inch at the widest part; cut off longer stems from the florets (use them in other dishes).

Sliced Vegetable Crisps

Makes 3–4 servings

This flexible recipe can be tailored to suit your tastes — and your vegetable supply. Use a mix of the vegetables listed, or just one type, and feel free to change the seasonings if you like. These snacks are dry and crisp; for a crunchier vegetable chip, see the recipe on page 292 for Vegetable Tortilla Chips.

- 4 heaping cups mixed raw, thinly sliced vegetables (see step 1): carrots, parsnips, golden beets, sweet potatoes, and/or turnips
- 1 teaspoon olive oil
- ½–¾ teaspoon salt
- ¼ teaspoon ground **coriander seeds**
- ⅛ teaspoon ground white pepper

1. Prepare the vegetables: They should be sliced ¹⁄₁₆ to ⅛ inch thick; if you're dehydrating a mix of vegetables, slice the carrots more thinly than the others because they take a bit longer to dry. Carrots and parsnips may be peeled or unpeeled; beets, sweet potatoes, and turnips should be peeled. Sweet potatoes, beets, and turnips should be halved or quartered vertically before slicing so the slices are not too large, especially if you're making a mix that includes narrower vegetables like carrots and parsnips.

2. Place the sliced vegetables in a large mixing bowl. Add the olive oil; toss with your fingers to separate the slices and coat all sides lightly with the oil. Sprinkle about half of the salt, coriander, and pepper into the bowl and toss well, then sprinkle the remaining salt, coriander, and pepper into the bowl and toss gently but thoroughly.

3. Arrange the slices on trays or racks. Dehydrate at 145°F, turning and rearranging slices occasionally, until crisp and dry, 4 to 6 hours.

Cashew Kale *(or Other Greens)* Chips

Makes 4–6 servings

These are delicious, and offer nearly as much crunch as fried potato chips.
Use kale, collards, turnip greens, chard, or other sturdy greens.

- 2 quarts torn greens, fairly firmly packed
- ½ red bell pepper, cored and cut into large chunks
- ¼ small onion
- 2 garlic cloves
- ½ cup cashews, raw or roasted, salted or unsalted
- 2 tablespoons sesame seeds
- ½ teaspoon **Chili Powder Blend** (see page 210) or purchased chili powder blend
- ¼ teaspoon salt
- ½ lemon

1. Prepare the greens: Cut or tear large leaves into pieces 2 to 3 inches across, pulling away and discarding any thick ribs as you go. Smaller leaves may be used without tearing. Wash the greens very thoroughly, lifting them out of the water so any grit stays behind. Spin the greens dry in a salad spinner, and place in a large mixing bowl.

2. Add the bell pepper, onion, garlic, cashews, sesame seeds, chili powder, and salt to a blender. Squeeze the lemon juice into a small bowl, removing any seeds, and add to the blender. Pulse a few times to chop the ingredients, then process on high speed until the mixture is smooth, adding a little water if necessary. Scrape the cashew mixture over the greens, and then toss thoroughly with your hands until each piece of the greens is coated with the cashew mixture.

3. Spread the greens on trays or racks, piling them very loosely.* Dehydrate at 145°F for about 2 hours, then rearrange and separate any pieces that may be stuck together and also unfold any pieces that were folded. Continue dehydrating until the greens are crisp and the coating is dry; total drying time is generally 7 to 9 hours.

---

* If you are planning to run your manufactured dehydrator at a lower temperature overnight, you won't be able to turn and separate the greens, so you need to arrange them in a single layer on trays to prevent them from sticking together and drying improperly.

Vegetable Tortilla Chips

Makes 5–6 servings

Unlike vegetable crisps that are made from thinly sliced raw vegetables, these are made with finely chopped vegetables; the finished product is wonderfully crunchy, very similar to baked tortilla chips. These tasty chips are vegan and gluten-free; for reduced-sodium diets, use salt substitute.

1	cup sliced carrots
¼	small onion, cut into 1-inch chunks
2	garlic cloves
¼	medium red bell pepper, cut into 1-inch chunks
2½	cups frozen corn kernels, thawed
¼	cup roasted, shelled sunflower seeds, salted or unsalted
¼	cup ground flax meal (must be ground, not whole flax seeds)
2	tablespoons cornmeal
2	tablespoons water
1	teaspoon salt
½	teaspoon **ground cumin seeds**
½	teaspoon ground paprika
¼	teaspoon freshly ground black pepper

1. Steam-blanching the carrots (an optional step) will make the carrots easier to process evenly. Steam-blanch the carrots for 3 minutes, then rinse in cold water and set aside to drain well. If you are not blanching the carrots, cut the raw carrot slices into ¼-inch pieces.

2. Combine the onion and garlic in a food processor, and pulse a few times until chopped. Scrape down the sides of the processor bowl with a rubber spatula. Add the carrots and bell pepper, pulse a few times to chop coarsely, then scrape the sides of the bowl. Add the corn, sunflower seeds, flax meal, cornmeal, water, salt, cumin, paprika, and black pepper. Pulse a few times, scrape again, then process on high until the mixture is fairly smoothly chopped but still has a little texture; add a little more water if necessary to help the mixture process evenly.

3. If using a manufactured dehydrator, line trays with solid liner sheets and coat lightly with cooking spray; you'll need two or three trays. If using a home-built dehydrator or the oven, the easiest thing to use is nonstick baking sheets that have been lightly coated with cooking spray; you'll need two standard-size sheets. Another option that works well is two large flexible cutting boards that have been lightly coated with cooking spray; clip the flexible boards to cooling racks or place them on baking sheets. You may also line baking sheets with kitchen parchment.

   Use a rubber spatula to spread the mixture thinly on the prepared sheets; it should be about the thickness of two stacked quarters. Take the time to spread the mixture evenly, smoothing the edges. If using baking sheets with kitchen parchment, trim any overhanging parchment off to prevent it from scorching.

4. Dehydrate at 145°F (140°F for a home-built dehydrator) until the mixture is dry on top and firm enough to peel from the sheets, 3 to 4 hours. Use a clean pair of scissors to cut the thin mixture into 2-inch-wide strips, then cut the strips into triangles. Turn the triangles over and place them, dry-side down, in a single layer on a mesh-lined tray; if using baking sheets, you can switch to a rack or simply continue drying on the baking sheets after cutting and flipping the triangles. You will need another tray or rack, since the chips take up more room once they're cut. Continue dehydrating until the chips are completely dry and crisp; total drying time will be 9 to 12 hours.

Grain- and Seed-Based Crackers

These crackers offer from-scratch goodness. Crackers dried in the dehydrator stay fresh for weeks in a tightly sealed canister and may be recrisped in the dehydrator or oven if necessary. Note: Don't try to use the dehydrator to "cook" cracker recipes written for oven-baking. It won't work properly and may be unsafe if the recipes include eggs.

Flax and Parmesan Crackers

Makes 4–5 servings

For additional interest, mix herbs into the dough or sprinkle the mixture with sesame or poppy seeds before dehydrating. Because of the Parmesan cheese, these crackers don't keep as well as the other crackers in this section.

    1   cup ground flax meal (must be ground, not whole flax seeds)
    ⅓   cup finely grated Parmesan cheese
    ¾   teaspoon **garlic powder**
    ½   teaspoon **onion powder**
    ¼   teaspoon salt
  ½–1   cup water

1. Combine the flax meal, Parmesan, garlic powder, onion powder, and salt in a mixing bowl, then stir until thoroughly blended. Add ½ cup water and stir until blended. Stir in additional water if needed until the mixture is smooth and somewhat stiff but still spreadable (the amount of water needed depends on the texture of your flax meal and Parmesan).

2a. **IF USING A MANUFACTURED DEHYDRATOR**, you'll be shaping the crackers on a solid liner sheet that is not positioned inside the tray. Mist the liner sheet with cooking spray, then spread the flax mixture out as evenly as possible with a spoon. Place a sheet of kitchen parchment over the flax mixture, then use a rolling pin to roll out to slightly less than ⅛-inch thickness. Peel off the parchment, then use a damp table knife to even out any rough edges of the flax mixture. Place the filled liner sheet onto the dehydrator tray, then cut the mixture into 1½-inch squares (or whatever size and shape you'd like).

2b. **IF USING AN OVEN OR A HOME-BUILT DEHYDRATOR**, you'll be shaping the crackers on a piece of kitchen parchment, then placing that on a baking sheet for dehydrating. Cut a piece of kitchen parchment that fits inside your baking sheet. Place the parchment directly on your work surface, then spread the flax mixture out on the parchment as evenly as possible with a spoon. Place a second sheet of parchment over the flax mixture, then use a rolling pin to roll out to slightly less than ⅛-inch thickness. Slide the parchment with the flax mixture onto the baking sheet, and then peel off the top sheet of parchment. Use a damp table knife to even out any rough edges, then cut the mixture into 1½-inch squares (or whatever size and shape you'd like).

3. Dehydrate at 145°F (140°F for a home-built dehydrator) until the mixture is dry on top and firm enough to remove from the sheet, 3 to 4 hours. Break the crackers apart, using a table knife to separate them on the lines you drew if necessary. Turn the crackers over and place them, dry-side down, on a mesh-lined tray; if using baking sheets, you can switch to a rack or simply continue drying on the baking sheets after separating and turning the crackers. Continue dehydrating until the crackers are completely dry and crisp; total drying time will be 10 to 12 hours, but you can dry them longer for additional crispness if you like.

Scandinavian Crispbread

Makes 4–5 dozen crackers (depending on size)

These are particularly good with jam but also work well with cheese or smoked salmon.

¼	cup whole golden flax seeds
¼	cup warm water
⅓	cup whole-wheat flour
⅓	cup rye flour
¼	cup sesame seeds
¼	cup roasted sunflower seeds, salted or unsalted
½	teaspoon kosher salt or sea salt
¼	teaspoon baking powder
¼	cup cold water
2	tablespoons sunflower oil or canola oil

1. Process the flax seeds in a clean coffee grinder or blender until they are coarsely chopped (not ground to a meal-like consistency). Transfer to a small bowl and stir in the warm water. Set aside for 45 minutes; the mixture will become pasty. Meanwhile, cut three sheets of kitchen parchment to fit your dehydrator trays or sheets (if your dehydrator is round with a hole in the center, cut two round sheets with holes in the center and one whole, rectangular sheet).

2. Combine the whole-wheat flour, rye flour, sesame seeds, sunflower seeds, salt, and baking powder in a mixing bowl. Stir with a wooden spoon until thoroughly mixed. Add the cold water, oil, and the soaked flax seed; stir until very well mixed.

3. Scoop half of the dough onto a sheet of parchment, then pat into a rectangle (for a round dehydrator tray, spoon portions of the dough around the circle of parchment). Top with another sheet of parchment and use a rolling pin to roll out very thinly; it should be about the thickness of the sunflower seeds. Remove the top sheet of parchment, then use a thin knife to score the dough into squares, triangles, or diamonds, whatever size you prefer; 1½ inches is a good average size. Transfer the sheet to the dehydrator tray. Repeat with remaining dough.

4. Dehydrate until crisp and dry, 5 to 6 hours at 140°F. Break along the score lines. Remove the parchment and return the separated crackers to the trays, turning the crackers over. Dehydrate for about an hour longer.

Swiss Cheese and Almond Crackers

Makes about 80 crackers

These melt-in-your-mouth crackers are rich enough to enjoy plain; they are also delicious when topped with a thin slice of apple.

½   cup blanched slivered almonds

1   cup all-purpose flour

½   teaspoon salt

¼   teaspoon onion powder

3 tablespoons unsalted butter, slightly softened but still cool

1½ cups shredded Swiss cheese (about 6 ounces)

Few drops liquid hot pepper sauce

3 tablespoons cold water, or as needed

1. Fit a food processor with the metal chopping blade. Add the almonds and pulse on and off until chopped to the texture of coarse sand. Add the flour, salt, and onion powder; pulse to mix. Cut the butter into 6 pieces and add to the food processor. Pulse until the mixture is somewhat coarse, with a few pea-sized pieces of butter. Add the cheese and hot sauce, and pulse until well combined. Add the water, a tablespoon at a time, processing after each addition, until the dough begins to come together and holds its shape when pressed. Scrape onto a large piece of waxed paper, forming into a log about 12 inches long. Roll up in the waxed paper, then roll the log on the counter until rounded. Refrigerate for at least 4 hours, or as long as overnight.

2. Line dehydrator trays or racks with screens. Unwrap the chilled log and slice into circles that are about ⅛ inch thick. Transfer the circles to the prepared trays. Dehydrate until crisp and completely dry, 7 to 9 hours at 140°F. These will keep for several weeks at room temperature; freeze for long-term storage, bringing to room temperature before serving.

Breakfast Cereals

HOMEMADE BREAKFAST CEREALS are delicious and far more nutritious than many commercially made ready-to-eat cereals. All the recipes below can be dehydrated at low temperatures for use with raw- and living-food diets. Salt can be replaced with lower-sodium substitutes or eliminated entirely for salt-restricted diets. The Whole-Wheat Flakes recipe is vegan; for the other cereals, you may wish to experiment with vegan substitutes for the eggs and buttermilk in the recipes. Store the cereals in tightly sealed canisters and serve with milk and sugar.

Whole-Wheat Flakes

Makes about 10 servings

- 1¾ cups whole-wheat flour, approximate
- ¼ cup wheat germ
- 1 teaspoon ground cinnamon
- 1 teaspoon ground nutmeg
- ½ teaspoon salt
- ¼ cup warm water
- ½ teaspoon baking soda
- ½ cup molasses

1. Have a large sheet of kitchen parchment and some plastic wrap handy; line dehydrator trays or racks with screens. Combine 1 cup of the whole-wheat flour with the wheat germ, cinnamon, nutmeg, and salt in a large mixing bowl; stir to mix. Place the warm water in a small mixing bowl. Add the baking soda, stirring until dissolved. Quickly stir in the molasses, mixing well. Add the molasses mixture to the flour mixture; stir until well combined, then add enough of the remaining flour to make a very stiff dough.

2. Scoop about one-quarter of the dough onto the kitchen parchment. Cover with plastic wrap, and then flatten somewhat with your hands. Use a rolling pin to roll the dough very thin. Cut the dough into 3-inch strips, transferring them to the screens as you cut each one. Repeat with the remaining dough.

3. Dehydrate at 150°F until crisp, 4 to 6 hours. Cool the strips completely, and then crumble into small, flaky pieces. Spread the flakes over the screens and dehydrate at 150°F for 2 hours longer, or until the flakes are very crisp. Cool completely and store in canisters.

Carrot Cereal

Makes about 10 servings

2	cups whole-wheat flour
1	cup cooked, mashed, and cooled carrots
¾	cup old-fashioned rolled oats
½	cup brown sugar, packed
¼	cup liquid egg substitute
1½	teaspoons baking powder
1	teaspoon vanilla extract
½	teaspoon salt

1. Combine the flour, carrots, oats, sugar, egg substitute, baking powder, vanilla, and salt in a large mixing bowl. Beat well with a wooden spoon.

2. Cover dehydrating trays or racks with kitchen parchment. Spread the batter thinly over the parchment. Dehydrate at 150°F until the top is firm and the sheets of batter can be peeled away from the parchment, 4 to 6 hours. Invert the sheets of batter onto separate trays that have been covered with screens, then peel off and discard the parchment. Continue dehydrating until the sheets are crisp and hard, 6 to 8 hours longer. Cool the sheets completely, and then crumble into small, flaky pieces. Spread the flakes over the screens and dehydrate at 150°F for 2 to 3 hours longer, or until the flakes are very crisp. Cool completely and store in canisters.

Nutty Cereal Nuggets

For a nice breakfast sundae, fill individual bowls with cut-up fresh fruit, top with a dollop of yogurt, and sprinkle a tablespoon of this cereal mixture on top.

Makes about 4 cups

- ½ cup buttermilk
- 2 tablespoons corn syrup
- 2 tablespoons pure maple syrup
- ½ teaspoon vanilla extract
- ¼ teaspoon salt
- ½ teaspoon baking soda
- ¼ cup hot water
- 1½ cups whole-wheat flour
- ½ cup chopped nuts, medium-fine

1. Preheat the oven to 350°F. Lightly grease a 9-inch round or square baking pan; set aside.

2. Stir together the buttermilk, corn syrup, maple syrup, vanilla, and salt in a large mixing bowl. Stir the baking soda into the measuring cup with the hot water, then stir that into the buttermilk mixture. Add the flour and nuts to the buttermilk mixture and stir until well blended; it will be like cookie dough.

3. Scrape the dough into the prepared pan, spreading evenly. Bake for 35 minutes, or until the cake springs back but feels firm when pressed. Cool the pan on a cooling rack for 10 minutes. Turn the cake out onto the cooling rack and cover with a clean dish towel; let stand until completely cool.

4. Cut the cake into 1½-inch squares. Add 5 or 6 squares to a food processor. Pulse a few times until coarsely crumbled. Be careful not to over-process; ideally, the chopped mixture should be in ⅛-inch or slightly larger crumbles.

5. Line dehydrator trays or racks with solid sheets. Spread the chopped mixture about ½ inch thick over the sheets, breaking up any large chunks you find. Dehydrate at 145 to 150°F, stirring occasionally with your fingertips and breaking up any large pieces you find, until hard and crisp, 2 to 3 hours; when the mixture feels hard and crisp, dehydrate for 1 hour longer. Cool completely and store in canisters.

"SUN" JAM

MOST JAM IS MADE by cooking the fruit with pectin, a commercial product that helps jams set. Pectin requires a specific amount of sugar and a specific amount of cooking time. Even jams that don't require added pectin require long, slow cooking to thicken the fruit.

"Sun cooking" has long been used for fruit jams — particularly strawberry. The process is very simple: Fruits are stirred with a small amount of sugar (far less than normally used in jam); no pectin is added. Some recipes use a brief cooking period, while others don't. The fruit mixture is put into wide jars or dishes and set in the sun; solar drying thickens the jam without the need for pectin. The result is jam with less sugar that sparkles with fresh fruit flavor. The instructions below provide information on this old-time jam-making technique.

For those of us who don't live in hot, sunny climes, the dehydrator or oven can be used to produce very similar results. This is a great use of the extra space at the bottom of a home-built dehydrator. Sun jam can be made in box-style dehydrators by removing extra trays; for oven-drying, simply find an unused spot on a rack (don't set the dish of fruit on the bottom of the oven, which will be too hot). Stacking-tray dehydrators don't work because there's not enough room between trays for the dish of fruit. Any temperature between 100 and 140°F will work, so you can prepare the jam almost any time you're dehydrating something else (don't put it in the same batch as onions, broccoli, or other vegetables that have a strong odor during dehydrating, though).

Although strawberries are the fruit that is most commonly prepared in this way, other juicy fruits can be used. Apricots, blackberries, blueberries, nectarines, peaches, and raspberries are all good choices. A blend of fruits is delightful; try combining strawberries and blueberries, for example. The recipe below makes a small batch, but it's easy to increase by using a larger dish or several dishes. For the most efficient preparation, the layer of fruit should be no more than 1 inch deep.

When the jam has been "cooked" to the consistency you like, transfer it to clean half-pint jars and store in the refrigerator; use it within a month. The sealed jars may also be frozen for long-term storage.

Sun-Style Jam

Makes 2 half-pints

1½–1¾ pounds strawberries, peaches, or other fruit; all one kind or a mix

1¼–1¾ cups sugar, depending on the sweetness of the fruit

2 teaspoons lemon juice

1. Place one-third of the fruit in a food processor. Pulse a few times to chop coarsely; the mixture should contain small chunks. Transfer to a large non-reactive saucepan; repeat with the remaining fruit, adding each batch to the same saucepan. When all the fruit has been added, add the sugar and lemon juice, then stir thoroughly. Let stand for 1 hour.

2. After the hour, heat the fruit mixture to boiling over medium-high heat, stirring constantly. Boil for 1 minute. Skim off and discard any foam. Transfer the fruit mixture to a 7- by 11-inch rectangular or 9-inch square glass baking dish.

3a. If using a **manufactured box-style dehydrator** or a **home-built dehydrator**, place the dish in the bottom of the dehydrator; remove a few trays from the box-style dehydrator to make room. Dehydrate at any temperature between 100 and 140°F, stirring the fruit every few hours.

3b. If **oven-drying**, place the dish on a lower rack but not on the bottom of the oven. Dehydrate at any temperature between 100 and 140°F, stirring the fruit every few hours.

3c. If **sun-drying**, position the dish in the sun-drying setup described on page 44. Make sure the dish is well protected from insects during sun-drying; the protective netting or cheesecloth needs to wrap entirely around the bottom of the dish to prevent insects from crawling into openings. Stir the fruit twice each day; bring the dish inside at night.

4. Dehydrate or sun-dry until the mixture thickens to a jamlike consistency; it will thicken somewhat as it cools, so it can be a bit loose. In a dehydrator running at 135°F, the jam will take from 9 to 12 hours; the times will change according to the dehydrating temperature you use. Sun-drying generally takes 1 to 3 days.

5. Spoon the jam into clean half-pint jelly jars; seal with clean lids. Store in the refrigerator for up to 1 month, or freeze for longer storage.

HOMEMADE PASTA

THE GROWING POPULARITY of pasta machines has made it easier than ever to have fresh pasta anytime. Most fresh pasta recipes are meant to be eaten immediately, but if you want to stockpile your favorites, the following procedure can be used. For those of you without the convenience of a pasta machine, this pasta recipe is easy to make by hand. You may also dry any other homemade pasta, as long as it doesn't contain fresh, unpasteurized eggs. A dehydrator (manufactured or home-built) or convection oven are the best choices for drying pasta.

Basic Pasta

Makes 3 cups dried pasta

This is a basic pasta recipe that demonstrates how to make and dry homemade pasta. Use the same steps for any other pasta recipe you like; always use liquid egg substitute or commercially pasteurized eggs if the recipe calls for eggs.

- ½ cup liquid egg substitute or commercially pasteurized eggs, beaten
- 1 teaspoon salt
- 2 cups all-purpose flour, approximate

1. Beat the eggs and salt in a large mixing bowl with a fork. Gradually stir in as much flour as possible, ½ cup at a time, then work in more flour by hand until the dough is very stiff. Cut the dough in half and roll out very thinly on a lightly floured work surface. Let stand for 10 minutes. Sprinkle with a little more flour, roll up as a jelly roll, and cut into thin crosswise slices. Repeat with the other half of the dough.

2. Spread the cut pasta in a thin layer over trays or racks. Dehydrate at 145°F until brittle throughout, stirring occasionally. This will generally take 4 to 6 hours in a dehydrator or convection oven.

3. Store the dried pasta in an airtight canister. To use, cook in boiling water until just tender.

Flavored Pasta Variations

The variations below let you create colorful pasta with extra flavor and nutrition. You will need to use a little more flour than in the basic recipe, particularly in the Spinach Pasta version.

CHILE PASTA: Add 1 tablespoon puréed cooked red bell pepper and ¼ teaspoon cayenne powder to the eggs.

HERBED PASTA: Add ¼ cup very finely minced fresh herbs to the eggs.

SAFFRON PASTA: Add ¼ teaspoon powdered saffron to the eggs.

SPINACH PASTA: Add ¼ cup puréed cooked spinach to the eggs; use an additional tablespoon of egg substitute.

TOMATO PASTA: Add 2 tablespoons tomato paste to the eggs.

VEGGIE BURGERS

HOMEMADE VEGGIE BURGERS are easy to make at home and can be customized to your preferences by using different beans or seasonings. Here's a mixture that's designed to be dehydrated so it can be stored on the pantry shelf, ready to go at a moment's notice. This tasty blend is vegan and gluten-free; for sodium-restricted diets, use a salt substitute or other salt-free seasoning blend, and be sure to use chickpeas you soaked and boiled yourself rather than canned beans, which are high in sodium.

Veggie Burger Blend

Makes enough for 4–5 servings

- 1½ cups cooked or canned chickpeas, drained and rinsed if canned
- ½ cup cooked brown rice, cooled
- ⅓ cup chopped walnuts

¼ cup coarsely chopped fresh parsley

⅓ cup shredded carrots

⅓ cup frozen corn kernels, thawed

¼ cup chopped fresh onion

¼ cup ground flax meal (must be ground, not whole flax seeds)

3 tablespoons shelled sunflower seeds

1 teaspoon olive oil or vegetable oil

½ teaspoon salt

¼ teaspoon **ground coriander seeds**

1. Combine the chickpeas, rice, walnuts, and parsley in a food processor. Pulse until chopped to medium-coarse texture. Add the carrots, corn, and onion. Pulse a few times until the carrots and corn are coarsely chopped; don't over-process, because the mixture should still have a fair amount of texture. Transfer the bean mixture to a bowl. Stir in the flax meal, sunflower seeds, oil, salt, and coriander, mixing very well.

2. Line two dehydrator trays with solid liner sheets, or cover a large baking sheet with kitchen parchment. Transfer the bean mixture to the sheets, breaking it up into clumps no larger than a tablespoon. Trim off any overhanging parchment to prevent it from scorching In the oven or home-built dehydrator. Dry at 135 to 145°F for 1 hour, and then crumble the mixture with your fingers. Continue drying, crumbling and stirring the mixture every hour, until it is completely dry and crumbly, 5 to 7 hours at 135°F; the finished crumbles should be no larger than pea-sized. Cool and store in a tightly sealed glass jar.

3. To prepare the veggie burgers, measure ½ cup of the crumbles for each burger you'd like to prepare. Place the total amount of crumbles you're preparing in a heatproof bowl. Add ¼ cup boiling water for each ½ cup of mix, stirring to combine. Set aside for 15 minutes, stirring frequently; add a little more water if the mixture seems too dry. Shape into patties and pan-fry in a little oil over medium heat until browned on both sides and heated through.

trail mix

gifts

CHAPTER 10

Dried-Food Mixes for Pantry, Gifts, and Camping

NOW THAT YOU HAVE A SUPPLY of delicious home-dried fruits, vegetables, and meats, you can pack up combinations that will make hearty soups, side dishes, snacks, and even desserts. A selection of these mixes is a tremendous boon in the pantry because you can prepare a wholesome, healthful meal with very little work and just a few added ingredients. Many of the pantry mixes also make great gifts. Finally, you can pack up special quick-cooking mixes to tote in your backpack (or car); they can be easily rehydrated and cooked at camp.

Mixes for Your Pantry or to Give as Gifts

WHEN YOU PACK YOUR OWN dried-food mixes for soup and other dishes, you can control the ingredients any way you like. Modify the spices to suit your family's preferences, or substitute one dried herb for another depending on what you have on hand. To make low-sodium mixes, use salt substitutes or eliminate the salt entirely. If you follow a gluten-free diet and are preparing a soup mix that calls for prepared chicken or beef broth, be sure to check the label of any broth you purchase, as some contain hydrolyzed wheat gluten.

The mixes in this section are best when stored in sterilized glass canning jars, which keep the dried foods from becoming battered and crushed, protect them from air, and also keep out insects and other critters. Whether you're packing these jarred mixes for yourself or as a gift, it's nice to layer the various ingredients in the jars so they are pretty to look at. For gift-giving, cut out a square or circle of colorful cloth that will generously cover the top of the jar; use pinking shears for a nice touch and to keep the cloth from fraying. Tie the cloth over the sealed jar lid with a pretty ribbon, and make up a tag that includes directions for using the mix.

Besides the following six recipes for gift-giving, you may also want to consider small jars of the herb blends on pages 236–238, the tea blends on pages 238–239, or a bottle of one of the seasoned vinegars on pages 240–241. Any cook would appreciate such a thoughtful gift, especially one that was prepared by your own hands from foods you dehydrated yourself. You can also create lovely potpourri for gift jars, or sachets for hanging in the closet or placing in a drawer, by following the instructions in chapter 11.

NOTE: If you have a vacuum sealer that can be used to seal canning jars, you can use it with some of the food mixes, as noted in the instructions; please read about vacuum-packing and food safety on page 30. Vacuum-packed mixes will stay fresh for a longer time than mixes that have not been vacuum-packed.

Minestrone Soup Mix in a Jar

For a gluten-free version, replace the barley with brown lentils and use pasta made from rice.

Makes 6–7 servings

- ½ cup **dried cooked or canned cannellini or great northern beans***
- 1 teaspoon **Dried Italian Herb Mix** (page 237) or purchased Italian herb blend

  A few **dried garlic flakes**

  A few grinds of fresh black pepper
- ¼ cup purchased dried split peas
- 3 tablespoons **dried diced bell peppers**
- 3 tablespoons **dried chopped onion**
- 2 tablespoons **dried celery slices**
- ¼ cup pearled barley
- ¼ cup **dried tomato pieces**
- ¼ cup **dried diced carrot**
- ½ cup **dried kale or other greens** (large crumbles)
- 1 **dried bay leaf**
- ⅔ cup uncooked macaroni or other small pasta shape
- 1 quart water
- ½ pound ground beef or bulk pork sausage, optional
- 1½ quarts beef broth or vegetable broth

1. **Pack the mix:** Place the beans in a widemouthed 1-quart canning jar, tilting to make an even layer. Sprinkle with the herb blend, garlic, and black pepper. Add the split peas, bell peppers, onion, celery, barley, tomatoes, carrot, and kale in even layers, following the order listed. Tuck the bay leaf along the side of the jar. Place the macaroni in a small plastic bag; seal with a twist tie, then tuck it into the top of the jar. Seal the jar tightly with a new lid; if you have a vacuum sealer that works with jars, this combination can be vacuum-packed. Store in a cool place until ready to use.

---

* Be sure to use dried beans that have been cooked or canned before drying (page 156); this recipe won't work with uncooked dried beans.

2. **To prepare the soup:** Remove the macaroni from the jar. Add the remaining contents of the jar to a soup pot; stir in the water. Heat to boiling, and then cover and remove from the heat. Let soak for 1 hour.

3. At the end of the soaking time, brown the ground meat (if using) in a skillet; drain excess fat. Add the browned meat and the broth to the soup pot. Heat to boiling, and then reduce the heat and simmer, stirring occasionally, for 30 minutes. Add the macaroni; cook at a gentle boil until the macaroni is tender. Remove the bay leaf before serving.

Mushroom-Barley Soup Mix in a Jar

Makes 4–5 servings

½ cup pearled barley

⅓ cup **dried mushroom slices**

3 tablespoons **dried chopped onion**

1 tablespoon crumbled **dried parsley leaves**

1½ teaspoons crumbled **dried dill leaves**

¼ cup **dried carrot slices or diced carrot**

1 **dried bay leaf**

1 quart beef broth, chicken broth, or vegetable broth

2 cups water

1. **Pack the mix:** Place half of the barley, the mushrooms, onion, parsley, dill, and carrot in even layers in a half-pint canning jar, following the order listed. Tuck the bay leaf along the side of the jar. Add the remaining barley. Seal the jar tightly with a new lid; if you have a vacuum sealer that works with jars, this combination can be vacuum-packed. Store in a cool place until ready to use.

2. **To prepare the soup:** Add the contents of the jar to a large saucepan; stir in the broth and water. Heat to boiling, then reduce the heat and simmer until the barley is tender, about 45 minutes. Remove the bay leaf before serving.

Curried Winter Squash Soup Mix in a Jar

If you use purchased chicken broth and are following a gluten-free diet, be sure to check the label, as some commercial broths contain hydrolyzed wheat gluten.

Makes 4 servings

1½	cups	**dried butternut or other winter squash pieces**
1	tablespoon	**dried snipped chives**
½	teaspoon	curry powder blend
		A pinch of ground cinnamon
		A few grinds of fresh black pepper
2	tablespoons	chopped **dried apple slices**
¼	cup	**dried diced carrot**
2	tablespoons	**dried chopped onion**
3	cups	water
1	quart	chicken broth
½	cup	sour cream

1. **Pack the mix:** Place half of the squash pieces in a widemouthed 1-pint canning jar. Sprinkle the chives, curry powder, cinnamon, and black pepper over the squash. Add the apples, carrot, and onion in even layers, following the order listed. Add the remaining squash pieces. Seal the jar tightly with a new lid; if you have a vacuum sealer that works with jars, this combination can be vacuum-packed. Store in a cool place until ready to use.

2. **To prepare the soup:** Add the contents of the jar to a large saucepan; stir in the water. Heat to boiling, then cover and remove from the heat. Let soak for 30 minutes.

3. At the end of the soaking time, add the broth. Place over medium heat and boil gently, stirring occasionally, for 30 minutes; the squash should be very tender. Remove from the heat, then mash with a potato masher until fairly smooth; add a little more water if needed. Stir in the sour cream and cook over medium heat until heated through.

Vegetable and Herb Dip Mix in a Jar

Makes about ½ cup of mix (enough for 8 batches of dip)

¼	cup **dried diced or sliced carrots**
2	heaping tablespoons **dried diced bell peppers** (any color)
1	tablespoon **dried chopped onion**
1½	teaspoons **dried celery slices**
5 or 6	**dried zucchini slices** or **dried cucumber slices**
4 or 5	small pieces **dried lemon zest**
1	**dried garlic slice,** or ⅛ teaspoon **garlic powder**
3	tablespoons crumbled **dried parsley leaves**
2	tablespoons crumbled **dried basil leaves**
1	teaspoon crumbled **dried tarragon leaves**
1	teaspoon **dried thyme leaves**
½	teaspoon coarse salt
¼	teaspoon sugar
⅛	teaspoon ground white pepper
	Sour cream as needed (¾ cup per batch)
	Mayonnaise as needed (¼ cup per batch)

1. **Pack the mix:** Combine the carrots, bell peppers, onion, celery, zucchini, lemon zest, and garlic in a blender. Process until very finely chopped; it should not be powdered but the flakes should be no larger than about ⅛ inch. Let the dust settle for about a minute before opening the blender, then transfer the mixture to a mixing bowl. Add the parsley, basil, tarragon, thyme, salt, sugar, and pepper; stir very well, then pack into a small jar and seal tightly.

2. **To prepare the dip:** Shake or stir the mix before measuring to distribute ingredients evenly. Combine ¾ cup sour cream, ¼ cup mayonnaise, and 1 tablespoon of the mix in a small bowl; stir together very well. Cover and refrigerate for at least 4 hours. Serve with fresh vegetables and crackers.

Swedish Fruit Soup Mix in a Jar (*Fruktsoppa*)

Makes 6 dessert servings

This unusual and tasty dessert is gluten-free, vegan, and low-sodium.

1	cup sugar
¼	cup quick-cooking tapioca
½	pound **dried plum slices or chunks** (or cut-up purchased prunes)
½	teaspoon finely chopped **dried lemon zest**
5 or 6	**dried orange slices**, peel removed before or after drying
½	cup **dried seed-free grapes** or purchased raisins
⅓	cup diced **dried apricot or peach pieces***
½	cup diced **dried apple slices***
⅓	cup **dried cherry halves**, or a mix of **cherries** and **dried currants**
1	stick cinnamon
2	quarts cold water

1. **Pack the mix:** Pour the sugar in an even layer into a widemouthed 1-quart canning jar. Sprinkle the tapioca over the sugar. Cut the dried plum slices into ½-inch pieces and add to the jar in an even layer; sprinkle evenly with the lemon zest. Place the orange slices in the jar, laying them flat and stacking as necessary. Add the grapes, apricots, apples, and cherries in even layers, following the order listed. Slip the cinnamon stick alongside the fruit in the jar. Seal the jar tightly with a new lid; if you have a vacuum sealer that works with jars, this combination can be vacuum-packed. Store in a cool place until used.

2. **To prepare the fruit soup:** Add the contents of the jar to a soup pot; stir in the water. Cover and soak at room temperature for 1 to 2 hours.

3. After soaking, heat the mixture to boiling, stirring several times, then reduce the heat and simmer, stirring occasionally, until the fruit is tender and the liquid has thickened somewhat. Serve as a dessert, either hot or cold; if serving cold, add a dollop of whipped cream to each serving, if you like. The completed soup can be chilled and refrigerated for several days.

---

* For the diced fruit, you may use dried slices or dried chunks; cut them into ¼-inch pieces before measuring. Kitchen scissors work best for cutting up the dried fruit.

Frosty Fruit Cluster Mix in a Jar

Makes about 4 cups (prepared)

This kid-friendly mix satisfies your sweet tooth and provides a good serving of healthful dried fruits.

- 1 cup white chocolate chips
- 1 cup whole-grain oat ring cereal
- ½ cup **dried syrup-blanched cranberries**
- ½ cup diced **dried pineapple***
- ⅔ cup dry-roasted or regular roasted peanuts, salted or unsalted
- ¼ cup **dried blueberries or huckleberries**
- ½ cup diced **dried mango or papaya***

1. **Pack the mix:** Place the white chocolate chips in a small plastic bag; seal with a twist tie and set aside. Add the cereal to a widemouthed 1-quart canning jar. Add the cranberries, pineapple, peanuts, blueberries, and mango in even layers, following the order listed. Place the bag of white chocolate chips on top. Seal the jar tightly with a new lid; if you have a vacuum sealer that works with jars, this combination can be vacuum-packed. Store in a cool place until ready to use.

2. **To prepare the snack mix:** Coat a baking sheet with cooking spray. Remove the bag of white chocolate chips and pour the fruit mix into a large bowl. Pour the chocolate chips out of the bag into a *completely dry* microwave-safe bowl. Microwave on 70 percent power for 45 seconds, then stir with a spoon. Some of the chocolate chips will be melted, but most will still be firm. Return to the microwave and heat for 15 seconds at 70 percent power, stirring again afterwards; repeat as needed until the chocolate can be stirred completely smooth. (As an option, melt the chocolate chips in the top half of a double boiler, stirring frequently until smooth.) Scrape the melted chocolate over the fruit mixture and toss with two spoons (as though mixing a salad) until evenly coated. Spread in an even layer over the prepared baking sheet and cool completely. Break into bite-size chunks; store in a plastic container or ziplock bags.

---

* For the diced fruit, you may use dried slices or dried chunks; cut them into ¼-inch pieces before measuring. Kitchen scissors work best for cutting up the dried fruit.

Mixes for Camping and Backpacking

ALMOST EVERY WELL-STOCKED sporting goods store has a display of packaged, freeze-dried meals developed especially for the camper, the backpacker, and the hunter. It's an appetizing array, including dishes like vegetable-beef stew, chicken noodle soup, peach cobbler, scrambled eggs and bacon, and potato soup. These meal-size packages are convenient for camping trips where there is no refrigeration and where keeping fresh foods is a problem. They're small enough for canoeing trips where there is little space for supplies and are light enough in weight for backpacking.

But those convenient little packages are expensive. A foil envelope containing the ingredients for a main dish of vegetable-beef stew intended to serve four costs as much as a fresh beef roast that would serve eight people. A single-serve pouch that will make scrambled eggs with bacon costs about the same as three cartons of fresh eggs. The packaged camping foods often make fairly small portions, too; a mix that's supposed to serve four could easily be eaten by two or three hungry campers who have been hiking all day. Furthermore, freeze-dried packaged meals are often too salty, too bland, or just not very tasty.

Home-packed dehydrated meals are a great solution. You can pack mixes that suit your tastes, in any quantity you want, for far less than the packaged meals from the camping store.

If you're traveling in an RV or car-camping, weight and bulk aren't usually a big problem, so you can use the jarred pantry mixes on pages 309–314. Backpackers, canoeists, and other campers who have to carry everything on their backs, however, need lightweight meal mixes that don't require large pots and a lot of time to cook. This section is written primarily for them, although the mixes here may also be used by RVers, car-campers, and even harried cooks at home.

Trail mixes and jerky are also traditional camping fare that can be made with your dehydrator. Take a look at Dried Fruit Snack Mix, Berry-Cherry Trail Mix, and Tropical Trail Mix (check the index to locate specific recipes), and a variety of jerky preparation techniques and recipes in chapter 7.

Packing and Preparing Lightweight Mixes

Some campers — especially those traveling in large groups — choose to carry dried foods and staples in bulk, combining them as each dish is cooked. That's great if it works in your situation, but smaller groups or individual campers are better off carrying packages that contain all the ingredients for a particular dish; that way, it isn't necessary to carry staples such as flour, seasonings, rice, pasta, and other ingredients separately. It's also dismaying to realize that the dish you're planning to prepare requires some ingredient you forgot to bring; if you pack all the ingredients for each dish together in one bag, nothing will be missing when you're miles from the nearest store. And in buggy, wet, windy, or hurried conditions, meal preparation will be much easier to manage with everything all pre-measured and ready to cook. You'll usually need to carry a few liquids such as cooking oil or maple syrup; use leakproof plastic containers that are designated for food storage, and pack them into several plastic bags as additional insurance in case one starts leaking.

Plastic food-storage bags work great for packing camping mixes. Use freezer-weight bags, which stand up better to jostling in the food pack. You can also rehydrate dried foods directly in freezer-weight bags, even if you're using boiling water; see instructions on page 318. Bags with ziplock-style closures — either the kind that pinch together or those that have a small sliding head — seal tightly and work far better for packing meal mixes than open-ended bags that need to be sealed with a twist tie. When the food has been prepared, the empty plastic bags can be rolled up and stowed in the bottom of the food pack; they often come in handy for other uses while you're camping, and can be reused for more meal mixes another time as long as they're clean and dry. Vacuum-sealed bags, sealed with a special vacuum machine (pages 29–30), work great too and are also waterproof, but they're not so easy to reuse.

The following recipes include instructions for both packing at home and preparing the meal at camp. Copy the cooking instructions onto a piece of paper and slip that into the bag with the food. Once the food is packed in the bag and instructions have been included, roll up the bag, pushing out as much air as possible, then seal the ziplock closure securely. Be sure to label the bag with the name of the recipe. It's helpful to pack the individual rolled bags of mixes into larger plastic bags according to the type of mix it is, keeping all breakfast mixes together and so on; that makes it easier to pull out just what you need when it's time to prepare a meal.

Because you're working with dried foods, you'll often have to rehydrate some ingredients before cooking. This can be done in any camping cookware you have, but since pots are often in short supply when you're traveling light, it's often more practical to rehydrate the food in its plastic bag. That way, you can have several types of food rehydrating at one time while you're preparing something else on the stove.

Rehydrating Dried Foods in a Plastic Bag

Step 1.

Remove the instruction sheet and any smaller bags that contain other ingredients. If you are going to rehydrate using boiling water, place the bag in a bowl, pot lid, or some other container that will support it.

Step 2.

Add enough water to just cover the dried food. Cold water may be used, but takes longer to rehydrate than hot or boiling water. ***Never add boiling water to a lightweight or standard-weight plastic bag;*** use boiling water only in freezer-weight bags. Seal the bag, leaving enough room for the food to expand as it rehydrates (and be careful when using boiling water so that it doesn't squirt out onto your hands). Let the bag of food stand until the food is tender and plump with no hard spot, or as directed in individual recipes; gently massage the bag once or twice to ensure that all pieces are covered with water, and add a little more water if it seems to need it.

Step 3.

If you've soaked vegetables that will be cooked and served plain, simply pour the rehydrated vegetables and their soaking water into a pot and simmer until the vegetables are tender. Most other foods need to be drained after rehydrating. To drain, open up just a small corner of the bag, then hold the bag over a bowl and squeeze gently until all the soaking water has run into the bowl; the small opening acts as a strainer. Use the soaking liquid in soup or stew. Fruit-soaking liquid is usually a tasty beverage on its own.

Recipes for Lightweight Camping Mixes

Here are some recipes for mixes that you can pack at home, and then easily prepare at camp using minimal equipment. (The recipes in this section were adapted from *The Back-Country Kitchen: Camp Cooking for Canoeists, Hikers, and Anglers* and have been used with permission.) Another option is to dehydrate prepared foods such as baked beans, thick soups, and sauerkraut; the dehydrated food packs easily because it is lightweight, and it's also easy to rehydrate at camp. See Dehydrating Prepared Foods on page 282 for more information. There are also several recipes at the end of this section for some camp versions of at-home favorites; these cook-and-dehydrate recipes have been specially formulated to make them easy to dehydrate and easy to prepare at camp.

Hot Cereal with Fruit

Makes 2–3 servings

- ½ cup granola
- ⅓ cup quick-cooking oatmeal or multi-grain cereal
- ⅓ cup diced **dried apricots**, **peaches**, **apples**, **pears**, or **plums** (all one kind of fruit or a mix)
- ¼ cup nonfat dry milk powder
- 2 tablespoons brown sugar, packed
- ½ teaspoon salt

1. **Pack the mix:** Combine the granola, oats, dried fruit, dry milk, sugar, and salt in a pint-size ziplock bag. Roll up the bag and seal.

2. **Camp cooking instructions:** Boil 1 cup of water in a medium pot. Stir in the mix. Cook for 5 minutes, stirring frequently, until the oatmeal is done. The cereal needs no additional milk or sweetening.

Hot Breakfast Nuggets

Each bag makes 1 serving

Use the ingredients list below to pack individual servings into small plastic bags, then carry as many servings as you need in a larger plastic ziplock bag. The individual servings have the milk and sugar included.

FOR EACH SERVING:

- ½ cup **Nutty Cereal Nuggets** (see page 300) or purchased nugget cereal
- 1 tablespoon plus 1 teaspoon nonfat dry milk
- 1 heaping tablespoon diced **dried peaches or apricots, dried currants,** or **dried grapes** (all one kind of fruit, or a mix)
- ½ teaspoon sugar
- ⅛ teaspoon butter-flavored sprinkles such as Butter Buds, optional

1. **Pack the mix:** Combine nugget cereal, dry milk, dried fruit, sugar, and butter sprinkles, if using, in a small plastic bag and seal with a twist tie. Pack the individual bags into a ziplock bag, then roll up the ziplock bag and seal.

2. **Camp cooking instructions:** Empty the contents of one small bag into an individual serving bowl or large cup. Add ½ cup of boiling water and stir well.

Borscht (Beet Soup)

Makes 3–4 servings

For this mix, you'll need a circle of dehydrated special tomato leather. Make the leather any time you have the dehydrator running for something else.

- 3 tablespoons tomato paste
- 1 tablespoon white vinegar
- 1 teaspoon all-purpose flour
- 1 cup **dried julienned beets**
- ¼ cup **dried ground beef**
- ¼ cup **dried julienned or shredded carrots**
- 1 tablespoon **dried onion flakes**
- 1 tablespoon beef bouillon granules
- 2 teaspoons powdered sweetened lemonade mix
- 2 teaspoons snipped **dried chives**
- 2 teaspoons crumbled **dried parsley leaves**
- Pinch of freshly ground black pepper

1. **Prepare the special tomato leather:** Stir together the tomato paste, vinegar, and flour in a small bowl. Spread out in a small circle on a sheet used for making leathers (see chapter 8). Dehydrate until dry and leathery, about 4 hours at 135°F.

2. **Pack the mix:** Combine the beets, ground beef, carrots, onion flakes, bouillon, lemonade mix, chives, parsley, and pepper in a quart-size ziplock bag. Cut the tomato leather into small pieces and add to the bag. Roll up the bag and seal. Keep the mix refrigerated or frozen until you're packing for your trip.

3. **Camp cooking instructions:** Boil 3 cups of water in a medium pot. Stir in the mix. Return to boiling, then cover and remove from the heat. Let stand for 30 minutes. Stir well, then heat to boiling. Reduce the heat and simmer, stirring occasionally, for about 10 minutes.

Camper's Corn Chowder

Makes 3–4 servings

⅔ cup instant mashed potato flakes

¼ cup nonfat dry milk powder

1 teaspoon cornmeal

1½ teaspoons **Mock Chicken Broth Powder** or chicken bouillon granules

½ teaspoon sugar

½ teaspoon celery salt or plain salt

⅛ teaspoon freshly ground black pepper

¼ cup **dried Canadian-style bacon strips**

¾ cup **dried corn kernels**

¼ cup **dried diced red or green bell peppers** or **pimientos**

1 tablespoon **dried chopped onion**

½ teaspoon **dried thyme leaves**

1. **Pack the mix:** Combine the potato flakes, dry milk, cornmeal, broth powder, sugar, celery salt, and pepper in a small plastic bag and seal with a twist tie; set aside. Cut the Canadian bacon strips into ¼-inch pieces and place in a quart-size freezer-weight ziplock bag. Add the corn, bell peppers, onion, thyme, and the small bag containing the potato mixture to the ziplock bag. Roll up the bag and seal. Keep the mix refrigerated or frozen until you're packing for your trip.

2. **Camp cooking instructions:** Remove and set aside the small bag containing the potato mixture. Add 1 cup of boiling water to the ziplock bag with the corn mixture (or stir the corn mixture and boiling water together in a pot); seal and allow to soak until the corn is almost tender, about 1 hour. Boil 2¼ cups water in a medium pot. Add the corn mixture and its soaking liquid. Cover the pot and return to boiling, then adjust the heat and boil gently until the corn is tender, about 15 minutes. Stir in the potato mixture; adjust the heat, and simmer until the mixture thickens, 2 to 3 minutes; if the mixture is too thick, add a little additional water.

Tabouli Salad

Makes 4 servings

- 2 tablespoons crumbled **dried parsley leaves**
- 2 teaspoons crumbled **dried mint leaves**
- ½ teaspoon salt
- ¼ teaspoon crumbled **dried oregano leaves**
- ⅛ teaspoon freshly ground black pepper
- 1 cup medium or fine bulgur
- ¼ cup **dried scallion slices**
- ¼ cup **dried tomato pieces or cut-up dried tomato slices**
- Fresh whole lemon
- 3 tablespoons olive oil

1. **Pack the mix:** Combine the parsley, mint, salt, oregano, and pepper in a small plastic bag and seal with a twist tie. Combine the bulgur, scallions, tomatoes, and the bag with the parsley mixture in a quart-size freezer-weight ziplock bag. Roll up the bag and seal. Carry the lemon and oil separately.

2. **Camp cooking instructions:** Remove and set aside the small bag containing the parsley mixture. Add 2½ cups of boiling water to the ziplock bag with the bulgur mixture (or stir the bulgur mixture and boiling water together in a pot); seal and allow to soak for 30 to 45 minutes. While the bulgur is soaking, squeeze 3 tablespoons lemon juice into a small bowl; stir in the parsley mixture and the oil.

3. When the bulgur is done soaking, drain the water out of the corner of the bag, squeezing to remove as much liquid as possible. Pour the lemon mixture into the bag and mix well. Let stand for at least 5 minutes before serving.

Green Bean Casserole

Makes 3–4 servings

- 1 (1.8-ounce) envelope white sauce mix (with the gravy mixes in the supermarket)
- 2 tablespoons sliced almonds
- 2 tablespoons nonfat dry milk powder
- ⅔ cup **dried French-cut green beans**
- 2 tablespoons broken-up **dried mushroom slices**
- 1 teaspoon **dried chopped onion**
- ⅓ cup broken potato chips, optional

1. **Pack the mix:** Cut open the top of the white sauce mix envelope, and add the almonds and dry milk. Roll-fold the top over and wrap a rubber band around the envelope. Combine the green beans, mushrooms, and onion in a quart-size ziplock bag. Add the envelope of white sauce mixture. Roll up the bag and seal. Carry the potato chips separately, if using.

2. **Camp cooking instructions:** Set aside the white sauce mixture. Boil 1½ cups water in a medium pot. Add the green bean mixture; cover and remove from the heat. Let stand for 10 to 15 minutes, or until the beans are tender. Add the white sauce mixture and blend well with a fork. Return to boiling, then reduce the heat and simmer, stirring frequently, until the sauce thickens, about 2 minutes. Top with the potato chips, if using.

Apple Skillet Bread

Makes 4 servings

This is a cross between a very thick pancake and a moist, fruity bread. It's wonderful served warm for breakfast, brunch, or dessert.

- ½ cup all-purpose flour
- ⅓ cup powdered egg (from the camping store)
- 1 tablespoon nonfat dry milk powder
- 1 tablespoon butter-flavored sprinkles such as Butter Buds
- ⅓ cup powdered sugar, optional
- ⅔ cup **dried apple slices**
- 1½ tablespoons butter

1. **Pack the mix:** Combine the flour, powdered egg, dry milk, and butter sprinkles in a small plastic bag and seal with a twist tie. Place the powdered sugar in another small bag and seal with a twist tie. Place the apples in a pint-size freezer-weight ziplock bag. Add the bags of flour mixture and powdered sugar, if using, to the bag with the apples. Roll up the bag and seal. Carry the butter separately.

2. **Camp cooking instructions:** Remove the two small bags from the bag with the apples and set them aside. Add ¾ cup boiling water to the ziplock bag containing the apples; seal and allow to soak for about 15 minutes, or until tender. Drain the soaking liquid into a measuring cup and set aside until completely cool.

3. Pour the flour mixture into a small bowl. Add ½ cup of the soaking liquid (adding additional water if needed to equal ½ cup) to the flour mixture, then beat well with a fork. Set aside for 10 to 45 minutes.

4. When you're ready to cook, stir the apples into the batter. Melt half of the butter in a medium skillet over medium heat. Add the apple batter. Cook until browned on the bottom and slightly dry on the top. Use a spatula to slide the bread onto a plate. Melt the remaining butter, then carefully flip the bread into the skillet with the uncooked side down. Cook for 3 to 5 minutes longer, or until the second side is browned and the bread is cooked through. Sprinkle with powdered sugar and cut into 4 wedges.

Cook-and-Dehydrate Recipes

Here are some recipes that you can cook in your home kitchen, and then dehydrate for use at camp — or even for those harried days at home. These mixtures are drier and less fatty than they would be if prepared to be eaten right away; this speeds dehydrating time and improves the storage qualities.

Sausage Sauce for Spaghetti

Makes 4–6 servings

To make it easier to dehydrate, this mixture is much thicker than normal spaghetti sauce. The sausage is also rinsed after cooking to reduce grease so the dried mixture keeps better.

8	ounces uncooked Italian sausage (remove casings if using cased sausage)
½	cup chopped green bell pepper
½	cup chopped onion
¼	cup chopped celery
2	garlic cloves, minced
1	(8-ounce) can tomato sauce
½	teaspoon salt
½	teaspoon crumbled **dried basil leaves**
¼	teaspoon crumbled **dried oregano leaves**
¼	teaspoon crumbled **dried chile (hot) pepper**, optional
6	tablespoons tomato paste

1. Cook the sausage in a large skillet over medium heat until no longer pink, stirring frequently to break up large clumps. Drain in a colander for a few minutes, then rinse with very hot water to wash off grease. Return to the skillet, then add the bell pepper, onion, celery, and garlic. Cook, stirring frequently, until the vegetables are just tender; if the mixture is sticking, sprinkle with a little water. Add the tomato sauce, salt, basil, oregano,

and chile pepper, if using. Cook for about 10 minutes, stirring frequently. Remove from the heat and stir in the tomato paste.

2. Prepare trays or racks as described in Solid Sheets to Hold Purées on page 272. Spread the sauce on the prepared sheets. Dehydrate until brittle and completely dry, breaking the mixture up as it dries. Drying time is generally 7 to 10 hours at 150°F. Cool completely and pack in heavyweight plastic bags or glass jars. Keep refrigerated or frozen for long-term storage.

3. To use, add the dried sauce mixture to 1½ cups of boiling water in a saucepan; stir well, remove from the heat, and let stand for 15 minutes. Add additional water if the sauce seems to need it, then simmer for 5 to 10 minutes. (You may also prepare a half-batch if you like; use ¾ cup water for the initial rehydrating in this step.)

Barbecued Beef for Sandwiches

Makes 3–4 servings

1	pound extra-lean ground beef
½	cup diced onion
¼	cup diced green or red bell pepper
¾	cup barbecue sauce
5	tablespoons tomato paste
	Pinch of sugar

1. Cook the ground beef in a medium skillet over medium heat, stirring frequently to break up, until the meat is beginning to lose its color. Add the onion and bell pepper. Cook, stirring frequently, until the ground beef is thoroughly cooked and the vegetables are tender. Drain in a colander for a few minutes.

2. Wipe out the skillet with paper towels and return the drained meat mixture to the skillet. Stir in the barbecue sauce, tomato paste, and sugar. Cook over medium-low heat for about 3 minutes.

3. Prepare a tray or rack as described in Solid Sheets to Hold Purées on page 272. Spread the beef mixture on the prepared sheet. Dehydrate until crumbly and completely dry, breaking the mixture up as it dries. Drying time is generally 5 to 7 hours at 150°F. Cool completely and pack in heavyweight plastic bags or glass jars. Keep refrigerated or frozen for long-term storage.

4. To prepare the beef for sandwiches, add the dried beef mixture to ¾ cup of boiling water in a saucepan; stir well, remove from the heat, and let stand for 15 minutes. Heat to boiling over medium heat, then reduce the heat and simmer for 5 to 10 minutes; add a little more water if needed. Serve in hamburger buns.

Hummus

Makes 4–6 servings

1	teaspoon olive oil
¾	teaspoon minced garlic
1	(15-ounce) can chickpeas, drained, or 1½ cups home-cooked chickpeas
1	tablespoon tahini (sesame paste), optional
2	tablespoons lemon juice
1¼	teaspoons salt
½	teaspoon freshly ground black pepper
½	teaspoon crumbled **dried parsley leaves**

1. Heat the oil in a medium skillet over medium heat. Add the garlic and cook, stirring constantly, for about 2 minutes. Stir in the chickpeas and tahini; cook, stirring frequently, until the mixture is dry, about 2 minutes. Stir in the lemon juice and cook for about a minute longer. Remove from the heat. Stir in the salt, pepper, and parsley. Mash with a potato masher until fairly smooth.

2. Prepare a tray or rack as described in Solid Sheets to Hold Purées on page 272. Spread the hummus on the prepared sheet. Dehydrate at 150°F for 1 hour, then reduce the heat to 135°F and continue drying until the mixture is dry and crumbly, breaking it up as it dries. Total drying time is generally 4 to 6 hours. Cool completely and pack in heavyweight plastic bags or glass jars.

3. To prepare the hummus, boil ¾ cup water in a small saucepan. Add the dried hummus; stir well, remove from the heat, and let stand until completely cool, stirring occasionally. If the mixture is too thick, stir in a teaspoon of olive oil or additional water.

CHAPTER 11

Other Uses for Dehydrating Equipment

ONCE IT HAS BECOME part of the household equipment, a dehydrator can prove to be a very convenient appliance. You'll find its low, warm temperatures ideal for a variety of jobs, both culinary and non-culinary.

Drying Small Batches of Grains and Corn

Freshly harvested grains must be dried before storage. Large, specialized grain dryers are used for crops grown for commercial use, but small batches of grains for home use may be dried with the smaller dehydrators discussed in this book. Grains such as wheat, barley, oats, rye, and buckwheat are harvested when the stalks are dry and yellow, but before the seeds scatter. Corn is dried on the stalk as long as the weather allows.

Grains and corn can be dried in a manufactured or home-built dehydrator at 115°F, but you won't get very much grain in each load. Sun-drying is a more efficient method because you can set up as many trays as you like. Oven-drying in a standard (non-convection) oven isn't recommended for drying grain or corn because it will take too long.

Ideally, grains should have a moisture content of about 10 to 12 percent to prevent mold and spoilage during storage. Moisture content can be estimated; consult your county extension agent for information.

HOME-DRIED GRAINS

DEHYDRATOR/CONVECTION OVEN

Use solid liner sheets on dehydrator trays; use a baking sheet for a home-built dehydrator or convection oven. Spread grains or corn in a thin layer on sheets. Stir occasionally and rotate trays several times during drying. Grains and corn generally take 12 to 18 hours at 115°F.

SUN-DRYING

Spread grains or corn in a thin layer on solid trays; large batches may be spread out on clean plastic tarps. Stir occasionally and take grains or corn inside at night. Grains and corn generally take 1 to 2 days. After the grain is dry, pasteurize as described on page 28 to destroy any insects or insect eggs that may have been deposited on the grain during drying.

DONENESS TEST: Small grains are dry when they have a hard, crunchy texture and a nutty taste when chewed. Well-dried corn kernels have a shriveled appearance or a dimpled end, depending on the variety.

YIELD: One cup of dried small grains yields about 1½ cups of flour. One cup of dried corn yields about ¾ cup of cornmeal.

TO USE: Grind dry grain or corn in an electric grain mill or hand grinder. If the grinder is adjustable, set it at fine grind for smaller grains or at medium-coarse grind for corn. An electric blender may be used to grind small amounts. Grind only enough grain to be used at one time. Ground grains lose flavor and vitamins in storage and are likely to turn rancid from the oil in the germ. Grains dried at the temperatures recommended may be used for seed.

Drying Breadcrumbs

Here's a good way to salvage bread or rolls that have gone stale. Store the dried breadcrumbs in glass jars in a cool location; they will keep for many months. Breadcrumbs made from rich rolls or breads such as brioche or challah won't keep as long as those made from standard bread.

The best way to make dried breadcrumbs is to chop the stale bread first in a blender. Cut or tear the bread into 1-inch cubes. Start the empty blender on medium speed. Open the lid about halfway and toss in a handful of bread cubes; re-cover the blender jar immediately because the cubes and crumbs will jump up and out of the blender jar with surprising vigor. Process the cubes on high speed until the crumbs are as fine as you like; remember that they will shrink as they dry.

HOME-DRIED BREADCRUMBS

DEHYDRATOR/CONVECTION OVEN

Use solid liner sheets on dehydrator trays; use a baking sheet for a home-built dehydrator or convection oven. Spread the crumbs evenly in a ½-inch layer on sheets. Stir the crumbs occasionally. Breadcrumbs generally take 2 to 3 hours at 140°F.

OVEN (NON-CONVECTION)

Use baking sheets, spreading the crumbs evenly in a ½-inch layer. Stir the crumbs frequently to prevent those on the outside edges of the sheets from burning. At 140°F, breadcrumbs take 1 to 4 hours; watch carefully as they become dry to prevent scorching.

DONENESS TEST: Dried breadcrumbs should be evenly fine and dry; if you press them, they should not stick together.

YIELD: 1 cup of chopped bread yields ½ to ¾ cup of dried breadcrumbs.

TO USE: Sprinkle the crumbs on casseroles before baking. Dip fish or other foods to be fried in breadcrumbs. Use in any recipe calling for dried breadcrumbs.

Miscellaneous Culinary Uses

Here is a short list of some other uses you'll find in the kitchen for your dehydrating equipment.

- **RAISING BREAD DOUGH.** Preheat a box-style or home-built dehydrator to 120°F. Turn off the heat and place a shallow pan of hot water on the bottom. Place a covered bowl of kneaded bread dough on the tray or rack directly above the water. Close the dehydrator and let the bread rise until doubled in bulk. Punch down and place in greased bread pans. Return the pans to the dehydrator until the loaves have risen again. The bread is now ready to be baked in the oven.

- **MAKING YOGURT.** Preheat a box-style or home-built dehydrator to 110°F. Meanwhile, stir together 1 quart of milk and ½ cup nonfat dry milk powder in a saucepan, and heat over medium heat just until tiny bubbles form around the edges of the pan. Remove from the heat and cool to 110°F. Add ¼ cup plain yogurt containing active live cultures, or 1 tablespoon yogurt culture; blend thoroughly. Divide the mixture into sterilized half-pint jars and place them on dehydrator shelves, then close the dehydrator. Keep the milk mixture in the dehydrator at 110°F until it thickens, generally 3 to 4 hours; check at 3 hours, and if it's not set yet, continue to check every 15 minutes until set.

- **MAKING CHEESE.** The low temperature of a dehydrator is ideal for ripening milk to be made into cottage cheese or hard cheese. The cheesemaking process is beyond the scope of this book, but if this is something you're familiar with, try using a box-style or home-built dehydrator, set at the appropriate temperature for each step, to ripen the milk and also to cook the curd.

- **RECRISPING CRACKERS, COOKIES, AND CEREAL.** These and other baked foods that have lost their crispness may be rejuvenated by spreading on drying trays and placing in the dehydrator. Dry at 145°F for 30 to 45 minutes, or until crisp.

- **DE-CRYSTALLIZING HONEY.** When a jar of honey crystallizes into a grainy mass, slip the glass jar into a box-style or home-built dehydrator. Heat at 110°F for a few hours, until the crystals dissolve. You'll have liquid honey again without any loss of nutrients or natural goodness.

- **CURING NUTS.** Walnuts, hickory nuts, butternuts, pecans, and hazelnuts (filberts) may be cured in days instead of weeks by drying them in a dehydrator or convection oven. Nuts keep best when cured in the shell. Before drying, remove the thick, spongy husks of walnuts, hickory nuts, butternuts, and pecans; this is often done by rolling the nuts underfoot on a concrete surface until the husks crumble off. Hazelnuts have thinner husks that are dry when the nuts are harvested; remove by rubbing with heavy gloves. Dry the husked nuts in the shell until the nutmeats are crisp, 8 to 15 hours at 100°F; crack a few open to check the nutmeats.

- **MAKING CRISPY BREAD SNACKS.** Slice day-old bagels or narrow loaves of French bread about ¼ inch thick; you can also use stale pita breads that have been opened, separated, and cut into quarters. Brush *very* lightly on both sides with olive oil, or mist with cooking spray. Sprinkle mixed herbs, garlic salt, or other seasonings over one side; dust lightly with finely grated Parmesan cheese. Place screens on dehydrator trays or racks, then arrange seasoned pieces in a single layer. Dehydrate at 150 to 160°F until crisp, generally 2 to 3 hours. Cool completely before storing in an airtight container.

- **DRYING PUMPKIN AND SQUASH SEEDS.** Dried seeds from pumpkins and other winter squash add great crunch to trail mixes and baked goods. Wash the seeds in a colander, freeing them from the pulpy, stringy material that surrounds them. Spread them out on solid sheets and dry until crisp, 3 to 4 hours at 135°F.

- **MAKING CROUTONS.** Toss ½- to ¾-inch cubes of bread with herbs or seasoned salt, or dry them unseasoned; don't use oil or butter for croutons meant for long storage. Spread the croutons on solid sheets and dry until crisp, 3 to 7 hours at 140°F. Use croutons to make bread dressing or poultry stuffing, or use them to garnish salads or soups.

Drying Flowers for Potpourri

Through the magic of drying, the fragrance of flower blossoms can be captured outdoors in summer, stored away in sealed containers, and enjoyed indoors in winter.

Dried flower petals may be used in potpourri mixtures, sprinkled over lingerie in dresser drawers, or crushed and added to bath water. Wherever they are used, their fragrance will spread and linger in a delightful way.

Dry any fragrant blossoms available. Some of the best are roses, especially the wild varieties; apple blossoms, geraniums, lavender, marigolds, rudbeckia, nasturtiums, and honeysuckle also make delightful choices. Tiny flowers such as chamomile and mint flowers may be dried whole, with just enough stem attached to hold the blossom together. Whether the petals have been plucked and dried separately or the whole blossom has been dried, the petals will become darker after drying, so you should plan your potpourri mixes to take advantage of the deeper tones. White flowers, unfortunately, often look fairly dreary when dried, but can be mixed with more colorful ingredients. Fragrant leaves, including herbs and geranium leaves, are also dried for use in potpourris.

Pluck the petals off just-opened flowers early in the day, as soon as the dew has been dried by the sun; for dried blossoms, pick whole flowering heads when the flower has opened fully. Discard any petals, blossoms, or leaves that are diseased or moldy; they can ruin an entire batch of good material. Use a manufactured or home-built dehydrator to dry potpourri materials; ovens will get too hot as they cycle, scorching the petals. Line trays or racks with screens. Spread the plucked petals, blossoms, or leaves in a thin layer over trays and dry at 110°F until brittle, generally 6 to 8 hours. (Although this technique does not use dehydrating equipment, you may also cut individual stems of roses and other flowers, then tie three or four together and hang in an airy room, out of the sun, as described for drying herbs in chapter 6. When the petals have dried and are brittle, pull them away from the heads, or cut small floral heads away from the stems.) Store the dried potpourri material in separate batches, placing them in tightly sealed jars or canisters in a cool, dark location until you've accumulated enough dried material to prepare the potpourri.

Making Potpourri Mixture

Step 1.

Assemble your ingredients. Make potpourri mixtures from any flowers, herbs, and spices you like. Pine needles and cones are often added for color and fragrance. Buy a bottle of ground gum benzoin resin or powdered orrisroot at a craft shop, health food store, or large drug store. These fixatives slow evaporation of the oils that give the petals their fragrance. You may also want to pick up a small bottle of fragrance oil from the same shop.

Step 2.

Follow one of the recipes on pages 338–339, or make your own blend using the same basic proportions of flower petals, dried herbs, and other ingredients as indicated in the recipes below. Combine all listed ingredients except the fixative mixture in a roasting pan or ceramic mixing bowl; use old or disposable cookware, because the fragrance oils may make the mixing vessels unsuitable for food. Mix gently with your hands. Combine all fixative mixture ingredients in another bowl and mix them well. Scatter the fixative mixture over the flower mixture, tossing everything gently with your hands until well combined.

Step 3.

Pack the mixture loosely into jars or canisters that seal tightly. Store in a cool, dark location for 5 to 6 weeks, stirring or shaking the mixture occasionally. This resting period allows the fragrances to mellow and meld together.

Step 4.

The potpourri is now ready for use. Pack into half-pint jars for gift-giving, or keep a supply for your own use.

Potpourri can be placed in a bowl, basket, or other attractive container and placed in any room to add fragrance and beauty. When the fragrance begins to fade, pour the potpourri into a small mixing bowl, add a drop or two of fragrance oil and a teaspoon or so of brandy. Mix gently, allow to dry, and the potpourri is ready to use again.

To make sachets, sew a small bag from pretty fabric, add a few tablespoons of the potpourri, and tie with a decorative ribbon; you could also just pile the potpourri in the center of a larger square of fabric, gather the material around the potpourri, and tie off the neck with ribbon. Place sachets in closets and dresser drawers to provide fragrance to stored clothes and linens; lavender potpourri is particularly popular for use in linen closets. Sachets make lovely gifts.

Rose-Geranium Potpourri*

1 quart dried rose petals

2 cups dried geranium petals

½ cup dried peppermint leaves

¼ cup dried lavender blossoms

FIXATIVE MIXTURE

1½ tablespoons gum benzoin or orrisroot

4 whole cloves

1½ teaspoons grated nutmeg

3 or 4 drops rose fragrance oil

Lavender Potpourri*

6 cups dried lavender blossoms

1 quart dried rose petals

1 quart dried nasturtium petals

FIXATIVE MIXTURE

3 tablespoons gum benzoin or orrisroot

4 or 5 drops lavender fragrance oil

Apple Blossom Potpourri*

1 quart dried apple blossoms

2 cups dried honeysuckle blossoms

1 cup dried rose petals

FIXATIVE MIXTURE

1½ tablespoons gum benzoin or orrisroot

3-inch cinnamon stick, broken into small pieces

4 or 5 drops citrus fragrance oil, optional

Pine Potpourri*

2 quarts pine, fir, or spruce needles

1 quart dried juniper berries

2 cups tiny dry pinecones, optional

1 cup dried sage leaves

1 cup dried parsley

2 tablespoons dried basil

3 dried bay leaves

FIXATIVE MIXTURE

2 tablespoons gum benzoin or orrisroot

4 or 5 drops pine fragrance oil

Geranium Potpourri*

1 quart dried geranium leaves

2 cups dried geranium flower petals

1 cup dried chamomile blossoms

½ cup dried mint blossoms or leaves

FIXATIVE MIXTURE

1½ tablespoons gum benzoin or orrisroot

2 tablespoons whole dried cardamom pods

2 teaspoons ground dried coriander seeds

3 or 4 drops rose fragrance oil, optional

---

* See page 337 for step-by-step instructions.

Simmering Mixtures

Potpourris are also used in special "simmering pots," small decorative vessels that are sold at stores specializing in decorative items for the home. You can get the same effect by placing a tablespoon or two of the potpourri mixture in a small saucepan of water and placing it over a very low burner on the stove. Here's a mixture that is similar to a potpourri, but it is designed specifically to use in a saucepan or slow cooker.

Simmering Spice Mix

PER PINT JAR

5 or 6 **dried orange slices**, preferably dried with peel on

4 or 5 **dried lemon slices**, preferably dried with peel on

⅓ cup dried rose petals

1 tablespoon whole cloves

1 teaspoon **dried marjoram**

1 **dried bay leaf**

2 cinnamon sticks

1. **Pack the mix:** Cut the orange slices and lemon slices in half. Arrange all ingredients attractively in a widemouthed 1-pint jar. Seal the jar tightly.

2. **Instructions for use:** Empty the contents of the jar into a small saucepan. Add 3 cups water. Heat to boiling and cook for 5 minutes. Adjust the heat so the mixture is barely simmering and leave on the stove for up to 3 hours; the fragrance will fill your home. You may also heat this in a very small slow cooker; when the mixture is simmering, open the lid slightly to allow the fragrant steam to escape. After use, the mixture can be stored in the refrigerator for up to a month; simply add more water each time you use it, then return to the refrigerator for the next time.

Miscellaneous Non-Culinary Uses

Here are a few more ideas that will put your dehydrating equipment to good use.

- **DRYING GARDEN SEEDS.** Seeds for the home garden may be dried without harm in a dehydrator or homemade dryer, if the temperature is kept at 100°F or less.

- **DRYING CRAFTS.** Whether you're into dough art or painting, you'll find the dust-free warmth of a dehydrator or homemade dryer ideal for drying.

- **POMANDER BALLS.** A box-style or home-built dehydrator works very well for drying these old-fashioned decorations, which also freshen closets. To make a pomander, pierce the skin of an orange, lemon, or lime with an ice pick and insert whole cloves into the holes. Dry at 100°F until the fruit is shrunken and hard, then tie a ribbon around it for hanging.

- **CINNAMON-APPLESAUCE ORNAMENTS.** Stir together ¾ cup smooth applesauce and 1 bottle (about 4 ounces) of ground cinnamon. Roll out ¼ inch thick between two sheets of plastic wrap. Cut into shapes with cookie cutters. Use a drinking straw to poke a hole for hanging at one end. Arrange on trays and dehydrate at 145°F until hard, generally 6 to 8 hours. Thread thin ribbon through the holes and tie on the Christmas tree or hang anywhere that holiday decorations are in order. Store the ornaments in tightly sealed plastic containers; they'll keep their wonderful scent for years.

Metric Conversion Chart

Unless you have finely calibrated measuring equipment, conversions between U.S. and metric measurements will be somewhat inexact. It's important to convert the measurements for all of the ingredients in a recipe to maintain the same proportions as the original.

GENERAL FORMULAS

Ounces to grams	multiply ounces by 28.35
Grams to ounces	multiply grams by 0.035
Pounds to grams	multiply pounds by 453.5
Pounds to kilograms	multiply pounds by 0.45
Cups to liters	multiply cups by 0.24
Fahrenheit to Celsius	subtract 32 from Fahrenheit temperature, multiply by 5, then divide by 9
Celsius to Fahrenheit	multiply Celsius temperature by 9, divide by 5, then add 32

APPROXIMATE EQUIVALENTS BY WEIGHT

U.S.	Metric
¼ ounce	7 grams
½ ounce	14 grams
1 ounce	28 grams
1¼ ounces	35 grams
1½ ounces	40 grams
2½ ounces	70 grams
4 ounces	112 grams
5 ounces	140 grams
8 ounces	228 grams
10 ounces	280 grams
15 ounces	425 grams
16 ounces (1 pound)	454 grams
0.035 ounces	1 gram
1.75 ounces	50 grams
3.5 ounces	100 grams
8.75 ounces	250 grams
1.1 pounds	500 grams
2.2 pounds	1 kilogram

APPROXIMATE EQUIVALENTS BY VOLUME

U.S.	Metric
1 teaspoon	5 milliliters
1 tablespoon	15 milliliters
¼ cup	60 milliliters
½ cup	120 milliliters
1 cup	230 milliliters
1¼ cups	300 milliliters
1½ cups	360 milliliters
2 cups	460 milliliters
2½ cups	600 milliliters
3 cups	700 milliliters
4 cups (1 quart)	0.95 liter
1.06 quarts	1 liter
4 quarts (1 gallon)	3.8 liters

Index

Other Storey Titles You Will Enjoy

The Beginner's Guide to Preserving Food at Home
BY JANET CHADWICK
Even first-timers can successfully preserve every common vegetable and fruit with these quick, easy, and encouraging instructions.
240 pages. Paper. ISBN 978-1-60342-145-4.

The Big Book of Preserving the Harvest
BY CAROL W. COSTENBADER
This is your go-to preserving book — a classic primer on freezing, canning, drying, and pickling fruits and vegetables, newly revised.
352 pages. Paper. ISBN 978-1-58017-458-9.

Drink the Harvest
BY NAN K. CHASE AND DENEICE C. GUEST
Savor every drop of summer by making and preserving your own juices, wines, meads, teas, and ciders.
232 pages. Paper. ISBN 978-1-61212-159-8.

The Pickled Pantry
BY ANDREA CHESMAN
Pickling isn't just for cucumbers. In this fresh, contemporary guide to pickling, you'll find 150 recipes for putting up everything from apples to zucchini.
304 pages. Paper. ISBN 978-1-60342-562-9.

Put 'em Up!
BY SHERRI BROOKS VINTON
Bright flavors, flexible batch sizes, and modern methods make up this comprehensive guide to preserving.
304 pages. Paper. ISBN 978-1-60342-546-9.

The Put 'em Up! Preserving Answer Book
BY SHERRI BROOKS VINTON
Find answers to your questions about safely canning, drying, freezing, fermenting, refrigerating, and infusing all kinds of foods.
256 pages. Paper with partially concealed wire-o. ISBN 978-1-61212-010-2.

Raw Energy
BY STEPHANIE TOURLES
Unprocessed, uncooked, simple, and pure: get an extra boost with more than 100 recipes for delicious raw snacks.
272 pages. Paper. ISBN 978-1-60342-467-7.

These and other books from Storey Publishing are available wherever quality books are sold or by calling 1-800-441-5700.
Visit us at *www.storey.com* or sign up for our newsletter at *www.storey.com/signup*.